ANTHROPOLOG

Anthropology, Culture and Society

Series Editors:
Dr Richard A. Wilson, University of Sussex
Professor Thomas Hylland Eriksen, University of Oslo

*Women of a Lesser Cost:*
*Female Labour, Foreign Exchange and Philippine Development*
SYLVIA CHANT AND CATHY MCILWAINE

*Ethnicity and Nationalism:*
*Anthropological Perspectives*
THOMAS HYLLAND ERIKSEN

*Small Places, Large Issues:*
*An Introduction to Social and Cultural Anthropology*
THOMAS HYLLAND ERIKSEN

*Anthropology, Development and the Post-modern Challenge*
KATY GARDNER AND DAVID LEWIS

*Power and its Disguises:*
*Anthropological Perspectives on Power*
JOHN GLEDHILL

*Anthropological Perspectives on Kinship*
LADISLAV HOLY

*Anthropology of the Self:*
*The Individual in Cultural Perspective*
BRIAN MORRIS

*New Directions in Economic Anthropology*
SUSANA NAROTZKY

*Human Rights, Culture and Context:*
*Anthropological Perspectives*
Edited by RICHARD WILSON

# ANTHROPOLOGY AND CULTURAL STUDIES

EDITED BY
STEPHEN NUGENT AND CRIS SHORE

Pluto Press
LONDON • CHICAGO, IL

First published 1997 by Pluto Press
345 Archway Road, London N6 5AA
and 1436 West Randolph
Chicago, Illinois 60607, USA

British Library Cataloguing in Publication Data
A catalogue record for this book is available from
the British Library

ISBN 0 7453 1136 9 hbk

Library of Congress Cataloging in Publication Data
Anthropology and cultural studies/edited by Stephen Nugent
and Cris Shore.
    p.   cm.
  Includes index.
  ISBN 0–7453–1136–9 (hbk.)
  1.Anthropology. 2. Ethnology. I. Nugent, Stephen (Stephen L.)
II. Shore, Cris, 1959–.
  GN25.A575   1997                                   97–28087
  306—dc21                                               CIP

Designed and produced for Pluto Press by
Chase Production Services, Chadlington, OX7 3LN
Typeset from disk by Stanford DTP Services, Northampton
Printed in the EC by Redwood Books, Trowbridge

# CONTENTS

# CONTRIBUTORS

**Joy Hendry** is Professor of Anthropology at Oxford Brookes University.

**Signe Howell** is Professor of Anthropology at the University of Oslo.

**Jeremy MacClancy** is Senior Lecturer in Anthropology at Oxford Brookes University.

**Stephen Nugent** is Senior Lecturer in Anthropology at Goldsmiths College, University of London.

**Alexandra Ouroussoff** is a Research Fellow at the London School of Economics.

**Cris Shore** is Senior Lecturer in Anthropology at Goldsmiths College, University of London.

**Gareth Stanton** is a Lecturer in the Media and Communications Department, Goldsmiths College, University of London.

**Pnina Werbner** is Lecturer in Anthropology at Keele University.

**Paul Willis** is Professor in the School of Humanities and Social Sciences, University of Wolverhampton.

# 1 INTRODUCTION: BROTHER, CAN YOU SHARE A PARADIGM?

*Stephen Nugent*

The chapters in this volume were first presented in an anthropology research seminar at Goldsmiths College, University of London, in the spring of 1995. Paper-givers (all anthropologists) were asked to consider anthropology's relationship with cultural studies.

Lurking behind the seminar were two issues: first, despite years of courtship, anthropology and cultural studies were still disarticulated; second, the impression that despite the numerous claims for the obviousness and naturalness of an alliance between the two fields there were unspecified (chalk-and-cheese, oil-and-water, etc.) incompatibilities which militated against easy melding.

More overtly, it seems that in weighing up opinion over the range 'good–bad–indifferent', there is not an obvious site (or key issue) of contention, yet the received view seems to be that there should be. Overall, there is less a sense of a clash of titans than a sense of bickering (cf. Sahlins 1994).

Several explanations for this (mildly) unsettled state of affairs suggest themselves. The first is that anthropology and cultural studies have been tipped to converge at a time when both are making fairly vigorous claims for being able to deal with new subject matter without outside assistance. In anthropology, for example, the arbitrariness and limitations of classical formulations of the object of analysis (the remote, isolated society) have long been challenged, and now that anthropology self-consciously operates within the complex, modern world, perhaps in the larger scheme of things, the field as previously formulated appears to have outgrown itself. An anthropology which addresses, for example, the range of subject matter displayed in the annual conference programme of the American Anthropological Association, is not an

1

anthropology which requires recontextualisation through an alliance with a new trail-breaker. Similarly, cultural studies, which draws on diverse disciplinary perspectives, can hardly be seen to be particularly dependent on the influence of one field. In the cases of both anthropology and cultural studies, professed competence in (relevance to) life outside previous academic constraints is plausible. The idea that an alliance is obligatory exposes the claims of both (putative) partners: what could a struggling partner bring to dinner?

Second, much of the passion and theoretical bluster which might have been expected to accompany discussion of the announcement of the impending union of anthropology and cultural studies – shotgun marriage or true romance – has already been expended in at least two decades of heated wrangling over postmodernism, post-structuralism and postcolonialism. This is hardly to deny that such engagements have produced much compelling work of great sophistication, nor to argue that unambiguous resolutions have been agreed, but it is to say that from both sides – anthropology and cultural studies – there may only be so many occasions for throwing Daniel to the lions.

Third, and a thread linking a number of chapters in this collection, is the fact that anthropology and cultural studies often use the same terms to describe very different concepts, phenomena, structures and processes. 'Ethnography', for example, is a key term in both fields, yet usage varies so widely as to defeat common purpose.[1] In complementary fashion, the valorisation of the triumvirate class/ethnicity/gender as the culmination of sustained late-modern critical scrutiny may also be regarded as an essentialist turn at odds with the professed aims in both fields to seek out hybridisation, borderlands and subalternity.

There is a fourth, and perhaps more prosaic – and perhaps narrowly local – reason, and this is that while in academic terms[2] anthropology is often more or less clearly defined by what it is not (for better or worse) – sociology or history, for example, despite the efforts in some quarters to efface such differences – cultural studies is more or less clearly defined by what it includes – literary theory, sociology, history, anthropology, for example. This leaves open the possibility that the union is analagous to, say, a market-recognisable tropical fruit drink – orange and mango, for instance – as well as the less likely, but in principle possible, turnip and grapefruit drink.

Despite the differences, and however inchoate the terms of engagement, a vital – and, I suspect, persistent and useful – link/tension between anthropology and cultural studies comes from the similarity of their synthetic ambitions. Anthropology, because of its 'others' worlds, others' lives' orientation and the fact that anthropologists can, through their field experience, claim (legitimately or not) a privileged and specialised grasp on their material, has largely been insulated from charges of diversity/promiscuity in terms of ignoring official disciplinary boundaries: an anthropologist may produce a monograph which covers kinship, politics, economics, animal husbandry, medical practices, cosmology and epistemology, not to mention economic botany, scarification, childrearing. . . and on and on; but precisely because this kind of engagement is 'out there', the basic fieldwork notion has not been subverted by an obvious objection: is it realistic for anyone to presume to cover such a range of topics; is there really, even in a mildly rigorous sense, an 'anthropological theory' which can cover all this? The lay defence for such breadth of purview (namely, that these are simple societies) is not available to the anthropologist because it is precisely the claim (and demonstration) that such societies are anything but simple that constitutes the distinctiveness of modern anthropology within the social sciences.

Cultural studies offers a parallel case in terms of multi-disciplinary diversity: is it realistic to attempt to join up literary criticism, social theory, ethnography and discourse analysis (to name but a few of the arrows in the quiver) in the name of the grand synthesis demanded by complex empirical material? Further, what is one to make of a field which raises significant theoretical banners – for example, post-structuralism and postmodernism – which because of their deconstructivist import would appear to subvert the very notion of a project?

While there may be some formal similarity in terms of the eclecticism (or disciplinary diversity) of the two fields, their connections may also be described in terms of the complementary unravelling of one field and consolidation of the other. Anthropology, for instance, has largely forsaken the idea of a central theory and is now comprised of a number of sub-fields or specialisms, while cultural studies is an emergent theory based on the pulling together of previously segregated fields.

The tension referred to above has led to two kinds of discussions, one epistemological (fair amount of literature), the other practical (not much literature). This volume is largely concerned with the latter. The authors are anthropologists who recognise that there is no easy contrast between anthropology and cultural studies, that the encounter between anthropology and cultural studies is neither clearly life-threatening nor necessarily life-enhancing and that, as yet, no formal agenda has emerged. Rather, as practising anthropologists, part of their remit now includes acknowledging that the disciplinary autonomy of anthropology is – not to put too fine a point on it – not so autonomous. This hasn't come about because of a direct challenge to anthropological authority (ethnography has become generic in a fairly desultory fashion, for example), but more because anthropology itself has become decentred and unable to articulate as clear a sense of purpose as was the case in earlier periods.

Reactions to this diminution of anthropological authority have been various. Marshall Sahlins, for example, offers the following in the context of an 'After-Dinner Entertainment' for the Fourth Decennial Conference of the Association of Social Anthropologists of the Commonwealth, Oxford, 29 July 1993, referred to earlier. Following an argument that objectivity is not essentialist, but the outcome of the comparison of all the empirical material available (that is, a contribution to epistemological literature referred to above) he says:

The same for ethnography. No good ethnography is self-contained. Implicitly or explicitly ethnography is an act of comparison. By virtue of comparison ethnographic description becomes objective. Not just in the naive positivist sense of an unmediated perception – just the opposite: it becomes a universal understanding to the extent it brings to bear on the perception of any society the conceptions of all the others. Some Cultural Studies types seem to think that anthropology is nothing but ethnography. Better the other way around: ethnography is anthropology, or it is nothing. (Sahlins 1994: 10)

To paraphrase: cultural studies is either redundant (anthropologists already do it) or it is out of the loop (practitioners are mistaken in thinking that what they do would be recognised by anthropologists as anthropology).

Others, however, are less sanguine. George Marcus, for example, enthusiastically embraces the virtue of anthropology's subsumption under cultural studies: as the conventional anthropological project (outward – other – oriented, empirically driven, comparativist) exhausts itself, and as globalisation continues to homogenise cultural difference, anthropology will be superseded by a cultural studies which will relocate anthropology in the core.[3] Although one of the few to provide a programmatic account of the desirability of this move (Marcus 1992), he has granted – through his editorship of *Cultural Anthropology* – a forum for the exploration of an anthropology/cultural studies synthesis not yet marked by clear tendencies. The best-of-*Cultural Anthropology* anthology, *Reassessing Cultural Anthropology* (1992), for example, is so inclusive (it even features denunciations of the whole project) as to suggest that the marriage of anthropology and cultural studies has already taken place and the nuptials are being announced after the fact.

While there has been sniping with anti-cultural studies overtones, much of this has been conducted covertly through critiques of post-structuralism,[4] postmodernism and the literary turn (see Sangren 1988), and a direct anthropology versus cultural studies encounter has been deferred. Disputes, for example, such as the alleged shift of editorial policy in *American Anthropologist* (from 'science' to 'anti-science'), have had airings, but no lasting consequences. In fact, the exercised (alleged) relationship between anthropology and cultural studies (and associated demons) has more often been expressed within exclusively anthropological circles (viz. Sahlins) than in more general domains. There is, for example, little acknowledgement in the mainstream cultural studies literature of anthropology's long-running 'absence of core theory' angst, yet were a merger actually imminent, it would be difficult for it not to address this crucial, dynamic issue: how do you merge with a field that is so self-doubting about a unified identity?

The obliqueness of anthropology versus cultural studies encounters has been illustrated in other domains. Terry Turner's analysis of the distinction between critical multiculturalism and identity multicul-turalism is one such example (1994). Another is Russell Jacoby's treatment of postcolonial theory (1995). In both cases, the point is made that regardless of the theoretical apparatus promoted by those who would claim to have moved beyond the parochialism of discipline-defined approaches, something crucial has been sacrificed, in Turner's case anthropology's critical political stance, in Jacoby's, the idea that social theory should attempt to explain, not merely outline an all-inclusive agenda.

It is hardly surprising that in the the present volume, in which questions of method are put to the fore, strong claims are made for the virtue of ethnography as practised by anthropologists, but it is useful to reflect on the recent commentary of Stocking to the effect that anthropology has traditionally overstated its ethnographic case. In *The Ethnographer's Magic* (1992), Stocking reveals the porousness of the method of ethnography, not its coherence. Rather than constituting distinctive techniques of anthropological practice, fieldwork methods/ethnography are shown to be ad hoc accommodations which, while serving various purposes (not least of which was the political goal of establishing anthropology as a distinctive professional adacemic field), do not lend themselves to presentation with much rigour; and if it is the case – as Sahlins declares – that 'ethnography is anthropology', where does this leave those – in cultural studies for example – who would seek to ally themselves with such an ethnographic tradition?[5]

That ethnography in principle does not match the claims made for it in practice is subject to a variety of readings, but two in particular illustrate that the symbolic appropriation of an anthropological notion of ethnography by cultural studies may not be all that unusual (although such symbolic manipulation may not bode well for a substantive anthropology/cultural studies alliance). The first of these is from Wolf who observes (too optimistically, according to Blok) that:

Offered a choice between biological determinism and literary criticism, most anthropologists have chosen to go about their work unencumbered by theoretical consistency. Luckily so, perhaps, for the strength of anthropology has always lain in its eclecticism, or – what may be the same thing – its respect for reality. (Wolf 1983, cited in Blok 1992: 16)

Implicit in this claim is the eminently reasonable notion that different kinds of research goals require different methods, but in the field as a whole – as Stocking documents at length – there has been a virtual fetishisation of fieldwork-as-method, a defining feature of the field despite its ineffability.

The second illustration comes from comments by Schneider (1995), also underlining the fetishisation of fieldwork. He notes that while anthropologists celebrate fieldwork as a hallmark of the discipline,[6] those modern anthropologists who have set the tone for the field are known mainly for their ideas, not their fieldwork. This is not to say that their fieldwork is impugned (although Lévi-Strauss has come in for unwarranted criticism, quite contrary to the facts), but that no one really pays that much attention to fieldwork *per se* if the ideas and arguments emerging from such work are not compelling. There is, as yet, little market in facsimile editions of field notebooks, and publishers' current enthusiasm for ethnographic monographs themselves is tepid to say the least.

In the context of a developing discussion around the prospects for some kind of alliance between anthropology and cultural studies, the chapters in this volume reflect on how anthropological notions of ethnography may be extended to embrace a subject matter whose definition is achieved by recourse to diverse disciplinary conventions, and it is not surprising that there is a flavour of territorial dispute. Nor is it surprising, given the strategic needs of academic disciplines in a period of funding crisis, that both proponents and critics of such a merger should appear to hedge their bets such that Marcus (1992: viii), for example, in describing the role of *Cultural Anthropology* can allude to both the revitalisation of the discipline and its simultaneous transformation: 'This alliance across the boundaries of the discipline made the critique both more provocative and more difficult to dismiss or marginalize among anthropologists.'

The question of territoriality, however, is also a question of perspective. Anthropologists are long accustomed to the charges of irrelevance and esotericism, and it would not be unreasonable to assume that an alliance with cultural studies would provide surcease, not least because cultural studies provides legitimation on the grounds that 'anthropology-at-home' is, acritically, more palatable than the study of dual organisation and political fission among the Kreen"akrore; but such aims have salience only within fairly narrowly defined professional domains. Generally, such claims have more to do with securing professional space within academia than they do with confronting broader issues of anthropology's relevance within public culture.[7] While in anthropology, territorial propriety was strongly challenged from within by an emergent critical anthropology in the early 1970s (see Asad 1973, Hymes 1974), such critiques – although widely cited – did not engage much of an audience beyond the professional. Cultural studies did engage such an audience.[8]

Mulhern (1995) has chronicled the rise and fall of a critical cultural studies in a concise and pointed essay and it is salutary to compare the trajectories of critical anthropology and cultural studies over the past thirty years. By Mulhern's account, cultural studies first presented

something along the lines of *kulturkritik*. This was followed by a
conformist phase in which the terms of 'culture' were extended to
include previously disenfranchised public voices. As a result of this
inclusion, the initial critique was domesticated. The political force of
*kulturkritik* was removed. And in the absence of a class and/or interest-
based analyis, the *critical* project of cultural studies was abandoned.

If one were to present as succinct an account of the rise and
accommodation/domestication of anthropology, it would be very
difficult to reach such a neat resolution (whether or not one agrees
with Mulhern's conclusions), and the reasons for this draw attention
away from the dominant areas of discussion – technical (for example,
is ethnography the same thing for anthropology and cultural studies?),
and epistemological (for example, can the notion of *kulturkritik* usefully
function in a culturally relativistic context, *pace* anthropology?), to a
more prosaic, but significant and neglected issue: cultural studies and
anthropology, while sharing many features, emerged under different
historical circumstances and in wildly different contexts such that
their seeming compatibility may be less than imagined, and attempts
to bind them together may be served by examining crucial differences
between the two fields rather than assuming a convenient elective
affinity. While the development of anthropology in the US in the post-
Second World War period, for example, was strongly shaped by the
effects of the GI Bill and the expansion of higher education, direct
and indirect effects of the Cold War (especially with regard to
restructuring of what then came to be called 'the Third World'), on
the back of massive economic expansion and concentration of capital,
cultural studies in the UK developed in a relatively insular, static
context (in terms of academic institutions, for example), in economically
constrained circumstances. These externalities (re: 'the fields') would
appear to have lost salience fifty years on (not least because national
cultural differences are obscured behind the flag of neo-liberalism),
but they are significant when considering how it is that two fields seem
to have reached points of mutual comprehension, yet still doubt that
they fully share the same sensibility.

Such matters will have to be taken up elsewhere (but see Lave et
al. 1992). For the moment, this volume represents outlines of the
problematic as seen by anthropologists who recognise that the synthesis
of anthropology and cultural studies is not simply a matter of announcing
that such a merger has taken place, and depends substantively not simply

on a rejigging of anthropological or cultural studies terms of reference as academic disciplines, but on ways of transcending them.

## NOTES

1. This is by no means counterproductive, nor is it meant to cast aspersions on non-standard usages. The assumption by cultural studies, for example, that there is an ethnographic method in anthropology waiting to be appropriated is misguided. As Stocking (1992) shows at length, the ethnographic method is ad hoc – but perhaps no less useful for that.
2. Especially given the – basically – single subject character of UK undergraduate programmes.
3. Core may be a misnomer in this context: one of the claims of cultural studies is that cultural homogenisation, globalisation and similar processes have eroded the boundaries between core and periphery.
4. In reality, though, post-structuralism has been so thoroughly domesticated that it serves to defend orthodoxy as well as contest it. For interesting discussion see Pavel (1989).
5. Paul Willis, whose ethnographic contributions within cultural studies are widely acclaimed, observed in Manchester in 1996, that despite claims for the centrality of ethnography in cultural studies, very little had actually been done. Indeed, he was quite scathing about the discrepancy between claims and reality.
6. Stocking – who did not do fieldwork – has some pertinent comments on the intimations of marginality befalling those who are thereby not quite in the club.
7. See, for example, Kahn's *Culture, Multiculture, Postculture* (1995).
8. It could be argued, though, that the public orientation of cultural studies was merely a starting point and that the actual trajectory was more conventionally academic: having valorised the study of culture/public culture, practitioners could then stake a claim to old-fashioned academic legitimacy. See in particular David Harris (1992).

## REFERENCES

Asad, T. (ed.) (1973) *Anthropology and the Colonial Encounter*. London: Ithaca Press.

Blok, A. (1992) 'Beyond the Bounds of Anthropology', in J. Abbink and H. Vermeulen (eds) *History and Culture: Essays on the Work of Eric R. Wolf.* Amsterdam: Het Spinhuis.

Harris, D. (1992) *From Class Struggle to the Politics of Pleasure: the Effects of Gramscianism on Cultural Studies.* New York: Routledge.

Hymes, D. (ed.) (1974) *Reinventing Anthropology.* New York: Vintage.

Jacoby, R. (1995) 'Marginal Returns: The Trouble with Post-Colonial Theory', *Lingua Franca* Sept./Oct.: 30–7.

Kahn, J. (1995) *Culture, Multiculture, Postculture.* London: Sage.

Lave, J., Duguid, P. and Fernandez, N. (1992) 'Coming of Age in Birmingham: Cultural Studies and Conceptions of Subjectivity', *Annual Review of Anthropology* 21: 257–82.

Marcus, G. (ed.) (1992) *Rereading Cultural Anthropology.* London: Duke University Press.

Mulhern, F. (1995) 'The Politics of Cultural Studies', *Monthly Review* 47 (3): 31–40.

Pavel, T. (1989) *The Feud of Language: A History of Structuralist Thought.* Oxford: Blackwell.

Sahlins, M. (1994) *Waiting for Foucault.* Prickly Pear Pamphlet No. 2. Cambridge: Prickly Pear Press.

Sangren, S. (1988) 'Rhetoric and the Authority of Ethnography', *Current Anthropology* 29 (3): 405–24.

Schneider, D. (1995) (with Richard Handler) *Schneider on Schneider: the Conversion of the Jews and Other Anthropological Stories.* Durham, NC: Duke.

Stocking, G. (1992) *The Ethnographer's Magic and Other Essays in the History of Anthropology.* Madison: University of Wisconsin Press.

Turner, T. (1994) 'Anthropology and Multiculturalism: What is Anthropology that Multiculturalists Should be Mindful of It?', in D.T. Goldberg (ed.) *Multiculturalism: A Critical Reader.* Oxford: Blackwell.

Wolf, E. (1983) 'Culture: panacea or problem?', *American Antiquity* 49 (2): 393–400.

# 2 IN DEFENCE OF *SAVAGE CIVILISATION*: TOM HARRISSON, CULTURAL STUDIES AND ANTHROPOLOGY

*Gareth Stanton*

As the burgeoning discipline of cultural studies imposes itself increasingly on the academic firmament it is hardly surprising that in areas of study which are more firmly established questions are being asked concerning this potential cuckoo in the nest. It is not hard to see that much is at stake here. Despite the occasional cross-dresser opinions are increasingly sclerotic. For the cultural studies adept, fully trained in the brief ancestor cult of its British variety, anthropology remains fully wed to oppressive structures of Empire. The sole redeeming feature is a method, ethnography, which is adopted and annexed, often with precious little understanding. For anthropologists it would seem that the agenda proposed by cultural studies is some form of elaborate joke – a concatenation of idiocies and ephemera. Both approaches ignore certain historical and intellectual roots. It is the purpose of this chapter to highlight some common ground and to reflect in some small way on the complex intellectual formation of this twentieth century. My starting point here, as elsewhere (Stanton 1996), is a British movement which sought to combine a science of the human derived from anthropology, with a study of 'ourselves'. In short, cultural studies *avant la lettre*. This movement, Mass-Observation, has recently been reviewed by MacClancy (1995). He is concerned to draw out the hidden links between Mass-Observation (M-O) and the surrealist movement in Britain whereas I am attempting to see in M-O the roots of a linkage between anthropology and cultural studies. It is this latter issue which I shall mainly be addressing in this chapter. Both MacClancy and I make the point that anthropology in all its recent incarnations has ignored the popular movement of the late 1930s which was given the name Mass-Observation by its founders. For MacClancy M-O is an example of 'popular anthropology' whereas for the founders of M-O it was to be considered the 'anthropology of ourselves' (Harrisson and Madge 1937: 10). It was, to use a phrase which Malinowski used in his preface to the ethnography of the Gikuyu written by Jomo Kenyatta (1938), 'anthropology at home'. This is a far from unfamiliar expression in British social anthropology and was, of course, the theme of the 1985 ASA meeting (Jackson 1987). The motives behind anthropologists' more recent turn to the home front, however, are rather different from those advocated by the founders of M-O. Nonetheless, it is clear that there are complex links between M-O, anthropology and cultural studies. In the first instance I shall outline the view of anthropology's development which is usually served up for anthropology students in Britain, that is to establish the founding moment of modern British social anthropology – an event generally associated with the work of the Polish *emigré* Bronislaw Malinowski. He has generally been regarded as the person who laid down the rules of modern anthropology as a discipline which required of its practitioners a spell of intensive fieldwork in close contact with the people under study. This new discipline, with its new methods became the dominant mode of British anthropology for many decades. For a variety of reasons, however, the Malinowskian citadel has recently been stormed. A new spirit of doubt stalks anthropology, a spirit which demands new ways of accounting for itself as well as new forms of self-expression. Such strategies as have appeared may be seen as a new movement within anthropology, albeit with nothing, as yet, approaching the dominance Malinowski's own brand of functionalism once possessed. How this movement relates to such trends as modernism, postmodernism or the realist tradition in literature remains an area of intense debate. It is becoming clear, however, that anthropology is increasingly drawing closer to cultural studies. For some (for example, Knauft 1994) this is regarded as a matter of some concern if not outright dismay. In this chapter I shall attempt to trace the development of a tendency that anticipated such concern, influenced by an anthropology then seen as part of a pioneering venture in academic cultural studies. This was the Mass-Observation movement.

The bridge between the two academic disciplines is a single text, *Savage Civilisation*, which appeared in 1937, yet has many of the distinctive – and now reclaimed – qualities sought after by some of the practitioners of the allegedly new forms of anthropology in the post-Malinowskian era. The author of this book, Tom Harrisson, was one of the co-founders of the Mass-Observation movement, the first movement in Britain to set out with the objective of documenting British cultural life in the broad sense implied by T.S. Eliot in his *Notes Towards a Definition of Culture* (1947). One of the methods used to achieve this objective was modelled on participant observation – quasi-Malinowskian principles used in order to arrive at an 'anthropology of ourselves'. The Mass-Observation movement itself became part of the cultural landscape and for a short period was the butt of jokes about snooping and prying. However, Malinowski himself lent the movement his support. I will argue that the history of the movement is a demonstration of the shared heredity of anthropology and cultural studies. This link has long been suppressed by both disciplines, but it should be to be recovered and recognised.

## A REVOLUTION IN BRITISH SOCIAL ANTHROPOLOGY?

In Anglo-Saxon circles the story of the development of modern anthropology is a fairly simple one, or at least it had been until the publication of Malinowski's field diaries in 1967. Up to that point it was generally held that a crucial part of the foundation myth of British social anthropology was beyond doubt. A young Polish scholar had, as a result of illness, taken to reading works of anthropology on his sickbed. Malinowski's acquaintance with the anthropology of the time, runs a version of the hero legend, led the Pole to give up his studies in chemistry and physics and head for the London School of Economics to study with scholars such as Westermarck and Seligman. The brand of ethnography these men practised was one which involved fieldwork, that is to say prolonged periods of time spent in the world of the ethnographic 'other', but the time spent was not usually restricted to a single localised region and bore, if anything, a close relationship to the nineteenth-century explorer/traveller tradition. The so-called 'armchair' anthropologists such as Frazer simply corresponded with people in the field (missionaries, colonial officials and so forth), creating their theories on the basis of such information combined with their knowledge of ancient mythology and folklore. Westermarck, himself also an *emigré*, but from Finland, serves as a paradigm of the model of researcher which is close to the explorer type, but which is approaching a model of fieldwork which would have been recognisable to the classic functionalist ethnographers. He travelled extensively in one country, Morocco, and worked in the vernacular, using 'native' informants.

In contrast to most earlier anthropologists, Seligman and Westermarck at least endeavoured to learn the languages of and make direct contact with the peoples they were studying. Malinowski himself went several steps further, or so myth has it. He insisted that his was the proper and only way to proceed, and laid down rules for the conduct of anthropological fieldwork, based on his own work in the Trobriands. For anthropologists this is well-trodden territory (see Young 1979). According to Malinowski, the goal is to grasp the way in which the 'native' views the world, his (for this tended to be the case) understanding of his reality. To sum up his attitude, Malinowski urged that:

The anthropologist must relinquish his comfortable position in the long chair on the veranda of the missionary compound, Government station, or planter's bungalow, where, armed with pencil and notebook and at times with a whiskey and soda, he has been accustomed to collect statements from informants, write down stories, and fill out sheets of paper with savage texts. (quoted from Malinowski's 1925 Frazer Memorial Lecture by Kuklick 1991: 287)

It has been suggested that the attitude fostered by Malinoski and his own personal self-agrandisement during his life led to a vision of the anthropologist as hero, but as Stocking has argued, the role of Malinowski is more complicated than simple versions of this myth might suggest:

The emergence of fieldwork was a multifaceted process to which many individuals before and after Malinowski contributed. But Malinowski's deliberate archetypification of the role of 'the Ethnographer' offered, both to prospective anthropologists and to various publics at the boundaries of the developing discipline, a powerfully condensed (yet expansive) image of the anthropologist as the procurer of exotic esoteric knowledge of potentially great value. (1989: 209)

Despite such nuanced appreciations of the development of anthropology it was certainly the case that, by the early 1950s, students of the functionalist founders of modern British social anthropology could reel off its purpose and objectives with some degree of clarity. Strong on method, however, Malinowski was often regarded as weak in respect of general theory despite which fact later commentators, such as Bloch, argue that British anthropology, although in theoretical disarray and almost entirely ignorant of intellectual currents such as Marxism, actually had its 'glory days' in the years 1920-60. British anthropology was unique, Bloch argues, 'for its detailed studies of actual societies in operation, and for relating whole varieties of phenomena to create a synthesis' (1983: 145), but this can only be understood as a reference to the methodological innovations introduced by Malinowski. That is not to suggest that certain problems with his prescriptions had not appeared previously. Malinowski himself recognised that the accumulation of data simply led to there being lots of data requiring interpretation in order to arrive at 'laws and generalisations'. It was precisely on this last point that M-O was to fail in the eyes of those anthropologists such as Firth who criticised the organisation at the time (see MacClancy 1995: 505). But I shall return to this point later.

Although this account is simplified, the consequences for the development of British social anthropology were as follows: one man, Malinowski, pronounced a revolution in method for the subject. He denounced all previous efforts as flawed and set out to produce a rationale for anthropology that was both scientific and humanist. Establishing a secure foothold within British academe (and the force of his charismatic personality has not gone unnoted) he was able to recruit and maintain a group of devoted acolytes who went forth and propagated his vision of anthropology. Although problems were acknowledged, most accepted Malinowski at face value and were prepared to follow the methodological path on which they thought he had embarked. Malinowski was even prepared to endorse the utility of anthropology on the home front. It is this latter issue that I shall develop in some depth by examining the work of a group of writers and investigators who, on the basis of Malinowskian principles, set out to generate an 'anthropology of ourselves' for the British context – the Mass-Observation movement. First, however, the Malinowski story must be brought up to date.

With the attenuation of colonialism, the discipline of anthropology has been forced to reconsider its own position given the close connection in relation to the whole colonial enterprise. Implicit in discussions of the relationship between anthropology and colonialism are what I would call a 'strong' critique and a 'weak' version. In a detailed discussion of a version of the 'weak' critique Kuklick (1991) makes a number of interesting observations regarding the Malinowskian 'anthropologist as hero' approach to doing fieldwork. Discussing the career of a typical colonial officer, she points out that careers were likely to start in rural areas often distanced from other colonial officials. In some respects, she suggests, it was the romanticised view they held that facilitated the triumph of functionalist anthropology. The descriptions functionalist anthropologists offered of their research methods 'were very like political officers' accounts of their administrative procedures' (1991: 189). Anthropologists could now be seen as 'kindred spirits' (ibid.). Kuklick's discussion of the compatibility between the 'hero' anthropologist and the colonial officer – and by extension the whole endeavour of colonialism – is an interesting one. It is impossible, however, to dispute that with the collapse of the colonial regimes, a certain animosity towards the figure of the anthropologist became evident. While an older nationalist leader such as Jomo Kenyatta actually sat in Malinowski's seminar at the LSE, others such as Nkrumah now viewed anthropologists with deep suspicion (Kuper 1983: 99). Kuklick's discussion, however, puts an interesting spin on Kuper's contention that there was, in fact, very little effective link-up between colonial finance and anthropological fieldwork, colonial administrators being more likely to regard anthropologists with disdain than anything else. In another context, Kuklick (1984) argues that the work of Malinowski-influenced functionalists 'may perhaps be better appreciated as a paean to the merits of egalitarian democracy than as an apology for colonialism' (Kuklick 1984: 76). This is clearest in Evans-Pritchard's work on the Nuer. As Renato Rosaldo has noted, the Nuer, in Evans-Pritchard's account, 'represent an ideal of human liberty, even in the midst of colonial domination' (1986: 96). The Nuer, in this sense, were simply portrayed as an idealised version of ourselves.

These 'weak' critiques of the relationship between anthropology and colonialism do not necessarily destroy the Malinowskian imperative, but critiques developed in the early 1970s were to take a much stronger position on the relationship. Anthropology came to be widely portrayed as the handmaiden of colonialism or imperialism, or indeed both. In the British context, the work which stated the line of argument most forcibly was Asad's *Anthropology and the Colonial Encounter* (1973). It was this work which laid much of the ground, within anthropology in Britain, for the latter's own encounter with political economy and

French structural-Marxism. This analysis of anthropology's role within the colonial system was to be joined in later years by a number of formulations initially coming out of comparative literary studies and utilising the rhetoric of Foucault (and others), trends which merged into a more general 'crisis of representation'. The plausibility of the critique was reinforced by the collapse of faith in the original Malinowskian formulation. This was a process which had been, in no small part, brought about by the publication of Malinowski's own fieldwork diaries in 1967. It is these to which I shall now turn.

Geertz's maverick assessment of the career of Malinowski hints that his revolution in anthropological methodology was suspect (Geertz 1988: 23). At the time of the diary's publication, Geertz described their author, in a piece in the *New York Review of Books*, as a 'crabbed, self-preoccupied, hypochondriacal narcissist, whose fellow feeling for the people he lived with was limited in the extreme' (quoted in Young 1979: 12). As Young comments, rather than anthropologist-as-hero we now have anthropologist as anti-hero, a fittingly dialectical progression. In what ways, then, had Malinowski transgressed? As Young suggests, expressions such as the following, 'As for ethnology: I see the life of the natives as utterly devoid of interest or importance, something as remote as the life of a dog', were likely to cause alarm amongst those who had taken his methodological prescriptions at their face value. Indeed, the whole tone of the diary could be interpreted as suggesting a degree of disdain wholly unfitting for one who built his career on championing rational 'Trobriand man' as a corrective to the naive formulations and speculations of earlier generations of anthropologists concerning the form and nature of 'savage' thought and mental processes. Certainly, his repeated references to the Trobrianders as 'niggers' were bound to create a stir (though it should be noted that Leach, in an early review in the *Guardian*, stressed the absurdity of translating *nigrami* as niggers rather than blacks, deemed a more acceptable usage by Leach [see Firth 1988: xxiii]). This point aside, and given the outbursts which no 'mistranslation' argument can dismiss, Firth noted, in his original introduction, that such moments reveal 'a darker side of the relation of an anthropologist to his human material' (Firth 1988: xvi). This very discussion of 'human material' might cause a shudder now, but Firth forgave Malinowski his lapses. Writing in a new introduction in 1988, Firth reviews the debate stimulated by the publication of the diary. Here he is prepared to grant that the publication of the diary destroyed the aura of 'Olympian detachment' which is given by the classic functionalist ethnographies, the view suggesting that 'the anthropologist came, saw, recorded and retired to write up the material, apparently untouched by his or her experiences' (1988: pxxviii). For Firth then, it is this element of detachment, rather than the notion of hero-anthropologist, that the diary destroyed. This, however, is but one view. As Stocking remarked (1986: 23), 'reaction to the diary has not got much beyond the disillusioning references to the Trobriand "niggers"'. Stocking himself was to attempt to probe the diaries in relation to Malinowski's encounter with Freudian psychoanalysis, but other writers were to take a somewhat different approach to the humanity of fieldworkers in general and attempt to transform the anthropological enterprise into a more reflexive, literary form.

A clue to this transition is given in Firth's 'review' of the reviews, provided in the second edition of Malinowski's diary. One figure who looms large is the American historian and cultural critic James Clifford, who, Firth remarks, has in his approach to ethnographic writings 'become fascinated by the notion of fiction and tends to treat any text with an element of personal subjectivity as "fiction"'. It is with the writings of Clifford and a number of his colleagues that we see the coalescence of a number of voices into something approaching a coherent movement in anthropology. If we were to put a finger on one moment in this process it would be the publication of the Clifford and Marcus collection *Writing Culture* in 1986. Clifford (1988), following the literary critic Steven Greenblatt, himself a writer who leans on anthropology on occasion, and his notion of Renaissance self-fashioning (Greenblatt 1980), discusses the Malinowski conundrum under the rubric of 'ethnographic self-fashioning'. The world in which we now live he describes as a 'syncretic', 'postcultural' one (1988: 94). Beginning with an epigram from Conrad's *Victory*, Clifford develops an extended comparison of the two Poles refashioning their identities in relation to the world around them. *Argonauts of the Western Pacific* (1922), Malinowski's first Trobriand book, Clifford argues, was part of this refashioning process, a text in which the diary is excluded and written over 'in the process of giving wholeness to a culture (Trobriand) and a self (the scientific ethnographer)' (1988: 112). This quintessential anthropologist of the ethnography would disintegrate with the revelations of the diary which 'once entered into the public record of anthropological science, shook the fiction of cultural relativism as a stable subjectivity, a standpoint for a self that understands and represents a cultural other'. For Clifford, the appearance of the diary made it possible for the late 1970s and 1980s to witness the appearance of new forms of ethnographic realism – both more dialogical than in the past and more resistant to closure – tendencies well-represented in the 1986 collection. Such works, he suggests, teeter precariously between realism and modernism, a suggestion, however, which leads us into murky definitional waters.

For Geertz (1988), the writing of Evans-Pritchard constitutes 'ethnographic realism', a form rigorously constructed to give the impression of reality. Geertz's discussion of the Malinowski diary, however, leads him to muse on what he terms 'I-witnessing' ethnographies of more recent vintage, writings which do not aspire to forms of realism used by such writers as Evans-Pritchard. He mentions a trio of American ethnographers who have worked in Morocco, Paul Rabinow, Kevin Dwyer and Vincent Crapanzano, whose work has frequently been cited in the context of new experimental ethnography or even under the rubric 'postmodern' ethnography. As one of its alleged proponents, Crapanzano is slightly sceptical concerning such developments. 'In the last few years', he writes, 'there has been much talk – salvationist talk – about developing experimental modes of writing ethnography' (1992: 1). Marcus and Fisher announced in 1986 that what is happening 'seems to us to be a pregnant moment in which every human project of ethnographic research and writing is potentially an experiment' (1986: ix). In more general terms, and following Rabinow, Fardon notes that the work of Clifford and his followers has meant that anthropological texts are being produced by means of texts rather than by fieldwork (1990: 5).

Such a description of the challenge to older versions of 'doing anthropology' does have some hint of the dispute which postmodernism has with forms of realism and rehearses Baudrillard's endless regression of meaning. For this 'new' anthropology, however, there do appear to be some problems. Indeed, there seems to be some confusion over what is modern or postmodern, as Robert Pool (1991) has demonstrated. A critic such as Scott can describe the collection *Writing Culture* as 'meta-anthropological' and postmodernist in atmosphere, claiming that postmodern anthropology proposes that culture is mobile, that it is unbounded and conjunctural (Scott 1992), yet Tyler, himself a contributor to the *Writing Culture* volume, writes that the collection is 'not post-modern, its authors neither invert the relationship between aesthetics and epistemology nor revolutionize the three-fold hierarchy of epistemology, politics and aesthetics' (1987: 50).

Scholte argues that the recent history of 'Anglo-American cultural studies' is largely defined by three movements: a 'critical anthropology' of which he cites Hymes (1974) as an early variety, though doubtless he would also include Asad (1973), and Wolf (1982); a feminist anthropology, for example, Shostak's *Nisa!* a recent classic; and finally symbolic anthropology, with which he lumps the developments surrounding the *Writing Culture* collection and the journal *Cultural Anthropology* (Scholte 1987). The core of this collection for Scholte, however, is a postmodern transition 'from a single idea of ethnographic authority to a multiplicity of descriptive experiments and interpretative paradigms' (1987: 37).

While it would be wrong to suggest somehow that 'experimental' ethnography (or whatever we choose to call it) has a total grip on the throat of anthropology in general, the denials of its importance in certain quarters suggests that there is something worth examining. As Knauft has remarked: 'There is a palpable if somewhat reactionary feeling among anthropologists that the intense development of cultural studies has usurped the anthropological notion of "culture" (1994: 133). Indeed, as the anthropologist Nicholas Thomas argues in an assessment of the current state of academic flux, recent work has 'almost created a post-disciplinary humanities field, in which histories, cultural studies, cultural politics, narratives and ethnographies all intersect and are all open to being challenged' (Thomas 1994: 19).

It is from within the predicament of such mergers and doubts that I shall examine the growth in Britain of the Mass-Observation movement. My starting point is a text which shares some features with the new experimental ethnographies. It is a work which takes a highly critical view of colonialism and cultural contact with the West and integrates, to some degree, the voice of the author into the body of the text, and yet was published in 1937. The author of the book, Tom Harrisson, was one of the founders of the M-O movement.

A TEXT OUT OF TIME? TOM HARRISSON'S *SAVAGE CIVILISATION*

Although this chapter owes much to Henrika Kuklick's patient research she wrongly gives the impression, perhaps unintentionally, that

Harrisson's work represents part of a genre of travellers' accounts which 'offered thrilling reports of explorers' physical heroism in the wilds of Empire' (Kuklick 1991: 13n). In her account this is to be distinguished from the anthropologists who forsook their armchairs in pursuit of scientific regularities rather than the merely exotic or curious. In fact, Harrisson had consulted a number of ethnographic 'authorities' and had read the account of Malekula written by Bernard Deacon, who had died in the field of blackwater fever. Deacon in turn had gone to the field with a large number of the field notes of John Layard, a maverick figure in the history of British anthropology (see MacClancy 1986). Harrisson, then, was not unaware of the state of anthropological knowledge of the region in which the book is set.

The book itself commences with a short series of epigrams entitled 'Seasaw', beginning with a quotation from Aldous Huxley: 'In every tropic land the poorest people are always the inhabitants' (a statement the validity of which he denies in the actual text, see Harrisson 1937: 290). Other authors quoted include T.S. Eliot, Nietzsche and Paul Robeson. What are, in effect, the acknowledgements are entitled 'Jigsaw' and here he describes how the book came about. He had been with the Oxford University Expedition to the New Hebrides and had stayed on in Malekula. When his funds were exhausted he 'went native', becoming a 'wandering unwhite whiteman'. Of the book itself he writes: 'This is not a story of decadence or despair but of inevitability; with oases in chaos' (1937: 6). There is then a short geographical interlude followed by a section entitled 'Persons', which deals with what would then have been described as 'natives'. Much of the material would certainly make its way into a 'classic' functionalist monograph dealing with the region. He talks at length of the people's attitudes to pigs (and their teeth) and the process behind the accumulation of these animals which lies behind competitive feasting. The real difference from an anthropological monograph, however, lies clearly in the fashion in which he has presented his material. It is written in the first person, as if Harrisson had indeed 'gone native': 'To us the great moments are those of the Na-Leng dances; the greatest interest is in our pigs, they come before food and sleeping. . .' (1937: 20). While this style might seem crude and naive in some respects now, at the time it represented a significant break with functionalist forms of presentation. This may well be a reflection of the fact that Harrisson was not linked in any formal way to the seminar system of Malinowski at the LSE and therefore avoided the pressures to conform to certain modes of presentation imposed by academic convention. However, there are several other points which make his work, in feel at least, closely resemble some of the recent efforts at a more 'literary' anthropology.

Appended to the section 'Persons' is a short commentary on the text. He discusses his attraction to the place, Matanavat, in which he stayed, and the 'balanced system of classless capitalism, typical of the New Hebrides, [that] came easy to me' (1937: 70). Before attempting to reconstruct a picture of that life before the arrival of the whites, however, he suggests that: 'Now it is time to welcome the advent of another type of culture that was peculiar particularly in morals and deaths' (1937: 71). Here, and this is a crucial break with the anthropology of the time, Harrisson goes on to talk about the history of the conquest of the New Hebrides. Weaving together various accounts, including that of Pedro Francisco de Quiros (the last of the 'great' Spanish navigators), he attempts to recreate, in ironic style, the early incidents of contact. From there he goes on to document the navigational virtuosity of the Polynesians and Melanesians in relation to the great navigators of the Western tradition, establishing the superiority of the former. With the explorations of the last European navigators Harrisson suggests:

The initiation of the native is now complete. A white man had been to all the main islands. He had fired off his stickshining and smoke after, with my brother crying out there on the sand shore as we took him and ran in our fear. . . to the hut where the in him went out, went without meaning, with no hate or pigs, – he had made no preparation. (1937: 121)

The book continues with a historical exploration of a number of aspects of the complex imperial/colonial nexus in this part of the Pacific: the sandalwood trade and the atrocities and deceits associated with it; the ravages caused by whalers in the region; the influence of the various competing missionaries, on village life and on matters such as dress – the appearance of 'Western' clothing styles (what Harrisson termed 'shirtism'); the development of pidgin in the region and a number of other items excluded from the functionalist accounts. An important subject in this respect is the nineteenth and twentieth-century use of Melanesian 'native labour' both in Fiji and on the plantations of Queensland – the process of transshipment which came to be known as 'blackbirding'. These movements Harrisson documents particularly for the nineteenth century, describing some of their effects on the men's home communities. He discusses the politics of 'white Australia' and Queensland's sugar industry. Indeed, he discusses the implications of the mass repatriation of blackbird labour which resulted from political pressures for a 'white Australia'. He notes the words of Rivers in 1913:

At the present moment there exists in Melenesia an influence far more likely to produce disintegration of native institutions than the work of the missionaries. I refer to the repatriation of labourers from Queensland which has been the result of the movement for a white Australia. (quoted in Harrisson 1937: 250)

He outlines the spread of white settlement, the depopulation of the region's native population. He applauds the good sense of *kava* drinking (the missionaries opposed it). He exposes the land-grabbing associated with the development of plantation agriculture and the copra trade. This latter he describes as a phase in the region's history which saw the 'native'

irrevocably harnessed to the wheel of making things which were to him pointless, things to be manufactured in other lands into stuff for which he had no use. . . things of our progress, the unessentials that build this staggering civilisation. (1937: 284)

The general tenor of the writing should be established by now and, indeed, its relationship to our foregoing discussion of Malinowskian brands of functionalism. The main point is that, in this last example, Harrisson actually draws the local actor, the native, into the nexus of the world capitalist economy, a connection which anthropologists were not to make for several decades, and one which some advocates of the the literary departure have only recently begun to pursue (as an alleged novelty) in their efforts to generate an anthropology which can deal with the microprocess of the local and integrate it into the global macro, without ironing out all forms of local difference (see Marcus and Fisher 1986).

Worth mentioning are the specific remarks which Harrisson makes with regard to anthropology. In his discussion of native decline in population he is dismissive of certain of Rivers's ideas concerning the Melanesian psychological 'will to live' being demolished by the onslaught of contact with the West. For Harrisson, the absence of immunological resistance to imported pathogens and the general depredations of the whites was perfectly adequate to explain the decline in population. More than this, however, he specifically criticises Rivers's *History of Melanesian Society*, published in 1914:

This has been regarded as a great scientific work. That is a mistake. It is only great prose. It is a brilliant piece of circular subjective reasoning and creative literature. It is the result of a short study, mostly among mission natives on board a mission yacht. (1937: 339)

Warming to his task, he suggests that it is the 'anthropologist's custom to detach his daily life from the people among whom he is working, to eat his own foods. . .' (1937: 343). It is , he suggests, an 'adolescent science'.

His period in Malekula made Harrisson wonder why it was that people had been financed to do work in exotic regions, but not at home among 'ourselves'. As far as he was concerned the crude contrast of 'savage' and 'civilised', which he had attempted to make in *Savage Civilisation*, was intended to undermine the very contrast itself, but the consequences of this needed to be pursued. What was there, he asked himself,

of Western civilisation which impacted into the tremendously independent and self-contained culture of those cannibal people on their Melanesian mountain? Only one thing, significantly in the mid-thirties: the Unilever Combine.
    Thus it happened that the trail led from the Western Pacific to the south of Lancashire. William Lever was born in Park Street, Worktown. . . . (Harrisson 1961: 25–6)[1]

Worktown was in fact Bolton, where Harrisson was to initiate a study into British social and cultural life. Initially he was alone, but soon he was to become one of the intellectual movers behind a populist experiment in the social sciences – the Mass-Observation (M-O) movement.


## AN ANTHROPOLOGY OF OURSELVES?

Underlying much of this discussion is the comparison which I wish to draw with the development of cultural studies in the British context. The founding moment of cultural studies is usually given as being the late 1950s (McGuigan 1992). I want to look back to the late 1930s and examine the development of the Mass-Observation project as a little recognised precursor to the development of academic cultural studies in Britain.

All too often, M-O is reduced in recent accounts of cultural studies, to a couple of sentences, if mention of it is made at all. McGuigan serves as an example of such treatment, largely ignoring the work M-O conducted. There are a number of reasons why this might be. In the first case, much of the work done by M-O never reached print and remained in archive form (the main archive is now based at the University of Sussex). Second, M-O was never formulated in explicitly political terms (although at the time of its founding, Charles Madge was a communist) so, from the distance of the 1990s (and in the light of Foucauldian perspectives on the 'panopticon') it takes on the veneer of having been just another ruse of the powerful – total surveillance, every dictator's dream. Indeed, it is possible to detect something sinister in the concept of the M-O project, as originally conceived by its founders Charles Madge and Tom Harrisson. This is understandable as the two, in an early pamphlet (Harrisson and Madge 1937), argued that Mass-Observation intended to work by a new method: 'Ideally, it is the observation by everyone of everyone, including themselves' (1937: 10), and as the popular Penguin edition of the first results of the study, *Britain*, trumpeted on the front cover, it was 'The Science of Ourselves' (Mass-Observation 1939). But it is possible to look beyond this essentially Orwellian reading of M-O. This is not *1984*. This fact was understood by many commentators at the time. Malinowski (1938), who was to become a member of the M-O advisory board, was to suggest that Mass-Observation was inconceivable in a totalitarian environment. Evidently he did not see a process of total control reminiscent of a police state in the objectives of M-O. The pursuit and availability of the information being sifted by M-O was, in his reading, essential to the workings of a healthy democracy. Malinowski clarifies this issue:

Mass Observation is invaluable in these days when power is in the hands of the masses who may remain free and allowed to express their own opinion, within limits, or else have to be gagged, dominated by gangs and pedagogues, who also have to work through the masses, but mass indoctrinated as well as intimidated. (1938: 120)

This view is endorsed by a more recent commentator on M-O, Tom Jeffery (1978). M-O, he suggests, 'was a political challenge of the man in the street, of us against them; it was a populist demand, that democracy should mean what it says, rule by the people, apprised of the facts' (1978: 4).

At the time of its founding, M-O attracted a great deal of publicity and much of this was of a hysterical variety. Indeed, the publicity it attracted was itself analysed by M-O. Ironically, that work was carried out by a young man who later in life was to have a hysterical voice all of his own in a British tabloid, Woodrow Wyatt. The terms of abuse heaped on M-O are extensive: 'maniacs, organisers of a cult, cranky, beastly, Groupey, Beaver players, inferior to Holman Hunt's "Light of the World," mass-mystics, spies. . .' (Harrisson and Madge 1938: 63). Such attitudes surfaced in various places. Graham Greene, for example, caricatures an Observer, the Indian, Muckerji, in his novel, *The Confidential Agent* (1971 [1939]). It is necessary, however, to look beyond such limited appreciations of the intentions of Harrisson and the rest of M-O. As I have indicated in my discussion of his Melanesian book, Harrisson's personal project was essentially anthropological in scope. Writing almost thirty years later, Harrisson summed up the objectives of Mass-Observation as seeking

to supply accurate observations of everyday life and *real* (not just published) public moods, an anthropology and a mass-documentation for a vast sector of normal life which did not, at that time, seem to be adequately considered by the media, the arts, the social scientists, even by the political leaders. (Harrisson 1976: 13)

On this occasion he describes the method as being two-pronged, one a self-documentary approach, coupled with a more observational approach and here he likens the study of Britons to bird-watching, which was one of his particular interests. Mass-Observation was to be a 'scientific study of human social behaviour, beginning at home' (1976: 13).

The structure of feeling of the time, if we can so describe it, is also revealed in the pamphlet *Mass-Observation* (1937). In some respects it indicates that the general mood of doubt at that time was similar to that evoked by certain brands of postmodernism. The pamphlet, its authors assure the reader, 'assumes that the contemporary attitude of doubt is not the end of the epoch of science, but the beginnings of a new epoch of science' (Harrisson and Madge 1937: 11). Calder and Sheridan (1984) explain the original impulse behind the formation of M-O. A letter to the *New Statesman* from a schoolteacher called

Geoffrey Pyke[2] in 1936 called for an anthropological study of the 'primitive' reactions to the abdication of King Edward VIII. The journal received a reply from Madge outlining that a group had already been formed for just that purpose. Madge thought that fieldwork would have to proceed in a more roundabout fashion than it did in such places as Africa. This was because British society was seen to be 'ultra-repressed' in the Freudian sense. Clues to unravelling all this might only be arrived at indirectly through the workings of coincidence. In this sense nothing could be ignored by prospective investigators, everything must be recorded – a necessity which could produce surrealistic lists of projects for investigation worthy of a Borges, ranging from such objects of study as the aspidistra cult, through the private lives of midwives to the objects on people's mantelpieces. This apparent surrealism was not in itself a coincidence. Both Madge and the film-maker Humphrey Jennings, who was also involved in M-O at this stage, were interested in surrealism. Jennings, in fact, was a member of the Organising Committee of the International Surrealist Exhibition which opened at the New Burlington Galleries, London, in June, 1936.[3]

In the vast amount of material which was generated by Mass-Observation, in contrast with some of the aspirants to a 'postmodern' anthropology, it is rare for the paid investigators to reveal themselves as subjective actors (volunteers, however, would allow the intrusion of personal opinion and feeling into their diaries and contributions), but the accounts did often introduce the presence of the observer. There was definitely the realist notion of the eye as a camera, albeit one with a particular slant, depending on the nature of the observer. As Madge and Harrisson wrote in *First Year's Work* (1938), 'Mass-Observation has always assumed that its untrained observers would be subjective cameras, each with his or her own distortion. They tell us not what society is like but what it looks like to them' (quoted in Calder and Sheridan 1984: 4–5). Harrisson wrote that: 'from the beginning film was of the highest interest to us. We were film minded. . .' (quoted in Richards and Sheridan 1987: 1). Much of the Bolton work had concentrated on cinema- and film-going, but the research results were not collated and published until 1987. This is, perhaps, one reason why cultural studies has paid so little attention to M-O. Of initiatives such as M-O and the Documentary Movement (Humphrey Jennings is a linchpin here, having been involved in both), Iain Chambers has observed of M-O's efforts: 'Optics, and the pragmatic limits of a liberal empiricist culture – the world is simply "there", to be observed, filmed and reproduced – are combined in a diffused "naturalism"' (Chambers 1986: 89). While Chambers's view has some validity, we need to probe more deeply. Certainly in the case of Jennings, the very writer who at first glance might be taken to give most support to the sort of view held by Chambers, this is becoming very clear. As Kevin Jackson has underlined in his introduction to a collection of Jennings's letters, poems and published works:

Jennings was never much interested in statistics and averages, and it does not take a very penetrating gaze to see that beneath its would-be scientific prose, Mass Observation – at least as conducted by Jennings – was really a kind of first cousin to surrealism. (1993: xiv)

There is clear evidence from his letters that Jennings saw himself as different from other members of the documentary movement. Writing to his wife Cicely, for example, he complains about criticisms he has received over the soundtrack for his film *This is England*. The comments, he writes, come 'of course from Rotha and other of Grierson's little boys who are still talking as loudly as possible about "pure documentary" and "realism" and other such states of self-advertisement' (quoted in Jackson 1993: 16).

The judgement of M–O normally held within cultural studies, then, obscures some of the factors motivating the work of M–O, but as the 'visionary' period for M–O was effectively the early war period, the whole emphasis drifted away from the 'visionary' and into the area of commissioned market research as many of the staff, including Harrisson, were gradually lost to the war effort. In 1947, Harrisson, the ornithologist and explorer, returned east to Sarawak, where he worked as curator of the island's museum. Madge meanwhile had split from the organisation in 1940 because of his disagreements with Harrisson over M–O and its wartime links with the Ministry of Information.

After the war, M–O continued to function, but increasingly it turned to more straightforward market research. In 1961, however, the energetic Harrisson was back with the outfit for a period to coordinate a re-study of some of the areas which M–O had been extensively working on in the late 1930s and early 1940s. This work resulted in the publication of *Britain Revisited* (Harrisson 1961). The absence of such re-studies in classical anthropology was, of course, one of the criticisms which Madge and Harrisson had levelled at the discipline – a criticism which Malinowski had refuted, citing various studies of American Indian groups (which he claimed, in effect, had been continuously under anthropological scrutiny since the Spanish conquest [Malinowski 1938]). If anything, by the 1960s, Harrisson's own views on anthropology had hardened into a bizarre doctrine, far distant from anything remotely innovative in contemporary terms. 'Observing' had indeed become the fetish that critics of the 1930s made it out to be in the caricatures such as that penned by Graham Greene. The original intention of M-O, Harrisson notes here, was 'to *observe* – to observe the *mass* and seek to have the mass observe itself. . .' (1961: 17). Here, Harrisson increasingly does fall foul of the critique put forward by Chambers and now his position represents an extreme rejection of any evidence other than the purely visual. Linguistic evidence is deemed inadmissible if the inquiry is to be dignified with the title science. In line with this proposition, he suggests that the best piece of technical equipment for the anthropologist is the earplug! Few anthropologists, from any epoch, are likely to endorse such a position. But his claim that such events as the St Bartholomew's Day 'Cow Head Festival' were only now being considered as suitable and worthy objects of scientific interest was true (traces of the event were sought out in the re-study; the original material was reported initially in *Britain* ([Mass-Observation 1939]). The orientation of M-O laid the groundwork for books such as Hoggart's *Uses of Literacy* (1957), with its 'anthropological' approach to the 'ordinary cultures' of 'everyday life', a seminal text for all students of cultural studies. Charles Madge, in a postscript to the re-study, adheres more closely to the original goals of M-O. As he remarks, the original objective of the group was to 'understand "ordinary people" in relation to the great issues of politics'. His modest proposal that the importance of M-O was that it assumed 'that a wide range of human phenomena had serious significance' could easily stand as a motto for more recent developments within academic cultural studies and in doing so resurrects cultural studies' links with anthropology. This, indeed, is the sense of culture as 'a whole way of life' which Raymond Williams found so laudable in T.S. Eliot's definition of culture (Williams 1958: 233). Hoggart prefaces his *Uses of Literacy* with a quotation from the American literary and social critic, Ludwig Lewisohn: 'The men of our age of critical realism, goaded by mass-stupidity and mass-tyranny, have protested against the common people to the point of having lost all direct knowledge and vision of it. . .' (1957: 10). This was precisely the sentiment which lay behind the formation of M-O.

## CONCLUSION

In this chapter I have argued that the Mass-Observation movement is worthy of serious study by any person interested in the historical developments of both anthropology and cultural studies in Britain. Indeed, considering M-O forces us to ask stern questions about the vaunted novelty of some recent approaches in both disciplines. I think MacClancy and I are in agreement on this score. Where we differ, however, is in our selection of essential texts. Whereas I have chosen *Savage Civilisation* as the platform on which to build my arguments he focuses on Jennings and Madge's book *May 12th 1937* (1937). It is for readers to rediscover both books and make their own judgement.

## NOTES

These arguments appear in an expanded form in Stanton (1996). Many thanks to the Department of Anthropology at Goldsmiths College and to my colleague David Morley.

1. On two occasions in *Savage Civilisation* Harrisson refers to projects dealing with 'copra and combines' (p. 298) and in a note in the bibliography he claims that he is working, with Oliver Bell, on a study of Leverhulme and Unilever (p. 439). On Harrisson's life, see Green (1970).
2. MacClancy (1995: 499) describes the author of this letter as a 'Cambridge scientist'. Whether or not the two descriptions are compatible I do not know.
3. As I stated at the outset, MacClancy (1995) has written in some depth of the connections between Madge and Jennings and British surrealism.

## REFERENCES

Asad, T. (1973) *Anthropology and the Colonial Encounter*. London: Ithaca Press.

Bloch, M. (1983) *Marxism and Anthropology*. Oxford: Oxford University Press.

Calder, A. (1985) 'Mass-Observation 1937–1949', in M. Bulmer (1985) (ed.) *Essays on the History of British Sociological Research*. Cambridge: Cambridge University Press.

Calder, A. and Sheridan, D. (1984) *Speak for Yourself*. London: Jonathan Cape.

Chambers, I. (1986) *Popular Culture: The Metropolitan Experience*. London: Methuen.

Clifford, J. (1988) 'On Ethnographic Self-Fashioning: Conrad and Malinowski', in *The Predicament of Culture: Twentieth-Century Ethnography, Literature and Art*. Cambridge, MA: Harvard University Press.

Clifford, J. and Marcus, G. (eds) (1986) *Writing Culture*. Berkeley: University of California Press.

Crapanzano, V. (1992) *Hermes' Dilemma and Hamlet's Desire: On The Epistemology of Interpretation*. Cambridge, MA: Harvard University Press.

Eliot, T.S. (1947) *Notes Towards a Definition of Culture*. London: Faber and Faber.

Fardon, R. (ed.) (1990) *Localising Strategies*. Edinburgh: Scottish Academic Press.

Firth, R. (1988) 'Introduction', in B. Malinowski, *A Diary in the Strict Sense of the Term*. London: Athlone.

Geertz, C. (1988) *Works and Lives: the Anthropologist as Author*. Oxford: Polity Press.

Green, T. (1970) *The Adventurers*. London: Michael Joseph.

Greenblatt, S. (1980) *Renaissance Self-fashioning*. Chicago: University of Chicago Press.

Greene, G. (1971 [1939]) *The Confidential Agent*. London: Heinemann.

Harrisson, T. (1937) *Savage Civilisation*. London: Victor Gollancz.

—— (1961) *Britain Revisited*. London: Victor Gollancz.

—— (1976) *Living Through the Blitz*. Harmondsworth: Penguin.

Harrisson, T. and Madge, C. (1937) *Mass-Observation*. London: Frederick Muller.

—— (1938) *First Year's Work 1937–38* (with an essay by Bronislaw Malinowski). London: Lindsey Drummond.

Hoggart, R. (1957) *The Uses of Literacy*. London: Chatto and Windus.

Hymes, D. (ed.) (1974) *Reinventing Anthropology*. New York: Vintage.

Jackson, A. (1987) *Anthropology at Home*. London: Tavistock.

Jackson, K. (1993) *The Humphrey Jennings Film Reader*. Manchester: Carcanet.

Jeffery, T. (1978) *Mass-Observation: A Short History*. University of Birmingham: CCCS.

Jennings, H. and Madge, C. (1937) *May 12th, 1937*. London: Faber.

Kenyatta, J. (1938) *Facing Mount Kenya*. London: Secker and Warburg.

Knauft, B. (1994) 'Pushing Anthropology Past the Posts: Critical Notes on Cultural Anthropology and Cultural Studies', *Critique of Anthropology*, 14 (2) pp. 117–52.

Kuklick, H. (1984) 'Tribal Exemplars: Images of Political Authority in British Anthropology, 1885–1945', in G. Stocking (ed.) *Functionalism Historicised: Essays on British Social Anthropology*. Madison: University of Wisconsin Press.

—— (1991) *The Savage Within: The Social History of British Anthropology, 1885–1945*. Cambridge: Cambridge University Press.

Kuper, A. (1983) *Anthropologists and Anthropology: The British School 1922–72*. Harmondsworth: Penguin.

MacClancy, J. (1986) 'Unconventional Character and Disciplinary Convention', in G. Stocking (ed.) *Malinowski, Rivers, Benedict and Others: Essays on Culture and Personality*. Madison: University of Wisconsin Press.

—— (1995) 'Brief Encounter: The meeting, in Mass-Observation, of British Surrealism and Popular Anthropology', *Journal of the Royal Anthropological Institute*, 1 (3) pp. 495–512.

McGuigan, J. (1992) *Cultural Populism*. London: Routledge.

Malinowski, B. (1922) *Argonauts of the Western Pacific*. London: Routledge and Keegan Paul.

—— (1938) 'Essay', in Tom Harrisson and Charles Madge, *First Year's Work*. London: Lindsey Drummond.

—— (1988 [1967]) *A Diary in the Strict Sense of the Term*. London: Athlone.

Marcus, G. and Fisher, M. (1986) *Anthropology as Cultural Critique*. Chicago: University of Chicago Press.

Mass-Observation (1939) *Britain*. Harmondsworth: Penguin.

Pool, R. (1991) 'Postmodern Ethnography?', *Critique of Anthropology* 11 (4) pp. 309–31.

Richards, J. and Sheridan, D. (eds) (1987) *Mass-Observation at the Movies*. London: Routledge.

Rivers, W.H R. (1914) *History of Melanesian Society*. Cambridge: Cambridge University Press.

Rosaldo, R. (1986) 'From the Door of his Tent: The Fieldworker and the Inquisitor', in J. Clifford and G. Marcus (eds) *Writing Culture*. Berkeley: University of California Press.

Scholte, B. (1987) 'The Literary Turn in Anthropology', *Critique of Anthropology* 7 (1) pp. 33–47.

Scott, D. (1992) 'Criticism and Culture: Theory and Post-colonial Claims on Anthropological Disciplinarity', *Critique of Anthropology*, 12 (4) pp. 371–94.

Shostak, M. (1983) *Nisa!* Cambridge, MA: Harvard University Press.

Stanton, G. (1996) 'Anthropology, Ethnology and Cultural Studies: Some Links and Connections', in J. Curran, D. Morley and V. Walkerdine (eds) *Cultural Studies and Communications*. London: Edward Arnold.

Stocking, G. (ed.) (1986) *Malinowski, Rivers, Benedict and Others: Essays on Culture and Personality*. Madison: University of Wisconsin Press.

—— (ed.) (1989) *Romantic Motives: Essays on Anthropological Sensibility*. Madison: University of Wisconsin Press

Thomas, N. (1994) *Colonialism's Culture*. Cambridge: Polity Press.

Tyler, S. (1987) 'Still Rayting', *Critique of Anthropology* 7 (1) pp. 49–51.

Williams, R. (1958) *Culture and Society*. London: Chatto and Windus.

Wolf, E. (1982) *Europe and the People Without History*. Berkeley: University of California Press.

Young, M. (ed.) (1979) *The Ethnography of Malinowski: the Trobriand Islands 1915–18*. London: Routledge.

## 3 'THE LION OF LAHORE': ANTHROPOLOGY, CULTURAL PERFORMANCE AND IMRAN KHAN
*Pnina Werbner*

### ANTHROPOLOGY AND CULTURAL STUDIES

The politics of difference – the essential object of cultural studies – also defines the contested terrain in which anthropology, deprived of its monopoly over culture, struggles to recover its own authenticities. Rather than re-enact this ritualised contest, however, I want to begin the present chapter by stressing not the differences between anthropology and cultural studies, but their affinities: the common discursive ground they potentially share. Of course, cultural studies is not one thing only: the theoretical impulse which guided cultural studies at Birmingham, under the directorship of Stuart Hall, has been increasingly obscured by the discipline's successful export to the USA. As a British product which has travelled, it has attracted many companions, from post-structuralism to feminist theory, to be reborn again as a massive academic movement. The discourses developed originally in Birmingham, modified in the course of this transplantation, have been fractured and transmogrified in this engagement with 'New Times'; with the postmodernist, feminist, postcolonial and deconstructive critical moment.

Two things need to be noted here: first, the theoretical underpinnings of both Cultural Studies Mark 1 and Cultural Studies Mark 2 are Continental and primarily French. Second, although Stuart Hall has in the meanwhile moved to the Open University, he continues to articulate what is best about this ever-changing field of discourse (for his own reflections see Hall 1992, 1996). In addition to Hall, two recent British exports to the USA, Paul Gilroy and Homi Bhabha, have gained an ascendant influence, while the boundaries between postcolonial and cultural studies have become increasingly blurred.

In this evolving field, the contested terrain that anthropology and cultural studies occupy is divided by different approaches to both method and writing. What we study, how we study and how we represent what we study are all at stake. And it is around the problem of how we study cultural events and performances, the theoretical tools we bring to bear on these performances, that I focus in the second half of the chapter. My chosen performance is cricket or, more specifically, Pakistani diasporic enthusiasm for cricket and for its iconic representation: Imran Khan, a charismatic figure with a mysteriously global appeal.

Historically, the CCCS under Stuart Hall was grappling with post-Marxist theory. In rejecting simplistic notions of base–superstructure and ideology-as-mystification, it drew upon Gramsci's theoretical critique of Marxism in his *Prison Notebooks* (1971). It joined this reconceptualisation of Marx with Roland Barthes' Marxist/structuralist, semiotic approach to the analysis of popular culture as a series of signifying practices. Culture was, in the Gramscian sense, a 'contested terrain' in which a 'war of positions' took place in 'civil society' for 'hegemony'. This war of positions included not the whole working class, defined in economic terms as the class exploited by capitalists, but 'class fractions' – youth, women, ethnic groups and so forth. 'Hegemony' was ideology which had become 'commonsensical', no longer openly coercive or the explicit political agenda of a single group, but organically embedded in a taken-for-granted way in everyday practices. So the war of positions was between class fractions using signifying practices to define themselves by contrast to current hegemonic discourses controlled by dominant class fractions. Through these signifying practices, exploited groups 'resisted' domination and subordination. In cultural studies discourse, the tools of this resistance were popular cultural, a subversive bricolage which utilised the 'bric-a-brac' of consumer society to invert 'magically' the hegemonic cultural message.[1]

A further feature of this Gramscian theoretical phase related to the notion of 'the organic crisis', the interregnums which Gramsci regarded as moments when the dominant forces were threatened by a workers' alliance and resorted to repressive measures to shore up their control. Each class, according to Gramsci, has its own 'organic' intellectuals who play a role in the organisation of society. The intellectuals of the capitalist class – cultural producers, technocrats and civil servants – act as its agents in sustaining elite hegemony in civil society and the state. Against these intellectuals, the working class has to create its own intellectuals, able to reach out and articulate the popular interests of the workers. Organic intellectuals thus transcend their class to build up effective alliances or blocs, challenging or sustaining a current hegemony (Simon 1982: Chapters 12 and 13).

This was the original framework within which the Birmingham Centre operated. It is reflected in Dick Hebdige's *Subculture* (1979), in *The Empire Strikes Back* (CCSS 1982), and in a very fine book on modern sport as popular culture considered here, *Sport, Power and Culture* by John Hargreaves (1986), which forms the cultural studies' backdrop to my discussion of cricket as performance. A further book *Policing the Crisis: Mugging the State and Law and Order* (Hall et al. 1978), although in my estimation the most important to come out of Birmingham, has received far less recognition by anthropologists. I return to this book below because it also relates directly to the question of cultural performance.

It is interesting that during this key formative period, from 1976, when *Resistance through Rituals* (Hall and Jefferson 1976) came out, until 1982, when *The Empire Strikes Back* was first published, the Centre appeared to have almost no awareness at all of the works of Michel Foucault or Mikhail Bakhtin. Althusser, Gramsci and Roland Barthes, along with various European Marxists, were its intellectual heroes. Foucault is mentioned once, in passing, in the introduction to *The Empire Strikes Back*, although his work was published in English from 1967 onwards, with *The Archaeology of Knowledge* coming out in 1972. It was Edward Said, in *Orientalism*, who first seemed to draw attention to the close theoretical resemblance between Gramsci's notion of 'hegemony' and Foucault's notion of 'discourse' or, more accurately, his notion of 'discursive formation'. Hence Said talks of 'the persistence and durability of saturating hegemonic systems like culture', a feature which he recognises that both Foucault and Gramsci, among others, want to illuminate (Said 1979: 14).

The resemblance between Gramsci's notion of 'hegemony' and Foucault's notion of 'discourse' within a discursive formation is striking. For both, the concern is with a dominant ideology – whether political or academic – which becomes progressively commonsensical and taken for granted, inscribed in practice, all-pervasive, embodied in institutions and in what Foucault calls 'technologies of power' which reproduce this discourse. For both Gramsci and Foucault, hegemonic discourses are seen to persist for very long periods of time as cultural givens of a taken-for-granted social order. Change is thus defined by both theorists as very unusual, highly disruptive, crisis-ridden and leading to a totally new order. Neither thinker proposes a theory of gradual change, of slow evolution or development. Social life is conceived of by Gramsci as an attempt to build up a network of cultural resistances, mostly unsuccessful, which may lead ultimately to revolution, and by Foucault as arguments within a discourse, the terms and concepts of which are altered only very occasionally, for historical reasons mainly to do with the rise of capitalism. Hence the problem for both scholars is to understand the 'structure of the conjuncture', the moment of paradigmatic shift.

I stress the affinity between the positions of these two thinkers because I believe that their notions of hegemony and discursive formation also bear affinity with Durkheimian assumptions about normativity and social control as underpinning structural continuities, produced by the interdependence of the social and the cultural. Against such monological approaches in anthropology, symbolic interactionist and phenomenological theories, derived especially from Alfred Schutz, defined common-sense knowledge as fragmentary, situational and inconsistent. Both these orientations have in one way or another implicitly guided the anthropological project since *Azande Witchcraft* and *The Nuer* (Evans-Pritchard 1940, 1976).

In anthropology, the problem of power and resistance was theorised by Gluckman in his essay on rituals of rebellion, grasped as cultural performances which articulated potential lines of social fissure, enacted in a ritual cycle of perennial resistance ('rebellion'). As in the Gramscian and Foucauldian versions, rebellion differed from revolution in that it sustained (or at any rate failed to undermine) relatively enduring social formations (Gluckman 1963: Chapter 3). From a different perspective, Bourdieu's ethnography of the Kabylia attempted to locate power struggles and individual strategising ('practice') within a French structuralist analysis of Kabylia culture and organisation which, again, was represented as inscribed bodily and relatively unchanging (Bourdieu 1977). Not surprisingly, given these pre-existing affinities to cultural studies, a whole literature of cultural resistance sprang up in the 1980s in anthropology. The best of that literature, however, went far beyond cultural studies.

The discursive space created by Gramsci's and Foucault's theories, potentially shared by social anthropology along with cultural studies, has been further expanded by postmodernist and deconstructive approaches brought into cultural studies through feminist critical writings.

Feminists drew on Foucault's work primarily in order to stress the constructed nature of cultural and linguistic categories, labellings, subjectivities, identities and modes of power – even those ostensibly describing natural or biological processes. Male dominance was the product of hegemonic constructions of gender, inscribed in the body and embedded in patriarchal relations of power and the domestic division of labour. This led to two further concepts which have become central to cultural studies. The first is the concept of 'subject positioning' and the second, the proposition that the 'personal is the political'. These conceptual additions to the cultural studies armoury were not entirely novel: they paralleled the Gramscian-inspired interest in the war of positions, in cultural politics and in culture as a contested terrain. The feminist-inspired shift has been from 'cultural politics' to 'identity politics' and with it has come also a Lacanian problematising of identity formation and a deconstructive questioning of essentialising discourses and labels (see Fuss 1990).

In anthropology, questions of moral personhood, the self and collective identity were first outlined by Marcel Mauss (1985 [1938]). In *Naven* (1958 [1936]), a study of ritual performance in New Guinea, Gregory Bateson highlighted the ambivalences of gender, sexuality, power and the nature of sociocultural interpretation, which have received renewed impetus in the discipline. From a materialist perspective on culture and power, Abner Cohen's work on political ethnicity anticipated some of the current discussions of cultural and identity politics (see Werbner 1996c). Once again, then, we find anthropology and cultural studies occupying a shared discursive space and, as in the debate on 'culture', here too the Foucauldian and psychoanalytic theorising of cultural definitions of personhood, identity, gender and sexuality as imposed, essentialising and often marginalising constructions, have challenged anthropologists to deconstruct unexamined dogmas.

What, then, is the difference in theory and practice between anthropology and cultural studies? In order to begin to answer this question, we need to make a further theoretical detour and examine the issue of text and textualisation. One of the distinctive features of cultural studies has been the preoccupation with texts – both literary texts, usually by contemporary novelists (preferably Third World, black or female authors), but also with all other forms of media – cinema, television, popular music, and sites of consumption such as malls or supermarkets, as well as with the signifying practices of youth, immigrant, gay, lesbian and other subcultures of marginalised social groups. The works of Roland Barthes, Paul Ricoeur and Jacques Derrida have liberated the 'text' from its moorings in the written word. Anything, any set of symbols, objects or actions serving as diacritical emblems to mark sociocultural difference, can be conceived of as a 'text' to be studied. The sudden abundance of new 'textual' material has released English and history departments from the shackles of a classical canon and enabled doctoral students to interrogate all the multifarious manifestations of contemporary culture.

This globalising textualisation, coupled with a Foucauldian/Lacanian stress on subjection, only served, however, to undermine any vestigial notions of agency contained in the notion of 'resistance'. Thus Gilroy speaks of an 'all-encompassing textuality' as spelling the 'death (by fragmentation) of the subject' and evacuating 'the problem of human agency' (1993: 77). Echoing this concern, Hall criticises the early Foucault for his inability to theorise resistance (1996: 11), that is, the capacity of subjects to produce the self as an object in the world within and *despite* normative regulation (ibid.: 12–13). Yet, the place of cultural performance is apparently revived by the later Foucault who envisages subjectivity as an 'aesthetics of existence', 'a kind of *performativity*' (ibid.: original emphasis).


THE REDUCTION OF PERFORMANCE

Yet despite its focus on texts, performances and signifying practices, and despite its theoretical elaboration, when it comes to cultural performance, it is anthropological works which set the pace. Cultural studies lacks a sophisticated sociological theory of action, emotion, power and authority, or of localised structures and transformative processes.

The grand narrative of industrial capitalism and modernity (and recently, postmodernity) provides the fundamental framework for analysis. The gap between the study of a text – that is, of signifying practices – and the social *explanation* of the text, its imputed sociological groundings, is thus necessarily bridged (despite disclaimers) by the basic Western modernist categories of 'class', 'race', 'gender' and 'nation', as self-evident markers of inequality and subordination. Here critical theorists revert to their Marxist origins with a concession made in the direction of ethnic and other marginalised groups.

Initially, of course, the Birmingham Centre for Contemporary Cultural Studies denied the power of ethnicity altogether, except as a white divisive strategy, and glorified instead the culture of the working classes. But as the list of subcultures recognised as authentic expressions of oppression expanded, ethnicity was reinstated as a social factor (for a discussion see Werbner, 1997a), and even more so since the migration of the discipline to America. Nevertheless, at its most reductive, the social cosmology of critical cultural theory remains materialist and Manichean: the implicit assumption persists that the genesis of all social texts is a singular dichotomy between, on the one hand, a hegemonic alliance of elites – capitalists, the bourgeoisie, international finance, ex-colonials, imperialists and white racists, usually lumped together; and, on the other hand, the working class and various subordinated gendered ethnic and postcolonial minorities. The presumed and unexamined motor of social action is Hobbesian self-interest (of the capitalists); the implicit theory behind the majority of studies that of maximising man. Social structure is defined by class, race and gender. The 'nation' is either an epiphenomenon of class and race within an international division of labour or, more subtly, as in Homi Bhabha's work, the liminal site of struggle between a hegemonic class and groups on its margins (Bhabha 1994: Chapter 8). Women, black people, ethnics and youth produce the counternarratives which fracture imaginatively the apparent homogeneity of the nation. Hence, ultimately, there are only three fundamental sociological parameters deemed relevant to the cultural interpretation of texts as positioned performances. According to such interpretations, subordinated groups are defined oppositionally; their cultural products are rarely if ever autonomous – their role is deconstructive rather than originary; they are merely, to cite Dick Hebdige (1979), 'subversive bricoleurs'.

Cultural studies is in constant danger of retelling the same narrative, an allegory of resistance to cultural domination which is also material exploitation, again and again and again. Such a danger can only be averted, as we shall see in Hargreaves's study, by drawing on alternative aesthetic theories to explain the cross-cutting ties that link elite and working-class fractions. But these theoretical borrowings underline the limitations of a Marxist aesthetics and its inability to theorise creativity (except as inversion) or the powerful ludic, symbolic and emotional underpinnings of culture as performance.

A focus on cultural studies' repetitive allegory of resistance provides the key to the irreducible gap between it and anthropology. Since anthropology's main work has been outside the industrial West, the discipline does not take social structure as a pre-given. On the contrary, the challenge anthropologists face is how to figure out the historical and cultural specificities of social organisation and sociality in any given, culturally distinct, locale. What are the unique terms of power, authority and value used by the people themselves? To answer this question requires a disclosure, first, of how cultural difference is celebrated, controlled, determined or constructed; and second, what concepts, rituals, events, modes of living, underpin authority and official discourses, as against unofficial and subversive discourses. What are the limits of power and social control? Who determines those limits? The study of cultural performance for anthropologists is a means towards recovering the very terms of struggle that produce and reproduce solidarities and inequalities. Some of these terms, 'caste', the 'gift', 'acephalous societies', develop into analytical substantives that 'travel', precisely because they appear to capture something antithetical to or beyond the West (see Strathern 1988).

Hence a cultural performance for an anthropologist, rather than being merely a cultural code to be deciphered in terms of the articulation (interpellation, suturing) of a pre-given set of categories – class, gender, race, nation – can only be understood in its full specificity once its intertextuality, that is, its placement within a wider context of other cultural performances in the same cultural locale, can be established. All those varied and different cultural performances, seen together, juxtaposed and contrasted, allow anthropologists to recover the unique heteroglossia of a particular field of action. Cultural performances are thus both creative and reflexive. While Fabian is right to propose that 'performance is the text at the moment of its actualisation' *not* a reflection of a pre-given social structure (1990: 9), this fails to acknowledge the further point that no single cultural performance makes sense outside the microhistory of other, related performances. Such a chain of performances is rarely reducible to race, gender or class in their multifarious disguises.


## SHIFTING SITUATIONS

I am aware, of course, of anticipating here a whole theoretical debate within anthropology itself. Before going on to talk about the cultural performances of diasporic cricket and Imran Khan, I want to draw attention to one further critical difference between cultural studies and anthropology or sociology, which I believe is often overlooked, and which relates crucially to the study of cultural performance.

One of the important conceptual tools of anthropological analysis, at least since *Azande Witchcraft* (1976), has been a recognition of the situational framing of cultural action. Both the analysis of cultural discourses in anthropology, and the analysis of performance, hinge on notions of situationalism – segmentary opposition, situational selection, shifting roles or identities, cross-cutting ties. Evans-Pritchard's early work was paralleled by Gluckman's *Social Situation in Modern Zululand* (1958 [1942]), an analysis of a situationally framed interracial encounter, and the subsequent development of the extended case method by the Manchester School. Pushed to its ultimate logic by Victor Turner's model of the social drama, this became one strand in an anthropo-logical theory of performance (on this and on Gluckman's essay see Parkin 1996: xvii). Gregory Bateson's work on enframing (1958 and 1973) and Goffman's on 'Encounters' (1961 see also McHugh 1968) later on pointed to some of the problematics of treating situations as givens. Social situations, these later works argued, were defined through contestation by interested parties. But the importance of the attention to social situations as the basic unit of social action was that it allowed for an analysis of broader complex and multiplex forms of social organisation; it allowed for the fact that collective identities were segmental and conflicting, that opponents in one context might be allies in another. It explained why common-sense notions and discourses are inconsistent and contradictory, and how they are reproduced despite, and indeed because of, these inconsistencies. It revealed the way that official ideologies could coexist with unofficial practices. It analysed how new cultural ideas could be produced and reproduced, not merely through sudden ruptures but through cumulative change over time. The work in anthropology paralleled work in sociology by symbolic interactionists and ethnomethodologists.

An important feature of situationalism was the fact that certain facets of a person's identity could be highlighted in one context, suppressed in another. Indeed, this was the theoretical basis for the possibility of institutional analysis of simple societies, where social relations were characteristically multiplex. A recent re-working of this position by Marilyn Strathern reconceptualises this situationalism from the perspective of ethnographic description itself as a matter of figure and ground (Strathern 1991). What is highlighted, objectified, configured, in one context, is suppressed in another. To my mind, this insight into the predictable fluidity and flexibility of social life – as well as of ethnographic description – is absent from cultural studies. Subject positioning (however multiple) is seen as ultimately fixed within a field of power and defined by the exclusive quadratic categories of race–gender–class–nation. In response to the feminist/minority rhetorical stress on fractured identities, the emphasis has shifted to ambivalence and hybridity (see my discussion in Werbner, 1997a and 1997b). But this masks a persistent tendency to rank identities within a logic of encompassment, a hierarchy of subordinations.

Dumont's (1972) analytic insight into the relation between segmentary opposition and value, which he terms 'encompassment', placed situationalism within a field of power relations or status differentials. Hence, if we take cultural studies as an example, cultural studies theorists work with a fixed idea of the encompassment, in descending order, of class, race and gender (see Figure 3.1). According to this logic, class (wealth, status, political power) is the principal determining value, followed by race (white), and gender (male). Ambivalent conjunctions are sometimes possible: an upper-class white woman may dominate a white, working-class man. But the impossibility of a black upper-class man's dominance is signified in white working-class racism, while the domination by an upper-class black woman of a white, working-class man is simply glossed as an impossible conjunction. The central thesis is that an upper-class white male is dominant in all situations while a working-class black female is always the victim. This is exemplified by Hargreaves's well-documented historical analysis of

popular sport in Britain, which traces the rise to dominance of the
English bourgeois classes over the working classes, of men over women
within the working class, and of working-class exclusions of ethnic
minorities in the name of a local patriotism (Hargreaves 1986:
Chapter 5).

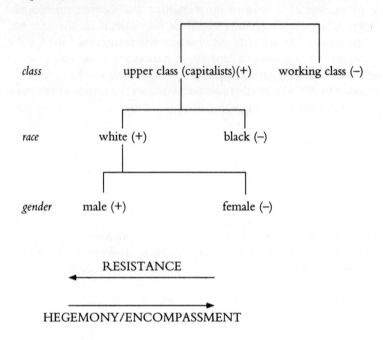

*Figure 3.1: The Structural Logic of Cultural Studies*

The logic of encompassment also signals the direction of oppositional
resistance. It further explains why Evans-Pritchard, an exemplary
'pure' white, upper-class male, is singled out in anthropological cultural
studies' discourses as the symbol of colonial oppression.

What needs to be recognised here, however, is that 'class', 'race',
'masculinity' (or 'femininity') and 'nation' may not be neutral discursive
constructs or analytic terms; they bear a historical legacy which makes
them deeply emotional labels of identity and non-identity. This was
made evident in the Ian Botham and Alan Lamb versus Imran Khan
libel case which took place in July 1996. The ambiguous status of an

upper-class black man who takes on an (ex-) working-class white man animated the case, not analytically but *emotionally*. In the words of Khan's defending QC, the case was 'emotionally charged. Issues of race, class and country move in and out like black clouds' (Engel 1996). Imran Khan, the upper-caste, Oxbridge 'Paki', was alleged to have said, alluding to Botham, that 'The difference in class and upbringing makes a difference. . . Look at those that have taken the rational side in the controversy [over the supposed cricket-ball 'scratching' by members of the Pakistani team and whether this counted as 'cheating']. . . They are all educated Oxbridge types' (Mark 1996: 17). As Mark argues:

By introducing 'class' and 'upbringing' into the ball tampering debate, Imran hinted that the old divisions [between amateur 'gentlemen' and professional 'players'] in English cricket still remain. (ibid.)

But Mark also recognises that:

the proud Pathan of an independent nation, mindful of past indignities on and off the cricket field, cannot bring himself to offer the unconditional apology that would have been automatic 60 years ago (ibid.)

(In actual fact, Khan had offered an apology, claiming he was misquoted in the press, but this was rejected by Botham [Chaudhary 1996].)

The fence-sitting posture and sarcastic tone adopted by the journalists reporting on the trial indicates how difficult it is for 'the English' to identify the true victim when class and race are no longer homologous. Class encompasses race hierarchically: in a kind of reverse snobbery, not a single journalist felt able to defend Imran Khan, too obviously the self-conscious aristocrat among the litigants, or celebrate his victory. Instead, it was glossed as 'something of a mystery', a tribute to the 'acting' skills of his QC, to his wife's superior fashion-sense or his clean-shaven appearance (juries, it seems, hate moustaches). Yet he was quite clearly the innocent victim who throughout had sought reconciliation and tried to avoid a trial he saw as a sad and costly 'exercise in futility'.

Class, race, gender, nation are emotionally charged cultural constructs which motivate people to action. Treated as analytic terms they become stop words which block analysis, obscuring the fact that at stake in this particular trial, for example, were serious legal, aesthetic and moral questions. These concerned not only emotive issues of identity but the limits of public debate, relations between competitors on and off the cricket field, culturally legitimate expressions of masculine conviviality, enjoyment and 'fun', and how to interpret the novel aesthetics of a ball that veers unpredictably off-course midway in flight, defying the laws of nature. Yet the complex implications of the trial were barely touched on by commentators. In their invocations of class–race–gender–nation they revealed their inability to disentangle their own feelings about these terms from the facts of the case itself, that the resistance to the logic of encompassment outlined here was one they shared with the protagonists.

## INTERPRETING PERFORMANCE: CRICKETMANIA AND IMRAN KHAN

The study of sport as performance lends itself to this logic of encompassment, but it also demonstrates the affinities between anthropology and cultural studies. John Hargreaves introduces his study by emphasising that a sporting encounter is an aesthetic performance which subsumes power, leadership, individuality, self-control, fair play, killer instincts, stamina and perseverance within a single dramatic space. Borrowing explicitly from Victor Turner and Mary Douglas, he defines sport as a highly ritualised form of popular theatre in which 'both players and audience can project their thoughts and feelings' (1986: 12). The symbols of sport are powerfully condensed and multivocal, narrating success and failure, good and evil. Sport is often, indeed, a 'political ritual' (ibid.) in which the body and its attributes are the most striking symbol of all (ibid.: 13). Not only does the body symbolise power but, Hargreaves proposes, 'power is literally incorporated or invested in the body' (ibid.). Moreover, the body in sport epitomises social conflict because sport is 'the site of social struggles' (ibid.). At the same time, 'the ludic element is inherently irreducible to programming for profit and control purposes. . . The ritualistic and dramatic character of sport is delicately constructed and does not automatically reproduce social relations' (ibid.: 222).

This recognisably anthropological stress on the power of symbols, set out in the introduction and conclusion, is, however, almost entirely divorced from the book's middle: a fine-grained analysis of the civilising process through which sport as culture was manipulated by bourgeois elites in order to draw working-class fractions into a hegemonic social order – by disciplining their bodies and controlling their leisure regimes in tandem with their work regimes. This is cultural studies at its very best: a social history of sport as popular culture which draws its inspiration not only from Gramsci and Foucault but from E.P. Thompson, Eric Hobsbawn and Raymond Williams, the ancestral founding fathers of cultural studies; a fascinating account of how sport in Britain comes to be articulated with class, gender, race and nation after the Industrial Revolution as a consequence of the reforming zeal of the new bourgeoisie. Within this account, culture is entirely subordinated to the materiality of capitalist production. Despite the disclaimers at the beginning and the end of the book, then, the analysis obscures rather than highlights the fact that the aesthetic is never fully reducible to the political. This reductive tendency is equally apparent in the Marxist aesthetics of Pierre Bourdieu, for example. What such an aesthetics cannot explain is why ritual and play become the sites of power struggles for control in the first place. As Geertz argued in relation to the Balinese cockfight (Geertz 1973), an aesthetic performance may move experientially and heighten consciousness without necessarily *doing* anything at all.

To explain diasporic Pakistanis' cricketmania for their national team or Imran Khan's charismatic appeal, one must start from that moment of identification with the team and its hero. In two recent papers (Werbner 1996a, 1996b) I argue that Imran Khan objectifies a peculiarly South Asian and Islamic idea: that of the exemplary person, and that he has fostered this image through what I propose to call here a Sufi critical discourse (on this discourse see Werbner 1995). Like the sportsman, the Sufi saint is an ascetic who, it is believed, has gained total control over his body, so much so that his body does not disintegrate at his death. His embodied self-denial 'opens' him up to divine knowledge which is thus embodied knowledge. World-renouncers in South Asia stand above and beyond politics or scholastic knowledge, and hence they claim the right to criticise elites and corrupt politicians (ibid.: 149–50). Theirs is, above all, a dissenting role. But this status of exemplary personhood, of cultural iconicity, is also granted to unique others. For example, Muhammad Ali Jinnah, Quaid-i-Azam, the Great Leader, founder of Pakistan, was described in Pakistani diasporic public meetings in Manchester as a man preordained before birth to accomplish the redemption of the Muslims of South Asia. In demonstrating his moral exceptionality, his physical courage was repeatedly stressed (see Werbner 1990a): he persisted with the battle to create Pakistan despite his knowledge, which he kept from the British, that he was dying of tuberculosis.

To gain the aura of a saint obviously thus requires more than physical genius on the cricket field. Yet Imran Khan was, from the start of my fieldwork, a celebrity and a star; an object of desire, tough, sexy, incredibly handsome. The cultural performances which gave me some insight into the special place cricket occupies for diasporic Pakistanis were public functions held in his honour or in honour of the national cricket team he captained. At the time he was also a county cricket player for Worcestershire. The first of these functions, a benefit dinner, was organised by two young Pakistani men. The second two performances, which took place several years later, were initiated by Imran Khan himself in his fund-raising drive for a cancer hospital in Lahore. This Imran Khan 'roadshow' included not only Khan himself but a whole posse of international film stars and entertainers.

Seen from a cultural studies perspective, there were obvious reasons for the wild enthusiasm for cricket stars which the visits to Manchester generated. The green Pakistani flags waved by youngsters during and after matches, the shouts of 'Pakistan' or 'Islam *zindabad*', live forever, the widespread subscription of diaspora Pakistanis to satellite stations broadcasting live international cricket, the development of Pakistani cricket leagues in several big cities in Britain, all highlight the link between cricket and nationalism which undoubtedly animates this adulation. In cultural studies phraseology, diasporic Pakistanis, positioned as working-class black males, deploy cricket (popular culture) to invert magically a hegemonic social order. The crackdown on this subversive bricolage by the dominant classes (white and male) was first signalled in an infamous speech by the Conservative MP, Norman Tebbit, in which he denied the right of British Asians to support their national teams. This was followed by media accusations of bribe-taking and ball-tampering by Pakistani international players; by an article in a long-established cricket weekly alleging the lack of commitment of (black) 'foreign' players for England; and finally, by the prohibition of green flags during matches. Additionally, of course, the triumphant winning by the Pakistani national team of the World Cup in Sydney, in 1992, can be conceived of in cultural studies terms as another inversion of the directionality of dominance. The empire had, quite literally, struck back.

The fundamental logic informing such an analysis is that of inversion: the new working-class Pakistani cricket patriotism reverses the terms created by their colonial and postcolonial masters, in a subversive postcolonial cultural bricolage. Hence cricket signals, simultaneously, both resistance and continued oppression.

Within these terms, the explanation for Imran Khan's charismatic appeal – both to his own people and to a wider Western public (as evidenced by the international media coverage he receives) remains, however, uncertain. One possible interpretation is to construct the ex-cricketer as a brown sahib, a product of empire (like Pakistani cricket itself). This interpretation fits well with the modernist narratives of empire, sport and cricket, exemplified in a whole series of studies. These focus on the conjuncture of sport, masculinity, class leadership and empire. Hence a cultural studies gaze upon Imran Khan would immediately recognise him as a *hybrid* subject, a typical product of empire.

Ashis Nandy's analysis of imperial masculinities underlines this conjuncture. He argues that imperial rule exaggerated a stress on masculinity implicit in the cultures of both English colonisers and Indian colonised. As a result, the Indian privileging of androgyny above masculinity (exemplified in the special status of gurus and spiritual men) was overturned, whereas the English Christian gentlemen who ruled the British empire were trained to deny their feminine side (Nandy 1983). Augmenting this view, Helen Kanitkar analyses the Victorian masculinities that produced these gentlemen fit to rule. She reports that Jawaharlal Nehru, the first Prime Minister of India, who went to Harrow, was advised by his father to learn to shoot, play cricket and ride (Kanitkar 1994: 186). The English sportsman was seen to be a man of honour (ibid.: 188), who takes risk in the call of duty (ibid.: 189). He is superior by class and race, selflessly bringing order and a sense of fair play to places of wild barbarism (ibid.: 191). He is imbued with a noble spirit of generosity for the poor and low castes (ibid.: 195). And, according to Kanitkar, although superficially, styles of masculinity have undoubtedly changed, these valorised representations of hegemonic masculinity continue to be 'rooted and reworked on the rugby field, in the club and around the boardroom table' even to this day (ibid.: 195).

As Hargreaves too notes, public school sports such as cricket and rugby, introduced in the 1830s:

incorporated a new demanding version of *noblesse oblige*: the new notion of service required those who were privileged to earn the position by paying continuous attention to duty and by displaying ordered, disciplined, restrained conduct as an example to the lower orders. (1986: 39)

The values associated with the civilising mission were 'loyalty, *esprit de corps*, self-sacrifice. . . moral excellence' (ibid.: 39–40), in what amounted to a 'cult of athleticism' (ibid.: 41). As Peter Parkes reports in his account of the transformation of polo during the colonial era, by 'civilising' the indigenous game, the English also created a hierarchical order which 'irrevocably divided the [indigenous] elites from their barely literate relatives' (Parkes 1996: 62).

What is important for our purpose here is that the narrative of empire, cricket, male dominance and the rise of the bourgeoisie is also a narrative of selfless *moral* dedication. Hence, In *Culture and Society*, Raymond Williams, one of the founding fathers of cultural studies, recalls his first encounter as a working-class lad with the English middle-class notion of service. With a touch of ironic wonder he comments that a 'large part of English middle class education is devoted to the training of servants' (1992: 329), an ideal of service he contrasts with the working-class ideal of solidarity. The service ethic trains a man 'not to think of his own interests. He must subordinate these to a larger good' (ibid.: 309). Ultimately, however, service exists within a 'larger selfishness', so that although the English ethic has been 'a major achievement which has done much for the peace and welfare of society' (ibid.: 328), it nevertheless serves also to perpetuate inequalities.

One possible explanation of the charismatic appeal of Imran Khan for both English and Pakistanis may thus be the way in which he epitomises these Victorian values. Indeed, in a recent book on empire and the imagining of masculinities, Graham Dawson traces the canonisation of Sir Henry Havelock, the British commander who repelled the Indian rebellion of 1857, as an English Christian saint-martyr (Dawson 1994: 122–4) whose exemplary life is enshrined in a series of 'hagiographies' (Dawson 1994: 124 *passim*). But is this an adequate anthropological explanation? To pursue this question fully, let me return first to the cultural performances I witnessed.

The intense competition between youth and elders to host the cricketer revealed cultural ideas among diasporic Pakistanis regarding elderhood and the rights associated with the status of being an elder.

There was also competition between different local elites to host the cricketer, reflecting the division between Muslim religious and westernised businessmen – expressed in moral disagreements over approved modes of celebration. As an anthropologist, I found, therefore, that 'cricket' was indeed a contested cultural terrain, but not simply between black and white, male and female, upper and lower classes. The identities foregrounded in the battle to host Imran Khan were more complex and less oriented to postcoloniality *per se* than a cultural studies approach might anticipate. But the battle nevertheless did seem to have something to do with being a migrant in a foreign country, with being a Muslim in an anti-Muslim social environment.

One of the striking features of cricket is that it is a discourse that has 'travelled'; it no longer 'belongs' to England. Indeed, it is questionable whether young Pakistanis associate cricket with England at all. But it is, like the English language, a shared discourse of the Commonwealth. Above all, like moka in New Guinea or Potlatch for the Kwakiutl, the game of cricket as a performance allows players and their supporters to humiliate an opponent utterly and totally without shedding any blood. Cricket, in other words, may be a substitute for war (although sometimes, as Jeremy MacClancy has pointed out in his introduction to *Sport, Identity and Ethnicity*, sporting contests may also be the *cause* of war [MacClancy 1996]). But beyond politics, it is also a form of aesthetic entertainment which is shared. This means that ordinary people, elites and working class alike, don't want to turn cricket into just one thing or another, to reduce it to politics. It is both shared and oppositional; a form of resistance against racist British domination or Islamophobia but also a bridge between communities, between Pakistanis, Indians, West Indians and the English. What is foregrounded from one perspective is situationally suppressed from another. Moreover, cricket allows for internal competition at the same time as it celebrates Pakistani and Muslim national identities. So it highlights identities situationally. Class is encompassed by ethnicity and not vice versa. But is this really so?

What would a cultural studies scholar make of Imran Khan himself? He is an upper-class, upper caste, black male. The ambiguity is compounded by his (past) reputation as a playboy, his numerous girlfriends (mostly white), his reputedly dissolute lifestyle and his pukka Oxbridge accent. His shock marriage to Jemima Goldsmith, one of the richest white (part-Jewish) multi-billionaire heiresses in

Britain, along with his born-again discovery of Islam, merely pile up
further layers of ambiguity. One possibility is to construct the cricketer
as a black with a white mask – a pretender, a hypocrite. This would
fit in well with our analysis of the creation of the Victorian gentleman.
Yet Khan's current transformation into a philanthropist, his apparent
embracing of Islam, the reputed Islamist connections of his new
political movement and his evident political ambitions – all these are
likely to create a problem for a postcolonial/cultural studies scholar.
Is he or she to privilege Khan's *class* membership or his racial identity?
If we choose to privilege class, the cricketer's roadshow has to be
interpreted as a manipulative charade staged by a man harbouring secret
ambitions to seize political power. By this interpretation most Pakistanis,
constructed as working-class black males, are blind victims, duped by
this black crossover, this brown sahib, who is really a stooge of the
West. The reverse option would be to construct Khan as a postcolonial
oppositional 'hybrid' hero returning to the fold through a conversion
process of self-realisation. This is becoming a more fashionable type
of interpretation for cultural studies, one which privileges postcolonial
identities (a version of race/nation) over class positioning. In this type
of interpretation all internal divisions within postcolonial/diasporic
societies are glossed over silently in order to stress the encounter with
the West. Appadurai's recent article on the indigenisation and verna-
culisation of cricket in India reflects this tendency (Appadurai 1995).
We find a similar kind of ambiguity in cultural studies analyses of the
Rushdie affair. Whereas some postcolonial scholars (such as Talal
Asad) condemn the author outright as a Western stooge (Asad 1993:
Chapter 8), others, mainly non-Muslims such as Homi Bhabha,
construct him as a postcolonial hero, but gloss silently over the attack
upon him by his fellow countrymen (Bhabha 1994: Chapter 11).
Either way, a theorisation of the complex divisions within ethnic
diasporas is evaded.

   Critical cultural studies, in other words, is not always very good at
dealing with apparent ambiguities in its essentialised social categories
of class, race and gender, despite its current stress on ambivalence
(Bhabha 1994). My own interpretation of Imran Khan's positioning
begins from an entirely different starting point. In order to understand
who Imran Khan is and was, I had to understand who his local
audience was and who the entertainers who came with him were. I
had to listen to the speeches, to take note of who was present and who
was absent. I had to record both the indexical dimensions of his visit,

that is, the power struggles over the right to host him, the whole razzmatazz of fund-raising as an index of status, and the symbolic and poetic dimensions of the event, seen as a cultural performance. I wanted to try to understand what identities were being projected by the audience and especially by speakers in this *particular* social situation, this particular historicised context; I had to try to establish what official discourses were enunciated, what unofficial symbolic modes of behaviour were allowed and how power and authority were constituted in this performance as against other performances I had witnessed.

Two things in particular intrigued me. The first, as already mentioned, was that Imran Khan was constructed by speakers as a Sufi saint – a 'friend' of God, pre-ordained for great deeds even before his birth. This meant that all his peccadilloes, his white girlfriends and nightclub crawling, were glossed over or joked about. Because of his philanthropic work, his selfless public service for the community (*khidmat* in Urdu), he was being reconstructed by speakers as an exemplary person, a leader who embodies the community in its moral perfection. I had heard similar rhetorical constructions of sufi saints but also of Quaid-i-Azam, Mohammad Ali Jinnah, the founder of Pakistan. The exemplar of all exemplars is, of course, for Pakistanis, as for all Muslims, the Prophet Muhammad, the 'perfect man', *insan el kamil*. I had come to the view that Pakistani political culture distinguishes between false politicians, the majority, and the exceptional leader who is conceived of as a redeemer. The cricket star, it was evident from the speeches, was being constructed in redemptive terms. When I read in the *Guardian* several years later that he was being defined as a saint and had embraced Islam I was not very surprised. The cultural performance in 1990, anticipated this personal, symbolic transformation. In a recent article in *The Times Higher* on the making of a film about Jinnah's life, the parallels between Imran Khan and the Quaid are explicitly drawn by Akbar Ahmed: 'Imran could achieve great things if he were to conform to the model of leadership epitomised by Mohammad Ali Jinnah' (Targett 1996: 15).

There was another feature of the event I witnessed, seen as a cultural performance, which intrigued me: some of the men present, who had paid large sums of money in order to be present, were the same men who, on other occasions, had been active participants in radical political Islamic meetings in the city. Recently, they had openly supported Saddam Hussein's invasion of Kuwait and calls for the death of Salman Rushdie. One might have expected them to disapprove of a performance which included whole families, men, women and children (including their own) and which tolerated instrumental music, singing, light-hearted joking and even discreet drinking of alcohol. It was an event, moreover, in which politicians and religious extremists were condemned (see Werbner 1996b). That all this was accepted as quite natural indicated the power of Imran Khan and the claque of Bombay film stars and entertainers he had brought along with him, to authorise and legitimise a hybrid synthesis of Islamic and South Asian popular culture. The official discourse of Islam encompassed South Asian dance, music and humour without being constructed as anti-Islamic. Moreover, the stress was on tolerance, internationalism and universal values. Yet when young men or women had tried in the past to convene such 'hybridised' events, they were castigated for being un-Islamic. Clearly, then, the legitimacy of discrepant discourses depends on the power of the convenor.

This type of analysis, stressing the indexical dimensions of cultural performance, and grounded in an 'ethnography of speaking' (Fabian 1990: 8), requires the kind of data and fieldwork which would, I think, be of very little interest to a cultural studies scholar; even worse, it would make him or her positively uneasy. Revealing internal divisions and discrepant discourses within a diasporic black or postcolonial community renders the primary identities – black–white, neocolonial oppressor–postcolonial oppressed – ambiguous. What is even more disconcerting is a focus on internal divisions which backgrounds the white neocolonial English altogether and creates a conceptual world in which they are rendered irrelevant. A sign of Paul Gilroy's integrity as a sociologist has been his willingness to tackle internal disagreements among black people over gender, emancipatory politics and the construction of ethnic authenticities, thus rejecting the defensive posture of 'cultural insiderism' (Gilroy 1993: 84) adopted by most postcolonial/cultural studies, Third World or black writers. The response of the editor of *Public Culture* to my paper on Pakistani cricket (which she rejected – it was later accepted by a sociology journal, see Werbner 1996b) was, however, a more predictable one of total incomprehension: she failed to see any point to an analysis of the religious politics of performance surrounding the cricketer's visit, and explained that the journal's purpose was to focus on the Western colonial/Third World colonised division. 'Public' culture was, it seems, restricted to this faultline. Imran Khan, represented as an indigenous Pakistani public figure or cultural icon, was of no interest.

There has, however, been a real change in cultural studies, associated with the work of Gilroy and of Homi Bhabha. Bhabha has introduced into cultural studies a rejection of all polarities which he views as always mediated by a third term, an in-between, liminal space that fractures and interrupts monological symbolic discourses (Bhabha 1994). In line with this stress on mediating polarities Dawson, for example, has argued that the adventurer heroes of the British empire need to be understood in the tension between pure masculinity and domesticity (Dawson 1994: 134–44). Seen from this sort of cultural studies perspective, Imran Khan constitutes and embodies the boundary, the space of liminality, the power of betwixt-and-between, of anomaly, crossover, hybridity, double consciousness. There are shades here, of course, of Victor Turner and Mary Douglas, as well as of Mikhail Bakhtin. The charismatic power of Imran Khan is the power of hybridity (on this power within the postmodern see Werbner, 1997b). The power of hybridity is embodied, to return to Foucault/Hall, in an aesthetic 'performativity of the self'. The ambivalence of the black sportsman for white viewers encapsulates a promise of pure power:

the black male body is a container of sexual desire, beauty, grace, portrayed in a rather animal-like manner. It is difficult to think of a white sportsman being filmed in such an erotic and beautiful manner. Is this a subtle kind of racism? (Horrocks 1995: 157).

## PERFORMANCE AND INTERTEXTUALITY

Of course, a cultural performance can be interpreted as a multiplicity of texts. The recognition of this fact has been one major anthropological advance since Clifford Geertz, inspired by Ricoeur, suggested that the Balinese cockfight could be interpreted as a 'text'. The problem with that essay was that the cockfight was essentialised as singular and repetitive; its indexical aspects were both asserted and ignored. It was construed as a paradigmatic event, beyond localised factional power struggles. What Geertz did importantly recognise, however, was its intertextuality: its experiential inversion of mundane reality. This was the source of its reflexivity. At the same time, what was obscured was the fact that the cockfight was also a symbolic and moral inversion of the Balinese temple rituals, seen as cultural performances. Appropriately, cockfights always preceded such rituals, with the slain cock constituting a sacrifice aimed at expelling demonic influences. Geertz, the anti-structuralist, preferred to see performances as comprising a loose 'library of texts'. More recent ethnographies, such as those of Lila Abu-Lughod or Janice Boddy, for example, demonstrate that cultural performances cannot be analysed in isolation: they constitute moral allegories or satirical commentaries about other cultural performances. Performances may be reflexive, conscious-raising events. But this is so precisely because discrepant discourses are connected and make sense only *vis-à-vis* one other. Hence, in her study of spirit possession in Northern Sudan, Boddy shows how through cultural performance women in the Sudan invert the official wedding ritual in order to reflect on and treat their disempowered position as too closed and pure (Boddy 1989). Similarly, Abu-Lughod shows how Bedouin unofficial poetic discourses of vulnerability highlight the fact that official Bedouin discourses of honour are voluntaristic and freely upheld (Abu-Lughod 1986). The complexity may be multiplied as, for example, in the case of Kalanga spirit possession, which inverts the terms of Kalanga sacrifice, itself a ritual containing anti-structural phases (Richard Werbner 1989).

What is evident from these examples is that the terms of performance, its sociological explanation, are culturally grounded and thus determined by the people themselves. The anthropologist must weave his or her analytic account into the conceptual framework that the people deploy, their own interpretations of their social world. To do so requires an intimate knowledge of the complex nature of social situations, the roles actors fulfil, their relative power in a local political arena and the signifying practices framing and marking their positions both in official and unofficial events and discourses. It is these arguments of identity between collective actors that animate performance. The end result of such an exposition is never simply reducible to essentialised categories of class–gender–race–nation or even to what is in between them. At the same time, because a performance is not one text but a multiplicity of texts, it can be interrogated from different perspectives. An example of this feature of performance is Alex Weingrod's fine study, *The Saint of Beersheba* (1990). Weingrod takes a single cultural event, the *hilula*, a commemoration of a Tunisian saint's death anniversary in modern Israel, and shows how it can be understood from different vantage points: in historical terms, as a variation on a more pervasive emergence of a cult of saints among North African Jewish immigrants to Israel; politically, as an expression of modern Israeli ethnicity; symbolically, as a contested ritual. In one of the classic monographs of the Birmingham Centre for Cultural Studies, *Policing the Crisis* (Hall et al. 1978) a single event, the mugging of an old man by two youths, is discussed as it is interpreted by the courts, the media, the police, the government – in other words, by all the forces of law and order. The book is modelled on Stanley Cohen's symbolic interactionist monograph, *On Folk Devils and Moral Panics*, which interrogates in similar fashion the clash on Brighton beach between mods and rockers (Cohen 1972).

The exercise reminds us of, but is not quite the same as, Bateson's experimental treatment of performance in *Naven* (1958 [1936]). What is shared is the fact that starting from a cultural performance is a strategy of textualising data which can reveal different perspectival ways of knowing: the complexity of social life is rendered transparent through analysis, as unlike allegories or conceptual vocabularies are brought to bear upon a single event.

Revealed, then, is a constant conceptual trafficking between cultural studies, literary criticism, psychoanalysis, philosophy, sociology and anthropology, which is both fertilising, but also oddly disturbing. Disturbing, because the political commitment of cultural studies to right the inequalities of race, class, gender and nation seems often to lead to a monochromatic world view which is disguised by conceptual complexity. The complexity arises from the need to grapple with ambiguities; these are constructed in Lacanian terms as the multiple subjectivities and subject positions from which the subject 'speaks' or 'reads' (see Fuss 1990: 33–4). But these multiple subjectivities/subject positions are always recognisably reducible to class–race–gender–nation, the cultural categories which have animated European societies since the advent of industrial capitalism.

This tendency towards sociological (if not psychological) reductiveness is highlighted by Aijaz Ahmad, the critical theorist, in a brilliantly lucid critique of Fredrick Jameson's proposal that all (sic!) Third World novels are 'nationalist allegories'. Reflecting on the Urdu critical-realist literary movement, Ahmad argues that although the movement did not ignore the 'Nation':

the categories one deployed for the sense of collectivity were complex and several, for what Critical Realism demanded was that a critique of others (anti-colonialism) be conducted in the perspective of an even more comprehensive, multifaceted critique of ourselves: our class structures, our familial ideologies, our management of bodies and sexualities, our idealisms, our silences. (Ahmad 1992: 118)

One scholar who has tried to walk the tightrope between critical theory and sociology has been Pierre Bourdieu and, despite some reservations about his work, it is worth examining his approach which seems to me to create a theoretical bridge via performance between anthropology and cultural studies. Bourdieu works with a metaphor of social 'space' as embodying social relations and modes of living or celebrating, and hence also as an expression of positioning, agency and identity, within and by contrast to a wider social field of competing interests, lifestyles and discourses. He argues that spaces, like people, cut across each other and are highlighted situationally. From my own point of view, as a student of immigrants, this conceptualising of social space allows for the possibility that new distinctive cultural spaces can be created and can be controlled autonomously by immigrants. In other words, the notion of space implies also a vector, a movement, a potentiality still to be realised. Unlike 'institutions', an analytical concept which seems to point to sets of relations which are unchanging and fixed, the metaphor of space evokes relations which have to be fought for and captured, constructed and defended. Moreover, the concrete embodiment of space is at once economic, political, ritual and so forth, an important feature of both simple societies and encapsulated immigrant groups, even if we do not accept totalising visions of the personal being the political.

Cultural performances create social spaces and are enabled by them. Imran Khan's roadshow created a new, distinctive, legitimate 'fun' space for fund-raising, philanthropy and popular culture which had not existed previously for Pakistani settlers in Britain, even though women and young men were struggling to create it. That space stood in marked contrast to the austere and puritanical spaces of political Islam in the city which were controlled by wealthy elders and religious experts. It challenged the hegemony of that particular perspective and lifestyle. The metaphor of space allows for a view of the social organisation of a society as determined not by fixed, unchanging categorical relations of class, ethnicity or gender, but of a constantly shifting constellation of culturally defined and valorised relations, alliances and oppositions. Rather than culture being merely a reflection of power or resistance to power, it can then be interrogated by anthropologists in its complex uniqueness, in terms of the categorical constructs deemed important by the people studied rather than those imposed upon other societies by academics located in the metropolitan centres of the West.

Imran Khan's charisma derived from his ability to create such a space for performance. This ability was rooted not in his 'hybridity', but in his tapping of authentically felt cultural sentiments. The key to Khan's charisma may thus lie in the East rather than the West, and in order to demonstrate this claim, I turn to Sara Dickey's fascinating anthropological study of Indian film star fan clubs in Tamil Nadu (Dickey 1993). As is well known, one of these film stars, M.G. Ramachandran, became a highly successful politician. Dickey's account returns us to the Sufi discourse of world-renouncers with its indigenous notions of dissent and service (*khidmat, sava* in Hindi). Fans described their stars as generous, courageous and powerful, as humble, strong and beautiful, stressing their physical brilliance and generosity of spirit (1993: 153, 155, 157).

Dickey shows, importantly, that the link between aesthetics and politics in Tamil Nadu is organisational: the fan clubs, although drawn from the poor and lower middle classes, engage in active philanthropy in the name of their admired guru. The stars themselves are said to:

want their fan clubs to act as instruments of service to the poor rather than as mouthpieces of praise. Generosity and ingeniousness imply a personality and an approach to the poor that are starkly in contrast to those of most powerful people known to urban lower class residents. (ibid.: 157)

The combination of compassion with physical (and political) potency is one attributed to saints and gurus. Ascetic bodily self-denial and generosity are the hallmarks of extraordinary, divinely blessed power in South Asia, performed within a hierarchical gift economy (see Werbner 1990b). The evident convergence with English notions of class, service and moral character begins to explain why Imran Khan can command admiration, respect and adulation globally, not because he is a hybrid, but because he seems to embody so fully the cherished values of two societies, each of which grasps him from a perspective grounded within their own culture. He is not an inauthentic, Third World, postcolonial crossover. Rather he appears to be an authentic public school/Oxbridge organic leader of men, and an equally authentic Pakistani cricket star-turned-saint-turned-politician. His interracial marriage adds mystery and the power to this conjunction of East and West, black and white, but in a context in which the cricketer already epitomises nobility, courage and beauty.

For young British Pakistanis, however, Khan was a hero from the start: because he was exceedingly handsome, sexy, glamorous, rich and physically powerful, but – above all – because he was a winner, a man who restored their pride and faith in their national origins. He was the lone cowboy in a real-life drama, who succeeded against the odds through sheer stamina, determination and physical brilliance; the 'Lion of Lahore' as he was dubbed by the English press.

To some extent, of course, Imran Khan's iconicity is a manufactured charisma (see Bilu and Ben Ari 1992). He fosters his image as a Pathan warrior of aristocratic origins, even though he is in fact a Punjabi Pathan whose father was an engineer (both sons were cricketers). A magnificently produced coffee-table book he authored, *Warrior Race* (1993), depicts his travels to his 'ancestral' home in Swat, illustrating this noble descent with large glossy colour pictures of the ex-cricketer visiting tribal people against the awesome backdrop of the jagged mountains of the North West Frontier Province. This book was sold as part of his hospital fund-raising drive. 'The British', I was told by a friend whose father had served in India, 'have always loved the Indian aristocracy.' Imran Khan has his own biographies/hagiographies. But equally important must be his legion connections to the press, a product of his cricketing, nightclubbing days. His marriage was front-page news in all the broadsheets, a coloured picture of the couple occupying most of the front page of the *Guardian*. It was a 'royal' marriage; no other cricketer has been featured so regularly and at such length on CNN, Sky TV, the BBC and ITV. Nor is this iconicity restricted to Britain – there have been articles on Khan in the *Los Angeles Times* and other American broadsheets, and he regularly fund-raises in the USA. He has been featured admiringly in *Q News*, a British Muslim weekly with Islamist tendencies, and in *Eastern Eye*, a British Asian weekly with none *(Eastern Eye*, 17 May 1996: 12). There is an Imran Khan page on the worldwide web which I found, surfing the net in search of academic articles about him (there were none). It gives (among other things) full details about the cancer hospital, why it was formed and its future plans, before explaining how to make donations in Britain, the USA and Pakistan. This page was set up by a Pakistani admirer living in Britain. Princess Di's preference to stay with her 'friend'

Jemima, rather than as a guest of the Prime Minister, was also front-page news. Whatever his media connections, clearly Imran Khan remains a cultural icon for Western as well as Eastern audiences, an object of postmodern/colonial desire.

Why have postcolonial/cultural studies scholars ignored him so far? Madonna as a cultural icon is a recurrent topic in cultural studies discourse. The issue of cultural iconicity is one that has been raised, especially because popular music and musicians are so central to the discourse; as are, indeed, questions of masculinity (there are 146 entries on masculinity in the University of Manchester's library catalogue, most of them post-1990). Perhaps Khan's image just seems too obvious; what are missed are the 'anthropological' dimensions of his persona which make him so interesting.

The question, of course, for Imran Khan, as for all saints-turned-politicians, is: can he sustain the critical Sufi discourse and the saintly image while sullying his hands in dirty politics? Zindapir, the saint I studied in the North West Frontier Province, told me he would never get involved in politics. 'God', he explained, 'is not elected, and to become a sufi you don't need to be elected.' 'The politicians', he continued, 'come here for *du'a* (supplicatory prayer), and I say *du'a* for them [i.e. ask God to help them win the elections], but they still have the thoughts of politicians – by coming to me they are making a demonstration to the people that they respect me, in order to gain their [the people's] support.' 'Why don't you like them?' I asked. 'Because they tell lies.'

Yet in his television interviews Imran Khan shines through as a man genuinely dedicated to his nation in its hour of need; a true patriot. Since the mysterious bombing of his hospital in April 1996, which seemed clearly to target him, he has also been reborn as a fearless warrior, willing to look death in the face for the sake of a wider cause – the redemption of his people. There have been other warrior saints in the past, not least the Prophet himself. Imran Khan speaks in the measured tones of a true statesman seeking 'justice' (*insaaf*, the name of his new political movement). His star-like qualities of integrity, sincerity and rationality draw the viewer to him. The more his opponents attack him, the more corrupt, violent and undemocratic they themselves appear to be.

Imran Khan needs his connections to the international media in his battle for survival in Pakistan, where the ruling elites use the state media in an attempt to muzzle him. The international press and media's concern to protect freedom of the press everywhere means that his political reformist campaign is necessarily grasped by the media as a global campaign. The postcolonial fable he enacts, of one man's civilising mission for the sake of the poor of his nation against the corruption and violence of Third World elites, captures the imagination. Here is a true, modern-day hero whom Westerners can identify with in the secure knowledge that their own nations are democratic and civilised.

In fact, however, Khan's moral agenda is a far more complex mixture of pro- and anti-Westernism. This makes him an enigmatic figure. One of his key platforms is the abolition of the elitist English-medium educational system which produced him as the public-schoolboy-hero and Victorian gentleman he is today. In the Pakistani press he articulates a complex rhetoric of selfless 'service' and Islamist reforming zeal, compounded by patriarchal attitudes. The latter appear to have created an unnecessarily and ultimately dangerous rift between him and feminist reformers, who have been for many years at the forefront of the battle for democracy and human rights in Pakistan (see Mumtaz and Shaheed 1987). In a recent article in *The News* of Pakistan, 'Protecting the Family System' (1995), Khan begins by extolling the Christian morality of Victorian England (!), now lost in the sinful West of sex, drugs and rock-n-roll culture. Feminists, he continues, 'devalue motherhood', and Pakistan is currently 'threatened by a small but extremely influential group of [feminist] zealots within our Westernised class. In TV dramas, we see a strange mongrel culture – a sort of mixture between India and the West.' Apparent here are the familiar cadences of political Islam – westoxification, women as icons of tradition whose place is in the home. The kind of universal tolerance expressed during the early fund-raising performances in Manchester has been lost. How would the Western press respond to Imran Khan, the reforming Islamist?

'Cricket', 'diaspora' and 'Imran Khan' are all performative texts to be approached from different theoretical and methodological vantage grounds. To reduce these texts to class–race–gender–nation is to gloss over the complex moral and aesthetic issues at stake in a cultural performance. Hence for me, personally, the reductiveness of most cultural studies writing is ultimately sterile, predictable and repetitious. The discipline's theoretical armoury is certainly impressive in its baroque elaboration, and now and then we also gain real understanding from a particularly insightful analysis, such as Hargreaves's on the history of British sport.

But such texts lose their repetitive predictable quality precisely if and when they reach out beyond the narrow definitions of cultural studies, in order to grasp the uniqueness of a performative 'text', produced by an anthropological fascination with social and cultural complexity.

## NOTES

This article was first presented at a seminar on Anthropology and Cultural studies at Goldsmiths College in February 1995. I wish to thank Peter Parkes, Cris Shore and Olivia Harris for their comments. Work on Imran Khan was carried out in the context of an ESRC project under my directorship: 'South Asian Popular Culture: Gender, Generation and Identity' and I wish to thank the Council for its generous support. Dr Bobby Sayyid, a postdoctoral research fellow employed by the project is currently working on cricket as a diasporic and postcolonial game.

1. For Gramsci 'resistance' was much more than merely 'subversive bricolage' but was about capturing an entire social space through the creation of a ramified network of socialist institutions, associations and bodies (Cris Shore, personal communication). An attempt to highlight one such space is Paul Gilroy's study of the emergence of Rock against Racism in the 1970s as an alliance with working-class youth (Gilroy 1987). None of this amounts, however, to an aesthetic theory which considers working-class culture as non-derivative.

## REFERENCES

Abu-Lughod, Lila (1986) *Veiled Sentiments: Honour and Poetry in a Bedouin Society*. Berkeley: University of California Press.
Ahmad, Aijaz (1992) *In Theory: Classes Nations Literatures*. London: Verso.

Appadurai, Arjun (1995) 'Playing with Modernity: The Decolonisation of Indian Cricket', in Carol A. Breckenridge (ed.) *Consuming Modernity: Public Culture in a South Asian World*. Minneapolis: University of Minnesota Press.

Asad, Talal (1993) *Genealogies of Religion: Disciplines and Reasons of Power in Christianity and Islam*. Baltimore: Johns Hopkins University Press.

Bateson, Gregory (1958) [1936] *Naven*. Stanford, CA: Stanford University Press.

—— (1973) *Steps to an Ecology of Mind*. St Albans: Paladin.

Bhabha, Homi (1994) *The Location of Culture*. London: Routledge.

Bilu, Yoram and Eyal Ben Ari (1992) 'The Making of Modern Saints: Manufactured Charisma and the Abu-Hatseiras of Israel', *American Ethnologist* 19: 672–87.

Boddy, Janice (1989) *Wombs and Alien Spirits*. Madison: University of Wisconsin Press.

Bourdieu, Pierre (1977) [1972] *Outline of a Theory of Practice*, trans. Richard Price. Cambridge: Cambridge University Press.

—— (1985) 'The Social Space and the Genesis of Groups', *Theory and Society* 14: 723–44.

Centre for Contemporary Cultural Studies (1982) *The Empire Strikes Back: Race and Racism in 70s Britain*. London: Hutchinson.

Chaudhary, Vivek (1996) 'QL Dismisses Botham Libel Action against Imran Kahan as "Hollow and Contrived"', *Guardian* 30 July.

Cohen, Stanley (1972) *Folk Devils and Moral Panics: The Creation of Mods and Rockers*. London: MacGibbon and Kee.

Dawson, Graham (1994) *Soldier Heroes: British Adventure Empire and the Imagining of Masculinities*. London: Routledge.

Dickey, Sara (1993) *Cinema and the Urban Poor in India*. Cambridge: Cambridge University Press.

Dumont, Louis (1972) [1967] *Homo Hierarchicus: The Caste System and its Implications,* trans. Mark Sainsbury. London: Paladin.

Engel, Matthew (1996) 'Hot Pitch', *Guardian*, 30 July.

Evans-Pritchard, E.E. (1940) *The Nuer: A Description of the Livelihood and Political Institutions of a Nilotic People*. Oxford: Clarendon Press.

—— (1976) [1937] *Witchcraft, Oracles and Magic among the Azande*. Oxford: Clarendon Press.

Fabian, Johannes (1990) *Power and Performance*. Madison: University of Wisconsin Press.

Ferguson, Euan (1996) 'Case of the Toff and the Barrow-Boy', *Observer* 21 July.

Foucault, Michel (1989) [1972] *The Archaeology of Knowledge*, trans. A.M. Sheridan Smith. London: Routledge.

Fuss, Diana (1990) *Essentially Speaking: Feminism Nature and Difference*. London: Routledge.

Geertz, Clifford (1973) *The Interpretation of Cultures*. London: Hutchinson.

Gilroy, Paul (1987) *There Ain't No Black in the Union Jack: The Cultural Politics of Race and Nation*. London: Hutchinson Education.

—— (1993) *The Black Atlantic: Modernity and Double Consciousness*. London: Verso.

Gluckman, Max (1958) [1942] *Analysis of a Social Situation in Modern Zululand, Rhodes-Livingstone Papers*, no. 28. Manchester: Manchester University Press for the Rhodes-Livingstone Institute.

—— (1963) *Order and Rebellion in Tribal Africa*. London: Cohen and West.

Gramsci, Antonio (1971) *Selections from the Prison Notebooks of Antonio Gramsci*, ed. and trans. Q. Hoare and G. Nowell Smith. London: Lawrence and Wishart.

Goffman, E. (1961) *Encounters*. Indianapolis: Bobbs-Merrill.

Hall, Stuart (1992) 'Cultural Studies and its Theoretical Legacies', in Lawrence Grossberg, Cary Nelson and Paula Treichler (eds) *Cultural Studies*. London: Routledge.

—— (1996) 'Introduction: Who Needs Identity?', in Stuart Hall and Paul du Gay (eds) *Questions of Cultural Identity*, pp. 1–17. London: Sage.

Hall, Stuart, Critcher, Chas, Jefferson, Tony, Clarke John, and Roberts, Brian (1978) *Policing the Crisis: Mugging, the State and Law and Order*. London: Macmillan Education.

Hall, Stuart and Jefferson, Tony (1976) *Resistance through Rituals*. London: Hutchinson.

Hargreaves, John (1986) *Sport, Power and Culture: A Social Historical Analysis of Popular Sports in Britain*. Oxford: Polity Press.

Hebdige, Dick (1979) *Subculture: the Meaning of Style*. London: Methuen.

Horrocks, Roger (1995) *Male Myths and Icons: Masculinity in Popular Culture*. London: Macmillan.

Kanitkar, Helen (1994) '"Real True Boys": Moulding the Cadets of Imperialism', in Andrea Cornwall and Nancy Lindisfarne (eds) *Dislocating Masculinity: Comparative Ethnographies*. London: Routledge.

Khan, Imran (1993) *Warrior Race*. London: Chatto and Windus.

—— (1995) 'Protecting the Family System', *The News* 15 December.

—— (1996) 'My Dream for Pakistan', *Daily Telegraph* 29 April: p. 34.

MacClancy, Jeremy (1996) 'Introduction' in Jeremy MacClancy (ed.) *Sport, Identity and Ethnicity*, pp. 1–20. Oxford: Berg.

McHugh, Peter (1968) *Defining the Situation: the Organization of Meaning in Social Interaction*. Indianapolis and New York: Bobbs-Merrill Company.

Mark, Vic (1996) 'England's Shining Knight', *Observer* 1 September 1996.

Mauss, Marcel (1985) [1938] 'A Category of the Human Mind: The Notion of Person; the Notion of Self', trans. W.D. Halls, in Michael Carrithers, Steven Collins and Steven Lukes (eds) *The Category of the Person*, pp. 1–25. Cambridge: Cambridge University Press.

Mumtaz, Khawar and Shaheed, Farida (1987) *Women of Pakistan: Two Steps Forward One Step Back*. London: Zed Books.

Nandy, Ashis (1983) *The Intimate Enemy: Losss and Recovery of Self under Colonialism*. New Delhi: Oxford University Press.

Parkes, Peter (1996) 'Indigenous Polo and the Politics of Regional Identity in Northern Pakistan', in Jeremy MacClancy (ed.) *Sport, Identity and Ethnicity*, pp. 43–68. Oxford: Berg.

Parkin, David (1996) 'Introduction: The Power of the Bizarre', in David Parkin, Lionel Caplan and Humphrey Fisher (eds) *The Politics of Cultural Performance*. Oxford: Berghahn Books.

Said, Edward (1979) *Orientalism*. London: Penguin.

Simon, Roger (1982) *Gramsci's Political Thought: An Introduction*. London: Lawrence and Wishart.

Strathern, Marilyn (1988) 'Commentary: Concrete Topographies', *Cultural Anthropology* 3: 88–96.

—— (1991) *Partial Connections*. Maryland: Rowman and Littlefield.

Targett, Simon (1996) 'Perspective: Refounding Father', *Times Higher* 31 May: 12.

Weingrod, Alex (1990) *The Saint of Beersheba*. New York: CUNY Press.

Werbner, Pnina (1990a) 'Exemplary Personhood and the Political Mythology of Overseas Pakistanis', *Social Analysis* 28: 51–69.

—— (1990b) 'Economic Rationality and Hierarchical Gift Economies: Value and Ranking among British Pakistanis', *Man* (n.s.) 25: 226–85.

—— (1995) 'Powerful Knowledge in a Global Sufi Cult: Reflections on the Poetics of Travelling Theories', in Wendy James (ed.) *The Pursuit of Certainty*, pp. 134–60. London: Routledge.

—— (1996a) 'Our Blood is Green: Cricket, Identity and Social Empowerment among British Pakistanis', in Jeremy MacClancy (ed.) *Sport, Identity and Ethnicity*, pp. 87–112. Oxford: Berg.

—— (1996b) 'Fun Spaces: On Identity and Social Empowerment among British Pakistanis', *Theory, Culture and Society* 13 (4): pp. 53–80.

—— (1996c) 'The Fusion of Identities: Political Passion and the Poetics of Cultural Performance among British Pakistanis', in David Parkin, Lionel Caplan and Humphrey Fisher (eds) *The Politics of Cultural Performance*, pp. 81–101. Oxford: Berghahn Books.

—— (1997a) 'Essentialising Essentialism, Essentialising Silence: Multiplicity and Ambivalence in the Construction of Race and Ethnicity', in Pnina Werbner and Tariq Modood (eds) *Debating Cultural Hybridity: Multi-Cultural Identities and the Politics of Anti-Racism.* London: Zed Books.

—— (1997b) 'Introduction: The Dialectics of Cultural Hyrbidity', in Pnina Werbner and Tariq Modood (eds) *Debating Cultural Hybridity: Multi-Cultural Identities and the Politics of Anti-Racism.* London: Zed Books.

Werbner, Richard (1989) *Ritual Passage, Sacred Journey: The Process and Organisation of Religious Movement.* Washington, DC: Smithsonian Institution Press.

Williams, Raymond (1992) [1958] *Culture and Society.* London: Hogarth Press.

# 4   UNWRAPPING JAPANESE CULTURE
*Joy Hendry*

Anthropological research in Japan concerns itself with many of the same issues addressed by practitioners of cultural studies. In a complex society, with a long history of literacy and documented artistic achievement, it is impossible to carry out a study bounded by the geographical limits of a village, or to devote attention only to participant observation in the daily lives of a particular social group. Japan has scholars in all the disciplines found elsewhere, often specialising in areas of interest chosen by any one anthropologist, and Japanese anthropologists have carried out research in their own country for as long as outsiders have. There is thus no problem in finding and engaging with the 'native voice'.

Within Japan, too, though it may be erroneously described by some as a homogeneous society, there are many of the same sub-cultures which have attracted the attention of the cultural studies schools in Britain (see for example, Lave et al. 1992). Working-class groups, sometimes distinguishing themselves physically by the use of tattoos, or particular clothes, have been the focus of research in Japan (for example, Allen 1994, Raz 1992), and there are many studies, approached from a variety of disciplines, of groups of women or youths, which could be called sub-cultures (for example, Dalby 1983, Sato 1991). Other scholars have discussed the role of the individual in society, and the dissenting voices to mainstream ideas and policies (for example, Goodman and Refsing 1992, Miyanaga 1991). Some of these scholars are anthropologists, some are not.

It is my contention, however, that social anthropologists practise research methods which are distinct from those of others interested in the same fields, despite the confusing use of the word 'ethnography' (originally the writings of the anthropologist about a people) to describe the 'qualitative' research of non-anthropologists. I argue that the 'quality' of the research of social anthropologists is different, too, and I will examine some of these methods and their results in this chapter. I propose to do this by a process of self-reflection, which will inevitably make the chapter rather personal, but this would seem to be the most effective way to make the point. My research was involved with the boundary between the arts and social science, just like cultural studies, and it was directly concerned with women in a class context.

## THE PROPOSAL AND THE RESULT

The original proposal for the research project in question was to make a study of 'speech levels in Japanese society'. Based on the experience of previous participant observation in a private Japanese kindergarten, and particularly, six months of quite intense interaction with the head of the establishment and her staff and their charges, I developed a plan to examine in further depth the use of the various polite and respectful forms which Japanese has to offer in the manipulation of social relations. Because of my own increasing age and academic position, I had found it necessary to use this earlier period, alongside the main purpose of investigating child rearing methods, to develop and improve my use of language appropriate to my situation.

Japanese language may be acceptably quite informal for students, especially if they are studying it at a youthful age, but, as a close Japanese friend, Kazuko, pointed out, 'when you are a university teacher, over the age of 30, you ought to be speaking more politely'. As it happened, my efforts to conform with this advice coincided with almost daily interaction with a mistress of the art. The head of the kindergarten in question used extremely polite language, and she trained her teachers to do the same. I joined the fray, with enthusiasm, and with some interesting results. I seemed to be engaged in a sort of serious competition, which I didn't often win, but I gradually became aware of the power the skilful use of language could command.

With hindsight, I realise that there was more to the success of this role model than I had anticipated when I planned my new research project, and the results went much farther than I could ever have planned. I did write some papers about polite language, and about the predominantly female society where I decided to make my investigations, but the book which followed is entitled *Wrapping Culture* (Hendry 1993), and it includes chapters about gifts, the materials used for wrapping them, the body, space, time, politics and art. I discovered that the famous, though little understood, Japanese tea ceremony epitomises many of the ideas I wanted to put across, and a class I took up casually as a form of relaxation became an integral part of my research. All very 'cultural' then, but how did my research proceed?

## SETTING UP THE PROJECT

As with any other research project, I began by reading the existing material on the subject I had chosen. I read the work of scholars foreign to Japan, including sociolinguistic theory, but I also tried to find as much work as possible by Japanese scholars, in Japanese and English. From the outset, an anthropologist is aware of the importance of the 'native voice', or more precisely, of course, native voices, and in a society as literate as Japan is, it is a major part of any investigation to be aware of written source material. The subject of 'speech levels', or *keigo,* to use the Japanese term, is part of the very fabric of social interaction[1] – reflecting social distinctions, hierarchy, relative intimacy and degrees of formality of an occasion – and ordinary Japanese people are so concerned with the subject of *keigo,* that I found a plethora of popular books about its use, as well as the scholarly tomes by linguists and others.

A Japanese anthropologist in Oxford helped me to gather and sift through this abundant material, and her implicit knowledge and experience was so valuable that I decided to build into the grant proposal a sum to engage her as a part-time research assistant. To investigate the use of language effectively requires more than a question-and-answer technique, and she would be returning to Japan to take up employment which involved much use of *keigo,* so she seemed an ideal 'mole'. Her investigations would avoid two inevitable pitfalls in studying a subject such as this in Japan: first, the difficulty for many Japanese of finding an appropriate way to place a foreigner for social interaction, and second, the fact that revealing the subject matter would affect people's use of language.

This problem also had its advantages, however, because I was interested in particular in the possibilities for manipulation of speech forms, and I decided to divide my own time between a close group which would know of my project, and a wider group which would not, a strategy only possible in a complex society where everyone does *not* know everyone else. To gain a maximum range in hearing the use of *keigo* I felt it was necessary to live in a community and engage in a wide variety of social activities. My reading had suggested that women in Japan use a greater variety of polite and respectful language than men, so for the more intensive interaction I decided to try and insinuate myself into a group of housewives. The need to take my school-aged children with me would help in this respect.

My long-standing friend of the 'now that you are 30' comment had set up the kindergarten contact, and she offered to help out again. There would certainly be an advantage to moving back to an area where I was known, but I was also aware of the regional differences in the use of *keigo*, and, with a few weeks before the children arrived, I decided to travel around a little and try and get a feel for the variation. I visited Kyoto, the ancient capital where I understood the most beautiful language could be found, and Sapporo, a relatively new city where there was said to be little use of *keigo*. I travelled back to Kyushu, to the site of an even earlier long-term project, where there is a strong local dialect, and I visited the English school in Kobe as a possibility for my children.

The trip was invaluable, for I managed to carry out a series of interviews in each location, but I decided I could not better the original offer. It was a town with a mix of inhabitants, from rural through provincial to those oriented towards Tokyo, only two hours away by train. My former Japanese professor at Tokyo University was now also teaching in a women's university known for its elegant language, and he had arranged for me to be attached to the Research Centre for Language and Culture at Keio University, headed by a well-known if somewhat controversial linguist, who agreed to support my work. My friend arranged for me to hire the bottom floor of a house from the local hospital where her husband worked. In time for the autumn term, my children arrived to join me, and the work of serious participant observation began.

## ESTABLISHING CONTACTS

The housewives' group was easy to identify since my friend, Kazuko, had a ready-made set of friends who welcomed me into their midst.

The day I arrived coincided with the birthday of one of her daughters, and they were gathered for the occasion. As is often the case, the mothers' group was defined by a range with children of similar ages. My children fitted the bill and we had plenty to talk about. Through these friends I was invited to participate regularly in a direct food-ordering scheme, a weekly tennis class, a bi-monthly cooking class, and sporadic events connected with the old kindergarten still attended by some of their younger children. Thus was established an important component of participant observation: a face-to-face group which I would meet in various different contexts. This proved extremely illuminating in observing different forms of language, for the informality of the tennis court provoked terms of address quite inappropriate for the more formal setting of a kindergarten PTA meeting.

In my efforts to set up other areas of interaction I followed various leads. In the time-tried tradition of anthropological investigation, I first set about making friends with the neighbours. Japanese neighbourhoods are usually quite integrated, for the maintenance of the surroundings are devolved to the local group, and there is a rota for sweeping the street and cleaning out the streams which run along their periphery. There is also a structure of responsibility, and I visited the head of our immediate vicinity to offer my participation. Apart from a few friendly individuals, however, I drew a bit of a blank. Our particular district was too poor even to support the local shrine festival, and there was little *esprit de corps*.

I paid my rent to the hospital, only a few paces away. There worked the husband of one of the housewives in our group and another employee who had been Kazuko's neighbour in the more friendly part of town where she had lived when I did my previous research. Through these contacts, I managed to extend the network, and the hospital became a useful source of observation, both of an established hierarchy, and the linguistic expression of a temporary loss of social status the patients seem to experience. I pursued my inquiries here by setting up a series of semi-structured interviews, during which I asked direct questions about the use of language.

Many hospitals in Japan are private establishments, as was this, despite being named after the town itself, and the manager/chief physician came of an interesting family which separated itself physically from its potential clients by living part of the week in Tokyo. The way the members used language reinforced this separation, for they spoke amongst themselves in a refined form of speech inaccessible to the local people, but switched to the local brogue[2] in communicating with patients and local staff. A relative of the family, who ran an associated rehabilitation unit, was a retired broadcaster, and he waxed eloquent on the subject of code-switching of this sort. He had first learned to do it when growing up in the town, as a defence mechanism to avoid teasing from his classmates.

Individual interviews in the neighbourhood also proved insightful. At the corner of the street stood a very smart eel restaurant, a remnant of the former days, no doubt, but well patronised in the town at large. The owner was quite explicit about the language he used with his customers, starting out politely, but growing intimate as they returned again and again, so that people would feel a welcome attachment to the place. The food was well prepared, of course, but it was also attractively presented, and served in surroundings that had been carefully designed. From the private dining room on the first floor, where we held the interview, one could glimpse a distant castle, and enjoy a slight breeze through the partially opened window. Such attention to detail was part of the package, it seemed.

Adjacent to our home lived a kindly couple who called me in to offer some old games their grown sons had left behind, and I chanced to meet their bed-ridden grandmother whose language was distorted by the stroke she had suffered. I persisted, however, and she proved to be a mine of local information. She had lived in the neighbourhood longer than anyone, and was able to explain its strange quality. The very house I was sitting in had been a cosy restaurant, like the eel shop, but more glamorous, and she had been the star performer. I don't believe this was rose-tinted memory. As it turned out, we had stumbled across a former red light district, whose small convenient love nests had been converted into social security accommodation. Hence the lack of wealth.

My children's schooling provided another source of interesting material for my research. The teachers were concerned to give the English visitors a good welcome, and relieved that their mother, at least, could speak Japanese, allowed me to spend some time settling them in. The language used amongst the staff was informative, since there is again a strict hierarchy of codes and the position of the higher-ranking teachers was reinforced by the arrangements of desks in the staff room. The head is separated altogether, in a room with photographs of former occupants, and he is addressed in a very formal style, even by his former equals.

This particular headmaster had previously been posted to Hong Kong, and he was keen to encourage international goodwill, so he called me into his inner sanctum for an interview. The occasion had mutual benefit, for he asked me about my research, and came up with a comment which significantly influenced the course of my research. He told me that he had visited England, where he had been taken to a number of schools, and he was impressed by their variety. He had even been to Eton, he said, and he wondered why the children of the British upper classes wear 'wedding garments' for everyday life. This apparent physical expression of a connection between ritual and superiority is echoed in the use of formal language in Japanese, since *keigo* is used by everyone for weddings and other formal occasions, but only by a few to mark their superior status.

In search of some new contacts, and an example of formal behaviour, I went out one day to seek an *ikebana* teacher. I found, only a short bicycle ride away, a house which advertised such classes at the gate, and I signed myself up for the following week. This would provide another group to meet regularly. It was still early days and I decided to keep on cycling, to get a greater feel for the area, and establish some wider bearings. It was a pleasant, sunny day, but the oppressive warmth of the summer had at last eased, and I travelled quite some distance. I was impressed by the number of shrines and temples I passed, and I began to feel that we might also have stumbled on quite a religious part of the country. The language of priests and their parishioners will be interesting, I mused, as will the language used to address gods.

I was drawn in to one particular compound, through an enticing archway, which brought me to another shrine building, but there was also a smaller path winding away up the hill. It seemed to be a kind of pilgrim's trail, with Buddhist statues every so often, marked with numbers. There was nobody around to provide information so, intrigued, I set off to see where it led. It was quite a climb and I was soon reminded that the heat was not that far gone. I persisted in my quest, however, and was drawn further and further into the woods which cloaked the hillside. The trail led downhill for a while, and the path seemed to curve around, but the numbers on the statues continued to climb. There was no recent evidence of offerings, and the undergrowth threatened to swallow up some of the route, which was also heavily draped with spiders' webs, so several times I considered turning back.

Eventually, I came across a small hut, possibly built as a retreat, and I approached it nervously in case someone was inside, but there was nothing to indicate any sign of human life, although I balked at testing the evidence. Indeed, the whole atmosphere was weird and lonely. Suddenly, I was surprised out of my reverie by voices, only a few yards away. I peered through a thick, bamboo grove, and found that, to my amazement, the path was now within sight of the main road. At first I was pleased, that I would not now need to retrace the overgrown path, but it soon became clear that there was no other way out. The tiny hut was effectively surrounded by an impenetrable natural barrier. I could see the cars of the civilised world passing by, but I could only reach them by returning along the long, winding path.

When I got back to my bicycle, I was greatly relieved. I had ventured out with bare legs, now very scratched, and the experience had been somewhat unnerving. Looking more closely at the entrance to the path, I found a map of the route, which had indeed covered a rather limited area. Cycling back, I passed a large Buddhist temple, with a graveyard, and an apparently inhabited dwelling adjacent to it. I thought I'd stop and inquire about the pilgrims' trail, and I called out a few times to see if anyone was at home. I was about to give up when an old man appeared, dressed only in a set of cotton underwear, which rather stifled the opportunity for further conversation, so I apologised and went on my way. Although I had no way of knowing it at the time, this man and his family were later to have quite an influence on my life.


## ATTENDING EVENTS – AND A MOMENT OF INSIGHT

During fieldwork in Japan, as elsewhere, people one encounters in the 'normal course of events' issue invitations to events. These may be proffered as a form of amusement, 'a break from all that study', they may be suggested as an interesting way to understand Japan, or they may form part of the obligations of a neighbour or age-mate. In any case, they usually provide opportunities to meet people, or to become better acquainted with those who perhaps unbidden, have helped make arrangements for one's stay. They are also sometimes occasions for unexpected contributions to the research of a social anthropologist, and I have rarely refused them. The district sports day, which I had thought would be a good opportunity to demonstrate my commitment to the neighbourhood, turned out to be something of a disaster because my children were whisked off to more pressing engagements of their own. A large festival, which I thought I had seen many times before, turned up some gems of material.

This particular festival drew participants from an area about the size of an English county (*gun* in Japanese) to a central Shinto complex dedicated to a powerful deity, also remembered at smaller shrines in many communities. Local people from these other shrines arrived from all directions, dressed in distinctive local costume. On the first day they carried in decorated portable shrines, and presented them, with much dancing and jumping about. On the second day, the first groups left, and heavy floats were pulled in by teams of people pulling on heavy ropes. There was much merriment and role reversal, and I only appreciated the full significance of the variety of language being used much later, but I did notice that each group had a distinctive local twang.

During the early months of my research, I regularly made time to discuss various findings with Kazuko, as well as with my research assistant in the city.[3] I also made copious notes as I attended these various events, and sometimes it was much later that things would fall into place. The practice of using language to protect and exclude emerged in many contexts, and the festival was another example, since the locals would communicate amongst themselves in their dialect, but switch to standard Japanese when speaking to outsiders. In fact this practice had played a serious role in Japanese history. Another practice I observed, that of tying a thin plaited rope around the part of town involved in the festival, did not find an easy interpretation until I came to write my book.

Another couple of events I was drawn into were less cheerful, but each interesting in its own way. The first was a funeral, a tragic situation where the father of a classmate of my 6-year-old son had taken his own life after being made redundant. There was a parents' channel of communication, and I was informed, and expected to pass on the news, so I inquired about the appropriate way to react. Several mothers were going along, and I joined them. To be honest, I was attending less to pay my respects, for I had not known the family, than to observe a funeral, but this is the role of the anthropologist. Nobody was offended, indeed, they were probably pleased, if they noticed, and I gathered some useful examples of formal language and dress.

Another funeral, which was held within a few weeks of the first, was quite different. This time it was the father of a very old friend of mine in Tokyo, a man whose family I had visited, and whose mother, as it turned out, remembered a great deal about me. I wasn't able to go to the funeral itself, but my friend, now married and living elsewhere, took me to call at the house. I presented a gift of fruit to the Buddhist altar, where the urn of ashes was still standing, and the father's picture was on display, and I repeated the formal phrases I had rehearsed. My friend's mother replied formally, but she also asked me to stay the night, and we spent the evening talking. She looked very thin and tired, and I was glad if I could ease her grief a little. I had no idea at the time how much her response would aid my research.

In fact, her response was a formal gift which she undoubtedly sent out to all the people who had expressed their condolences. Many of these had been accompanied by money, wrapped in envelopes appropriate to the occasion, and she had shown me an enormous pile, so I didn't receive special treatment. It was just that the arrival of her gift provoked a moment of insight in the course of my thinking. Such moments are impossible to predict, and they could never be incorporated into a research design, but the seemingly nebulous nature of participant observation allows for a change of focus, and this is what transpired from the day that her gift arrived.

The contents of the package were quite charming – five tiny dishes for individual servings of sauce – but it was the way they were wrapped which drew my attention. To proceed from the parcel which was delivered to my door, I had to remove no fewer than seven layers of packaging to reveal the contents. Some had a clear purpose: protection of the breakable material, paper marked with symbols of death and the afterlife, and an outer covering to transmit the gift through the mail, but there was no functional explanation which could account completely for the seven layers. A few days later I attended a low-key, but politically important shrine rite to give thanks for the harvest. Again I received a formal gift. Its wrapping seemed much more significant than the contents.

In the following weeks I began to pay greater attention to wrapping, and I began to notice the use of wrapping materials, such as paper, cloth and straw, in other ways. In reading, and in discussions about the use of language, I discovered a neat connection between the use of polite and formal language and the use of other markers, such as wrapping, to express the same sentiment. The Japanese word for politeness, *teinei*, also means 'care', and care for an object, through the appropriate use of wrapping, expresses care for the person to whom it is presented. The same care is expressed by the use of language which 'wraps' words in a form appropriate for a particular occasion. This might lend formality for a special occasion such as a wedding or a funeral. It might also 'wrap' a group of people and distinguish them from others.

This is clearly not the place to detail all the developments of the research, but it is worth mentioning one further event which opened up a fruitful line of comparison. My flower-arranging teacher enjoyed the prestige of having a foreign student in the class, and she asked me to participate in a Culture Festival which was being held in the town. In practice, she chose the blooms, and their container, and I merely copied her example, but this is the way one learns in an art such as this, and she was able to display the end-product with a foreign name attached.

She was dressed in a beautiful kimono, and she was keen to introduce me to her acquaintances. It was possible to take part in a tea ceremony, another art she taught, and I followed her around, on my very best behaviour, stretching my formal language skills to their limits. Later, in discussion with Kazuko, I commented on the way language seemed to be notched up by people wearing kimono, and she replied, with physical illustration, that one can hardly leap about informally when tied up so firmly The kimono is a package, too, I realised, and it was hardly even a surprise to discover that the most formal one, worn in the ancient court and by the bride at imperial weddings, had no fewer than twelve layers. I also began to have an explanation for the extremely informal language used by my housewifely group in their short skirts on the tennis court.


SOME SPECIALIST FEEDBACK

My ideas about 'wrapping' were exciting, and fun to discover – although it is important not to get carried away – and my connection with the Japanese academic community in Tokyo allowed me to consider them in another setting. Life continued in the community, and I had plenty to occupy my time, but I did travel to Tokyo about once a month to attend a seminar series organised by my linguistics sponsor, and towards the end of my stay, I was invited to give a couple of seminars, at one of which I decided to present what I came to call the 'wrapping phenomenon'. This was, for me, a major trial, and I consulted some local specialists before I committed my research to the academic community.

Social anthropology is concerned with thought patterns, and systems of classification which underpin the way people behave, and in any society there are various influences which shape a world view. Spoken language is of course an important component of a classificatory system, but it is not the only one, and what I had been identifying were means of communication which employ other symbolic forms. Japanese speakers obviously draw on their linguistic traditions, but they also draw on other historical influences, and I decided to have a look at one or two of these in more detail.

My first port of call was a Zen Buddhist priest whom I seemed to encounter in various contexts. First, in following up the language associated with classes of instruction, I had asked to interview a *koto* player whom I had met at a concert. She was willing, and invited me to her home. Second, my older son was invited to a birthday party by a classmate, held in her home. Both turned out to be in the family house of the Buddhist temple where I had first encountered the grandfather in his underwear. The father of the family was my consultant. He was also a *shakuhachi* player, and he joined his wife and me for tea after my interview with her. The atmosphere was quite formal, and there were some very elaborate cakes which seemed to add to the occasion. I noticed that their form was a kind of wrapping, so I raised the subject.

This Zen Buddhist musician was particularly interested in a kind of depth of communication which he felt was available to artists through their work, whether it be painting, music or other art forms, and I found his whole argument a little too deep for my stage of understanding. He was, however, able to introduce me to some ideas which fitted my developing theory when he talked of the chanting which accompanies Buddhist rites for the dead. This chanting is drawn from mantras incomprehensible to most lay Japanese, but his parishioners insist that the chanting be of an appropriate length for the occasion they commission. Thus, the words apparently have a power which goes beyond their meaning, and it was not too difficult to term this communication a kind of 'wrapping' whose form outweighs its content for most participants. Much of the formal language in Japanese seems to play a similar role.

Later, his explanation was borne out by a Shinto priest at an important local shrine whom I interviewed about the language of communication with the deities. Again, on a ritual occasion, words which have no direct meaning to the lay person are considered appropriate, he explained, showing me some of the ancient and difficult scripts used for formal prayer. For a human to communicate directly with gods, however, no words are necessary, he went on. The communication is from the heart, with no 'wrapping' at all. This surprised me at first, for I had thought, with my Christian background, that there might be some special form of respect language, akin to that used for people in high-ranking positions. The language used to address members of the Imperial Family is very formal, for example. There was a nice parallel to be observed in the shrine, however, for the offerings used to communicate with the gods are properly presented entirely devoid of wrapping.

Shinto shrines also offer a parallel with 'wrapping' in their use of space, I observed, for they are approached by passing through one or more special archways, and the path is also sometimes marked by statues and carved stone pillars. Sometimes these archways are hung with a plaited straw rope, thicker than the one which encircled the area of the festival I attended, but also serving as a sacred marker. In front of the building, there may be further straw rope, hung with fresh, white paper, of a quality similar to that used to wrap the most formal of gifts. The inner sanctum contains a sacred object, but this is not the goal of the visitor, who is usually expected to pray outside the shrine, at the appropriate layer of spatial wrapping. In any case, the inner object is said often to be a mirror, which would reflect the image of the viewer back again.

There was much food for thought here, and I was turning these things over in my mind when I began to write my paper for the seminar. There had been other examples of spatial 'wrapping', with linguistic parallels: first, in the eel shop, then in the school staff room. The pilgrim's trail had been a carefully constructed example of spatial wrapping, too, and the tiny hut at the centre was possibly a place of retreat, separated symbolically from the rest of the world if not actually very far away.

To seclude oneself in a small hut like that is an ascetic practice known as *komori*, discussed by Carmen Blacker (1975) and, long before, by Origuchi Shinobu, whose paper points to a link with the power of 'wrapping' (1945: 267).

At a PTA meeting at the school, I had also begun to observe a 'wrapping' process in the order of proceedings. They began formally, offering fixed polite phrases with little content which merely referred to the busy lives people must have left to come along (whether they were busy or not). Then the agenda was laid out, again quite formally, but this time leading up to the real business of the meeting. Eventually, there was time for discussion. I noticed that language became much more relaxed at this point, and the local dialect slipped out here and there. To bring the meeting to a close, those in charge merely needed to notch the phraseology up a bit, and everyone knew it was time to go home.

My paper followed something of the same pattern. It started formally, because I wrote it out roughly, with Kazuko correcting my style and vocabulary so that it would be appropriate for an academic seminar. Our preparation time ran out before the day, however, and the second part of the paper was much more colloquial. The final paragraphs were cobbled together on the train, where they almost became loosely connected notes. As I was presenting this before the assembled company of anthropologists and their students, I realised that I had unintentionally unwrapped myself as I went along. At the end I appealed for them to comment in kind, sparing their polite formality, which would be of little help in the process of developing the research.

The ploy worked, and they were very forthright, quite unusual for a Japanese seminar. One or two made negative comments. I had not yet understood the depth of significance of the religious wrapping, according to one professor, and another was not sure about my extension of the linguistic material to express social distinctions. On the whole, however, the audience was most encouraging. They liked the ideas. They thought that the parallels worked well, and they spent the rest of the evening, in a nearby hostelry, furnishing me with enough further examples to keep me busy for days. The fact that I was sick the next day was probably more to do with the tension of the occasion than the beer we consumed.

## CONCLUSIONS: RESEARCH METHODS USED

So what, in all this happenstance and serendipity, can be concluded about the research methods of social anthropology? In this last section, the material might be scrutinised for some general principles, and these, I will argue, are clearer and more concrete than may at first glance be apparent. The reader would have to turn to the more detailed results of the research to follow up all the leads which have been thrown out here. For the time being we will concentrate on the methods.

The planned part of the work is not inconsiderable, of course, and the results of planting a 'native mole' have not been pursued here, though they were of course valuable. The material gleaned from the regional interviews, again, proved useful, as did the interviews held in the town. A conscious effort was made to cover a wide range of people in different occupational groups, and attendance at events was prioritised to cover different situations and contexts, formal and informal, ritual and mundane. Throughout the research period, careful notes were kept, as was a detailed diary. All this, however, is directly comparable with the methods used in other fields.

For a social anthropologist in a society separate from his/her own, there is immediately an important difference in the *total absorption* of the situation. It is never possible really to cut out from the project. Even in the privacy of our own home, we could be telephoned or called upon, and, as it happened, our neighbours were so close that we could often hear their voices. We went on holiday, but the language of the air stewardesses on our internal flight was fascinating, as was the treatment we received in our hotel. We took time out together as a family, but we never knew when some little incident might prove vital to the research. The diary is necessarily always at hand.

In the case of this project, I had another intangible advantage, in that I had already spent two long periods of research in Japan, equally absorbed. Things which I had learned then came back to me in this new framework, and I was able to follow them up. During the second and third periods of fieldwork I travelled back to the first site, partly for this very reason. To discuss ideas with people whom one already knows allows for a quality impossible with short-term contacts, and one is in a position to encounter and observe people at different stages of their lives. Thus, the research I was engaged upon could be called long-term fieldwork.[4]

Maurice Bloch has analysed the cognitive development of an anthropologist working in the field, and he describes the knowledge acquired, often intuitively, as 'chunked mental models' which allow for *post hoc* interpretation. This 'non-linguistic' learning he compares to the acquisition of the skills necessary to drive a car. Once absorbed, one no longer needs to think about every stage of the procedure. An anthropologist picks up a huge amount of knowledge and information simply through coping with daily life, and this is subsequently available, not only for social interaction in the field, but also for analysis and writing-up. At this stage, he points out, we are expected to find 'more academically acceptable evidence' to explain the people with whom we have worked, but he encourages anthropologists to have confidence in their new cognitive constructs (Bloch 1991).

Bloch's theory is quite in keeping with Japanese ideas about learning. Above I mentioned the *ikebana* class, where study is largely made through copying the work of the teacher, and this is no deviation from usual procedure. Moreover, a great deal is thought to be communicated simply by being around experts and in their working environment. Carpentry apprentices, for example, may expect to spend years sweeping up before they are even allowed to touch the tools of the trade (Coaldrake 1990: 8). In like fashion, doing fieldwork as a housewife in a Japanese town brings one into contact with all kinds of situations which may contribute to an understanding of non-linguistic communication. The *implicit knowledge* acquired in this way was, in this case, not only germane, but central to my research.

Those who have been born and brought up in a particular society will of course be the experts in negotiating daily life, and there is a school of thought which advocates that only members of a society can adequately speak on their own behalf. This is another area in which a social anthropologist is often in a situation quite different from other researchers, for anthropologists are usually not only learners in the society of their research, they are 'experts' elsewhere. Even anthropologists working 'at home' usually choose a part of society which is different from that of their upbringing, but they have another advantage. Social anthropologists, in their training, learn of many different societies, so they are aware of a range of possibilities, which provide a context in which to interpret their findings.

Japan provides another good illustration of the point being made here, by the abundance of works which demonstrate the pitfalls encountered by people attempting to speak for 'themselves'. There is a genre known as *Nihonjinron*, or 'theories of Japaneseness', which includes works which typically compare Japan with a nebulous entity described as 'the West'. Japan is perceived as unique, not surprisingly or unreasonably, but Japan in this genre is uniquely unique, and the reasons range from her climate, through her rice production, to the wiring of Japanese brains.[5] This genre is itself material for anthropological analysis, and it has been described as a form of 'cultural nationalism' (Yoshino 1992; cf. Befu and Manabe 1990).

My own sponsoring linguist, an eminent professor at one of the best universities in Japan, is a contributor to this genre and his work is lively and interesting, but it is not anthropology. His firm belief in the unique qualities of Japanese language, the subject of my own study, made him an excellent informant, but there are aspects of his work which border on the fringes of a claim to racial superiority. He did not believe that a foreigner could ever understand Japanese properly, even if her grammar were perfect, for she would be incapable of identifying the 'real intent' of the speaker, he said. Perhaps not, but an outside anthropologist, with the collaboration of Japanese ones, can bring a greater degree of objectivity to her research, as has been pointed out by Yoshida Teigo (1987: 21–3).

A similar point was made some years ago by Victor Turner, who argued that anthropological analysis can go beyond the explanations of the people under study, even to the extent of disagreement with them, because the anthropologist is capable of (or compelled to adopt) a wider view (1967). Those who are involved in witchcraft accusations can never see the overall situation from the outside, he argued, and those who are committed to a religious view are bound to view their own creed differently from that of non-believers.

Identifying the principles of 'wrapping' was partly a consciousness-raising exercise, but once the principles are grasped they can be applied more broadly. In Japan, the notion of 'wrapping' accords particularly well with other aspects of the system of classification, and there is a level of awareness about these principles which allows for their conscious manipulation in many areas of life. Several Japanese writers have written about this (for example, Ekiguchi 1986, Nukada 1977, Oka 1967, 1988) even in Western languages, and there have been displays of packaging in many different parts of the world. In other societies, other principles of order may play a greater part at the conscious and unconscious level, and the special ability of an anthropologist is to place such principles in a broader context.

Ideas about 'wrapping' incorporate language, material culture, art, literature,[6] religion and politics, at the very least, so they are very much concerned with culture. Indeed, wrapping could be seen as a way of describing culture itself. This case has been particularly apt, then, to make a comparison between the disciplines of anthropology and cultural studies. I have concentrated on the anthropological side, but I hope that I have shown that this kind of research goes beyond what is often referred to elsewhere as 'ethnographic' or 'qualitative'.


## NOTES

1.  The well-known practice of exchanging name cards in Japan is vital to establish appropriate language for subsequent interaction, for example.
2.  In this area there is no strong dialect, as such, but there is a definite twang to the speech, and there are words distinctive of the area. Most people do not use a great deal of *keigo* in everyday speech, indeed they become tongue-tied if confronted with it (for more detail see Hendry 1992a).
3.  The relationship with Kazuko became more complicated than I had anticipated, and contributed to the research in an unexpected way, but I have written up this aspect of the fieldwork experience elsewhere (Hendry 1992b).
4.  Some of the advantages of this long term view are discussed in Okely and Callaway (1992), specifically in the papers by Caplan and Kenna, and in an earlier work by Foster (1979).
5.  None of these examples is exclusive to Japan of course. The climate is not particularly unusual, rice growing is found throughout Asia, and since the wiring of the brain is related to learning the written language, if it were true it would be shared with Koreans and, possibly, Chinese.
6.  Literary examples of Japanese wrapping were discussed by a Korean writer studying in Japan, namely O'Young Lee, who identified differences between Japanese and Korean verse forms (1984).

REFERENCES

Allen, Matthew (1994) *Undermining the Japanese Miracle*. Cambridge: Cambridge University Press.
Befu, H. and Manabe, K. (1990) 'Empirical Status of *Nihonjinron*: How Real is the Myth?', in A. Boscaro et al. (eds) *Rethinking Japan*. Sandgate: Japan Library, pp. 124–33.
Blacker, Carmen (1975) *The Catalpa Bow*. London: Allen and Unwin.
Bloch, Maurice (1991) 'Language, Anthropology and Cognitive Science' *Man*, 26 (2) pp. 183–98.
Caplan, Pat (1992) 'Spirits and Sex: A Swahili Informant and his Diary' in J. Okely and H. Callaway (eds) *Anthropology and Autobiography*. London: Routledge, pp. 64–81.
Coaldrake, William H. (1990) *The Way of the Carpenter: Tools and Japanese Architecture*. New York: Weatherhill.
Dalby, Lisa Crichfield, (1983) *Geisha*. Berkeley: University of California Press.
Ekiguchi, Kunio, (1986) *Gift Wrapping: Creative Ideas from Japan*. Tokyo: Kodansha International.
Foster, G.M. (1979) *Long-term Field Research in Social Anthropology* New York: Academic Press.
Goodman, Roger and Kirsten Refsing (eds) (1992) *Ideology and Practice in Modern Japan*. London: Routledge.
Hendry, Joy (1992a) 'Honorifics as Dialect: The Expression and Manipulation of Boundaries in Japanese', *Multilingua*, 11(4): 341–54.
—— (1992b) 'The Paradox of Friendship in the Field: Analysis of a Long-Term Anglo-Japanese Relationship', in J. Okely and H. Callaway (eds) *Anthropology and Autobiography*. London: Routledge, pp. 163–74.
—— (1993) *Wrapping Culture: Politeness, Presentation, and Power in Japan and Other Societies*. Oxford: Clarendon Press.
Kenna, Margaret E. (1992) 'Changing Places and Altered Perspectives: Research on a Greek Island in the 1960s and in the 1980s', in J. Okely and H. Callaway, *Anthropology and Autobiography*. London: Routledge, pp. 147–62.
Lave, Jean, Duguid, Paul, Fernandez, Nadine and Axel, Erik (1992) 'Coming of Age in Birmingham: Cultural Studies and Conceptions of Subjectivity', *Annual Review of Anthropology* 21: 257–82.

Lee, O'Young (1984) *Smaller is Better: Japan's Mastery of the Miniature*, trans. R.N. Huey. Tokyo: Kodansha International.

Miyanaga, Kuniko (1991) *The Creative Edge: Emerging Individualism in Japan*. New Brunswick and London: Transaction Publishers.

Nukada, Iwao (1977) *Tsutsumi*. Tokyo: Hosei Daigaku Shuppansha.

Oka, Hideyuki (1967) *How to Wrap Five Eggs: Japanese Design in Traditional Packaging*. New York: Weatherhill; Tokyo: Bijutsu Shuppansha. 1988 reprint, Tokyo: Meguro Museum of Art.

—— (1988) 'The Embodiment of Spirit: Reflections on Japanese Packaging Traditions', introduction to *The Art of Japanese Packages*, catalogue for Canadian tour of an exhibition of the same name, Quebec: Musée de la Civilisation.

Okely, Judith and Callaway, Helen (eds) (1992) *Anthropology and Autobiography*. London: Routledge.

Origuchi, Shinobu (1945) 'Reikon no Hanashi', *Origuchi Shinobu Zenshu*, vol. 3. Tokyo: Chūōkōronsha, pp. 260–74.

Raz, Jacob (1992) 'Self-presentation and Performance in the *Yakuza* Way of Life: Fieldwork with a Japanese Underworld Group', in Roger Goodman and Kirsten Refsing (eds) *Ideology and Practice in Modern Japan*. London: Routledge.

Sato, Ikuya (1991) *Kamikaze Biker: Parody and Anomy in Affluent Japan*. Chicago: University of Chicago Press.

Turner, Victor (1967) *The Forest of Symbols*, Ithaca and London: Cornell University Press.

Yoshida, Teigo (1987) 'Is Japan a Secular Society? A Report on the Third Japan Anthropology Workshop Conference', *Japan Foundation Newsletter* 15 (1).

Yoshino, K. (1992) *Cultural Nationalism in Contemporary Japan*. London: Routledge.

# 5 RESEARCHING CULTURE IN THE BASQUELAND

*Jeremy MacClancy*

Long-term intensive fieldwork, based on the impossible ideal of participant observation, is the characteristic research method of social anthropology. Realising its intellectual potential is what has made anthropology, among its cognate disciplines, both distinctive and prestigious. Fieldwork has become so central to anthropologists' sense and image of themselves that carrying it out has long been a necessary *rite de passage* for any doctoral student who wishes eventually to be accepted as an equal by the professionals who control the discipline. There are, it is true, some tenured anthropologists who have never left the library but, for better or worse, they tend to be looked down upon by many of their colleagues and, chances are, they found it much more difficult to get a job.

It is also true that fieldwork is no longer unique to anthropology but has been taken on board by a variety of disciplines either within or allied to the social sciences. While this spread in its popularity might make anthropology a slightly less distinctive discipline than it once was from those closest to it, most anthropologists regard this taking-up of their method as reflecting well on the discipline. If others wish to borrow from us, the reasoning seems to go, it must be because we have something worth borrowing. In these circumstances, some anthropologists continue to pride themselves that since the notion of fieldwork maintained within their discipline is highly developed and very fine-grained, others will continue to look to anthropology for methodological insights and suggestions.

In this chapter, I wish to probe the nature of contemporary fieldwork in a modern European setting by discussing aspects of my own continuing research in the Basque Country of northern Spain. This

will allow me to pursue three general aims. First, I wish to underline
the role of dialogue in the production of anthropological knowledge.
'Dialogue' is a simple concept employed in a complex manner. As I
will reveal in an extended example, an academic of social life comes
upon and enters into a variety of dialogues, any of which may be relevant
to her aims. Also, these constant conversations with others may throw
up unanticipated questions and reveal unexpected contexts for the
exploration of meaning. This fluidity and open-endedness, where
contexts are not always set but frequently shifting and constantly
evolving, is a distinguishing consequence of fieldwork compared to
other methods of research and fledgling fieldworkers who aim at even
a basic level of competence must be intellectually supple enough to
exploit these opportunities when they appear.

Engaging in dialogue makes the fieldworker as much a social actor
as a social interpreter. This is a further distinctiveness of fieldwork,
for in order to study social and cultural relations, anthropologists must
enter into social relations with the people they are studying. This
complicating factor is neither simply a boon nor a hindrance. It is, above
all, a fact of the fieldworking life of which fieldworkers must take
account, obliging them to reflect on the nature of the information they
have helped to generate and *how* they have helped to generate it.

Second, I wish to explore the limitations of a focus on textuality.
Those who fail to situate sufficiently texts within their institutional
and social settings, or to pay adequate attention to the nuanced analysis
of the production and reception of texts, construct accounts which
are only lightly anchored in the social. Analysing *texts* without
grounding them in a thoroughgoing manner in *context* is like trying
to prove an equation by dealing with only half of it. An essentially
'textualist' account of the world is ultimately a very meagre one. The
nature of culture that anthropologists study is the fabric and content
of social relations, and one cannot really attempt to understand these
relations without becoming subjectively involved with the people one
wishes to study and whose view of the world one wishes to comprehend.
Thus fieldwork, by its very nature, forces researchers to position
themselves squarely within the field of research, and that interaction
and engagement may well generate significant research findings which
cannot be substituted by an approach which concentrates on the
analysis of representations-at-a-distance.

Third, I wish to demonstrate the impoverishing restrictiveness of any approach which fastens on the contemporary, in the process forsaking various historical dimensions. According to Colin McCabe (1995), when Richard Hoggart wished to set up a 'Centre for Cultural Studies' at the University of Birmingham, certain academics complained that the university had already been doing cultural studies for years. As far as they were concerned, the subject already existed, under the name of classics. Hoggart took the point and named his centre one for 'Contemporary Cultural Studies'. Yet in doing so, Hoggart and his followers cut themselves off from one of the most important dimensions of cultural life. The point here is that just adding a historical chapter to the beginning of one's study simply will not do. Rather, what is required is the thoroughgoing integration in one's study of the various local forms of the social production of histories.

## TEXT, CONTEXT AND DIALOGUE

Having done my doctoral research in island Melanesia, I chose to do postdoctoral fieldwork in Europe for several reasons. The academic reasons were that I liked the challenge of working closer 'to home' in a complex culture with a glorious and lively tradition of literature and a strong sense of history – since the 1820s Spain has suffered four civil wars and undergone several changes, not just of government, but of system of government.

I also relished the test of working in an area where anthropologists compete against novelists as fellow students of social life and so are forced to do finer-grained fieldwork if they wish their cultural characterisations to be ethnographically credible. Literate natives can all too easily crab what they consider to be caricatures. They do not want to be remembered in print as unsophisticated handlers of crudely defined concepts. In these settings the Other is not radically different, and fieldworkers, by studying and living with people so culturally similar to themselves, come to a more detailed understanding of their own social selves. The careful consideration of this narrow cultural gap is a test both for the individual and for the discipline. For if anthropology has little to report about our own societies, then what exactly *can* it say?

The original aim of my research was to study the culture of a nationalism, until then an undeservedly neglected topic. A stereotyping statement about postwar British anthropologists was that they ignored culture for the sake of social structure. Rather than repeat the sins of my predecessors, and keen to demonstrate the blinkered approach of political theorists of nationalism (such as Gellner), I wished to examine the manifold roles of cultural aspects of nationalism in the production and maintenance of a nationalist community. A Spanish anthropologist passing through Oxford told me that Basque, Catalan, and Galician nationalisms were already well studied and that the Andalusian variety 'isn't really nationalism'. He said the northern province of Navarre nursed a regionalism worthy of investigation. This would complicate my project, in an intellectually interesting way, for I now intended to research the cultural consequences of the ideological conflict, in Navarre, between left-wing Basque nationalism and right-wing Navarran regionalism. Fieldwork in Navarre had the added attraction of enabling me to do some work on Carlism, a very long-established legitimist movement still alive in the area.

I went to live in the Old Quarter of Pamplona for nine months in order to improve my Castilian and to learn more about the local scene. After gaining a research fellowship, I returned to Pamplona where I attended an intensive course in the Basque language (Euskera). Three months later I went to live in 'Uli Alto', a small aesthetically pleasing Navarran village. I lived there for the next 21 months and have since returned to the village at least once every year.

It is true that I read texts, thousands of them, in a variety of formats (newspapers, magazines, comics, pamphlets, manifestos, books, novels, songsheets, catechisms, hymnals, devotional literature, political flyers, posters, television and radio programmes, and so on) and from a variety of sources (I consulted, for example, familial, municipal, parochial, judicial, episcopal, regional, national and party political archives). But my understanding of all these physical texts would have been very greatly impoverished if I had not been able to engage in dialogue with the broadest possible spectrum of locals. Investigating text outside of context would have been an intellectual con, and I wasn't into hoodwinking.

Clifford, in a highly influential paper (1980), has tried to portray fieldwork as essentially a process of dialogue where the anthropologist complicitly participates with a huddle of key informants in the fabrication of an intersubjective, intercultural text. On the basis of my own experience, I can state that his portrayal, though highly suggestive, is ultimately meagre and, to a significant degree, misleading. I did come, I openly confess, to value highly the words and opinions of a few key friends. But they were only a shifting inner circle, to my Ego, of a extensive network of friends, acquaintances and colleagues, all of whom I valued in different ways.

Let me be more specific. Dialogue began from Day One, with my pestering my Pamplonan flatmate and his friends about what I was reading in the local papers or observing in the streets. Those conversations occurred during the evenings on our bar-crawls. During the day, I chatted with the shopkeepers I assiduously patronised, with off-duty barpersons I had come to know, with the students to whom I taught English, and with the drivers who picked me up when I decided to hitchhike around the province. Getting to know expatriate Anglophones helped to round out my expanding circle of acquaintance and provided another avenue into the social life of the city. By the end of my first stay in Pamplona, the majority of my friends were in their 20s or 30s, left-wing to a varying degree, and, if employed, held down jobs in schools or City Hall, on factory floors or behind a bar.

I gained entry to Uli Alto thanks to a journalist acquaintance who knew the village poet. He introduced me to his neighbours who had a near-empty house three doors down the street. I moved in a fortnight later, now already knowing two local families. That Saturday the poet had me made a member of his age-grade's weekly dining group. It was members of the poet's family, my landlord's family, and of the dining group who were to become my closest friends. These were the people to whom I constantly turned, even though I eventually got to be on speaking terms with everyone in this settlement of 400 people.

My friends and many of the villagers made frequent, and often spontaneous, commentary on events they knew I was interested in. My landlords, for instance, used the television news programme we dutifully watched every lunchtime as a stimulus for discussions with me about contemporary politics or the state of the nation. My landlady would come in to quiz me about what other villagers whom I had just interviewed had revealed. She would then provide her own context to, and evaluation of, what they had said. Her daughter would visit me at other times and often give me a somewhat different version. When I spent the day in a Pamplonan archive, she and her husband would inquire over supper what I had been reading and would then pass judgement on the information I reported. Their statements I could begin to evaluate by provoking other villagers to give their opinion on the same topic. I was also able to contrast and contextualise village views by speaking to my urban-based friends in Pamplona. At the same time I discussed my work with local academics (above all, regional historians) and with archivists who guided me through their collections, frequently passing (often hilarious) comment on the material they found in the stacks.

European societies are complex ones and I did not want to reproduce in a blinkering fashion the sort of closed community study that epitomised the classic ethnographies of my Europeanist predecessors. That was one reason why I had deliberately chosen a research topic whose boundaries went far beyond any village and why I was so keen to maintain my Pamplonan contacts. It was for the same reason that, for my Carlist research, I interviewed not just villagers but provincial, regional and national leaders of the movement as well. I wished to follow the evolution of Carlism at different levels and to clarify the perception of what constituted the movement held by people at different rungs on its hierarchy. For this reason I journeyed to the capitals of other nearby provinces and to Madrid, where, once again, I engaged in a series of dialogues, provoking commentary by telling Carlist leaders what villagers thought of the movement and of their actions, and (back in Uli Alto) vice versa.

A few years after my major stint of fieldwork, I was asked to contribute to a conference on 'Biological and Social Aspects of Ethnicity' (published as MacClancy 1993). This invitation led me to explore a further dimension of the complexity of anthropology in Europe: regarding one's peers as ethnographic material and entering into dialogue with them as fieldwork subjects. For what I had to do was not just to assess the biological information available on the prehistory, genetic polymorphisms and physical characteristics of the Basques, but to attend, as well, to the work done by Basque anthropologists over the last hundred years into the nature of their compatriots. I needed to examine the nature of the social concepts they employed and the uses, academic and political, to which their work was put. In other words, what I was doing was looking both at the biological anthropology of the Basques and at the social anthropology of Basque biological anthropology. To that end I spent some time doing an abbreviated fieldwork in *and of* the Departamento de Biología Animal y Genética of the Universidad del País Vasco. The more I learnt, the more I discussed what I learnt with certain members of the department, and with other academics in other departments of the same university. I valued the comments they made on my drafts.

That last procedure was (and is) standard in my fieldwork. For I do not regard the dialogues I have mentioned so far as terminating with the plane home. From my very first day in Uli Alto I was as open as possible with the villagers about the nature and aims of my work and declared that I would return with my manuscript for them (or at least some of them) to comment on. So far the procedure has worked well and I have adapted my work somewhat when given, in my opinion, good reason to do so. The villagers to whom I read out sections of the manuscript agreed with the general frame of my analysis but disputed various details or shades of interpretation. The advantages of this procedure are obvious: the power of the ethnographer to represent the locals however she likes is, to a certain degree, mitigated, and the ethnographer gains a more fine-grained account in the process. Indeed, if anything, the procedure has worked suspiciously well and I wonder at times if the villagers are not, once again, treating me with the perhaps over-great respect they display towards academics.

Dialogue may also emerge in unexpected ways and may be stimulated in an unforeseen manner. This is to draw out the importance of being physically present in a fieldsite and of participating physically in certain activities. While living in the Old Quarter of Pamplona, I was forced to be present at (or at least be very aware of) the frequent skirmishes between police and nationalist demonstrators which took place in the narrow labyrinthine streets of the Quarter. Later on, in a bar, I would discuss the details of the demonstration with my friends. It was a topic of conversation and I did not give the matter much importance. I only became conscious of the significance of these urban battles when, that summer, I ran with the bulls.

Hemingway made Pamplona famous by writing a novel about Sanfermines, its annual fiesta. And, thanks to his obsessive interest in bullfighting, the particular event within the week-long fiesta which has become most renowned is the daily running, at dawn, of the bulls from one of the city gates to the bull-ring. Until the day I ran, I had discussed the matter with experienced friends who had told me how best, and where, to run. But, on the evening of the day I ran, I realised that the questions that they now asked me ('Where did you run? How often? For how long? How close did the bulls get?') were remarkably similar to the questions they had put to me after a street battle. For the riot police are commonly called bulls. At the same time, I also realised that people run, on both occasions, along the same streets of the Old Quarter.

Wishing to follow this interesting lead, I decided to pursue the matter and began assiduously to observe demonstrations and to discuss their form and significance with friends. It rapidly became clear that the meeting between the police and a crowd was almost as ritualised as the encounter between bulls and runners in Sanfermines. Demonstrators would provoke reaction by gathering in the main Plaza of the Old Quarter, shouting slogans and spilling the contents of bottle-banks across one of the entrances to the square. The police-vans would then arrive, to the patent expectation of their opponents: I once heard the crowd *cheer* when the vans belatedly turned up; friends told me they had seen demonstrators impatiently stamping their feet while waiting for their adversaries to appear. The police would push open their van doors and charge towards the fray. The demonstrators would run to the relative safety of cars pulled out across the street, or stay behind smelly barricades of burning bags of rubbish. The police would use tear gas, rubber bullets and long rubber truncheons. Those behind the barricades would shout slogans, whistle, maybe let off firework rockets horizontally, and smash small drain-hole covers against marble shopfronts to make stones for throwing. The taunting, challenging nature of their jeers was patent. I heard demonstrators cry, '¡*Vago!* ¡*Vago!*' ('lazy, indolent') when the police paused in their firing. The police would charge again, the demonstrators would retreat, and so on, until the crowd was finally dispersed.

The runners in both demonstrations and Sanfermines come from predominantly the same social groups: local male youths. It is generally recognised that running with the bulls is something a young Pamplonan male does, at least once in his life. It is an opportunity to display speed, agility and bravery, especially if one is daring (and fast enough) to run 'between the horns', 'with the bull's breath on your back'. Similarly, some young nationalist activists told me that demonstrating was a necessary *rite de passage* for radicalised teenagers. As one put it: 'You have to suppress your fear.' I thought at first that tourism would be a source of major difference between the two events, as thousands of young foreigners occupy the city during Sanfermines, many of them with the aim of running at dawn. I was therefore surprised during my second winter in Navarre to meet a group of young Scandanavian tourists who were rapidly becoming locally notorious for their evident enjoyment of participating in demonstrations.

Both police and people recognised the similarities between bull-running and demonstration, but the unpaid participants in these duels emphasised to me that they run because they are against the police. If they enjoy it, they stressed, that was merely a secondary benefit. The fight may have had ritualistic elements; it was still a fight for political ends.

As I was piecing this information together I also began to notice that demonstrating was actively promoted by *Egin*, the daily newspaper produced by Herri Batasuna, the radical nationalist, revolutionary socialist party which has links with ETA, the Basque terrorist organisation. Since elected representatives of Herri Batasuna did not attend any of the national or regional assemblies, they manifested their political clout by the number of activists they could rapidly mobilise into the street. These demonstrations could be seen as doubly democratic because they were a way for 'the people', without the aid of any political representatives, to state their politics with their feet (and often their fists), and because everyone within the demonstrating crowd was equal – there was no apparent hierarchy within their number during the event. The street was openly recognised by all politicians as urban territory to be contested. As *Egin* put it, demonstrating was almost the duty of an *abertzale* (active Basque patriot); it was part of their necessary performance if they wished to be regarded as such. When, in 1987, a particular member of ETA died in prison (of natural causes) *Egin* followed its usual pattern of devoting several pages to the life of the dead man. Amidst the general panegyric typical of such events, the paper emphasised the athletic ability of the late terrorist. He had been nicknamed 'El Olímpico' ('The Olympic runner') because, in one well-known demonstration seen on television, an armed policeman swinging a truncheon had chased him for several hundred yards but had not been able to reach his target. By participating in the demonstration and getting so close to the police that one of them singled him out, El Olímpico had acted like a true *abertzale* and had done so in an exemplary, swift-footed manner.

The observed parallel between bull-running and demonstration was also exploited by another hard-left radical nationalist party, Batzarre. In a television advertisement for the party, broadcast during an election campaign, clips from riots in the Old Quarter were interspersed with shots of the crowd being chased by bulls in Sanfermines. When I asked a leading member of Batzarre, why these aspects of these two events had been juxtaposed, he replied, 'Because they show the reality of Navarran life today.'

I hope the point of this extended example is clear, that is, that I came to this understanding of the possible relations between bull-running and demonstration because of a fieldworking process of dialogue between series of participants which then enabled me, however tentatively, to place texts produced by political parties in some of their contexts. Above all, however, the process was stimulated by the fact that I had physically participated in both kinds of performance. It is, of course, possible that I might have been stimulated in the same direction by simply having listened to the conversation of my friends and others around me, but I doubt it greatly.

During fieldwork I also learnt that dialogue may be stimulated in an unforeseen manner, in a way which revealed the influence of my presence on the contexts I was studying. In the last fortnight of my extended residence in Uli Alto, I attended, for the second time, the village's annual fiesta. As usual, in the small main square, a hired band played music for people to dance to, starting at 8 in the evening and ending, after two lengthy breaks, at 3 in the morning. One night, as the music was ending and the drunkenness of the remaining revellers was becoming evident, I was suddenly cornered by a well-built, angry man about my own age. He began to berate me for having spent so much time with him and fellow nationalist radicals in the village yet without committing myself to their cause. I tried to defend myself and so we initiated a public debate which lasted over an hour. During our discussion he emphasised the prestige I held in Uli Alto because I had received so many years of education. He was angry about the inequity of our position: I was going to write about the Carlism of the village, and because I was a qualified scholar, my book would be published. I tried to answer his comments by pointing out that my book would not be a final statement and that it was not immodest of me to think that, when it appeared, it would, like almost all other books published on the area, be reviewed in the regional press. The reviewer and any correspondent who felt so inclined could state what they liked about it and I, if I felt so inclined, could reply to their comments. In this way, if the debate were sufficiently important it could come to be part of the ever-evolving context of Carlism. In other words, my forthcoming ethnography of the movement would itself become an ethnographic text for any subsequent ethnographies. To put that another way, I would become part (albeit a tiny part) of the context I was studying. This is not conceit. I had already seen similar debates in the local papers and had observed how people had then discussed them, while my work on native anthropologists of the Basques had shown me to what extent anthropology could become part of nationalism itself. In such a highly politicised area as the Basqueland, it is often difficult for students of local life to pretend not to be components of it.


## HISTORY

History is not singular but plural. This is not just to state that there are different 'histories', competing accounts of the same past period. It is to observe that people live in historical time, are influenced by historical factors, and have consciousness of the past. To typify matters somewhat we might say that there are three main different forms of history: chronology, historical consciousness and historiography. These are key aspects of any people's way of life and any study of the culture of a people which did not take them into account must be judged inadequate. The classical ethnographies of British social anthropology have been strongly criticised for precisely this reason. And, for exactly the same reason, modern ethnographies of any Western European people are thoroughly historicised, or else face the prospect of being damned by reviewers.

Let me give an example. Navarre is nationally famous as the home of Carlism, a populist, legitimist movement which has lasted over 150 years and has been a major participant in several Spanish wars. Known as 'Europe's most enduring lost cause', its heartland is that particular part of the province where I had gone to live. In order to comprehend Basque nationalism in anything like a rounded manner, I needed to look at Carlism, especially its evolution since the Civil War of 1936–39. In that conflict Carlists had fought, and fought memorably, on the side of Franco. But in the 1950s and 1960s Carlism was transformed from an ultra-orthodox Catholic, legitimist movement of the extreme right into a secular centre-left party with terrorist sympathies headed by a socialist pretender to the Spanish throne. In the 1970s many of its members passed over to the side of the Basque nationalists.

The accounts of Carlism produced by professional historians have tended to portray the movement only from the 'top down'. Writing chronicles of kings and their courts, they have usually concerned themselves with the machinations of the Carlist leaders, the programmes they elaborated, and the courses of the wars they initiated. And none of them had studied its postwar evolution. Thus if I were to study Carlism, I had to work out, as best as I could, the series of events and processes which marked the evolution of the movement, at both the national and village levels, from the beginning of the Civil War to the present. In order to elucidate villagers' historical consciousness and form of historiography, I asked them what Carlism meant to them, why they had (or had not) become Carlists, and how they had learnt about it. In order to come to an understanding of how the controlling elite of the movement represented its past, and its past in the present, and how those representations changed, I read as many relevant documents, articles, histories, novels (especially bad novels) and war memoirs, mainly Carlist but also non-Carlist, as possible. 1 also interviewed members of the elite (including its royal family) in order to ascertain why the evolution in the nature and representation of the movement took the courses they did.

My repeated discussions with Carlist veterans and with their neighbours revealed, as one might expect, that there is no single history to Carlism, that Carlists occupying different structural positions within their movement do not hold the same conceptions of the Carlist past. Members of its elites and of its rank and file have related, but identifiably distinct, notions of what it means to be Carlist and of what the Carlists had done. Their accounts, organised in narrative form, are in some aspects complementary to each other, in other aspects conflicting. In this sense, there is no one 'history' of Carlism, but a plurality of histories.

But Carlists' sense of history may be different not simply because of the structural positions they occupy. Lisón-Tolosana (1966), drawing on the ideas of Ortega y Gasset, has already demonstrated in his ethnography of an Aragonese village that people's conceptions of their history may differ because of the particular social generations to which they belong. Similarly for Carlists, their perception of the historical time within which they live may colour their vision of

Carlism and lead them to interpret it in a distinctly different way to members of earlier, still extant generations. The youthful Carlist progressives who emerged as a political force in the late 1960s and early 1970s were too young to have experienced the war but were old enough to comprehend the effects of Francoism in Spain and to be able to compare it with the rapidly developing economies and social life of other West European states. Their ideas of Carlism, of what its past signified and of how it should be understood were, to an important extent, a consequence of the chronological time they lived in. Thus in order to reveal the varieties of Carlist histories, I needed to look at the groups within the movement both socially and historically.

The histories produced by these different Carlist groups – members of the elites and of the ranks, conservatives and progressives – are couched in overlapping discourses. 'Discourse' I take to be a usefully vague term, one which Sherzer (1986: 296) characterises as 'an imprecise and emergent interface between language and culture. . . It is discourse which creates, modifies, and fine tunes both culture and language and their intersection.' Since much of my analysis is concerned with the production of histories, I had to examine that fluid interface. Since there is no simple, stable relation between discourses and the social activities through which they are produced, I had to look, in a sustained fashion, at the practice of discourse over time: how, where and when it was produced, and for what reasons; what can be said, and what cannot be said, at what times, at what places, and by whom. Both discourses and their associated social activities may change, as may the relations between them. Key terms may remain the same, though their contents alter; key terms, and the narratives which they constitute, may change in step with the development of the social activities which produce discourse. Holders of, or aspirants to, power may utilise certain discourses in order to legitimate their positions; others may use their position to legitimate their discourse. There is no fixed, prescriptive set of connections between discourse and power. I had to follow the course of their varying interrelations wherever Carlist chronology took me.

History is uttered through discourse. It may also be performed, through ritual. Though much of ritual can be regarded as a form of statement, it is at the same time a form of act, a set of embodied routines carried out in time. I analysed the central, annual ritual of Carlism, the 'pilgrimage' to Montejurra, in this dual way: as a memorial and celebration of the Carlist past, one which is constituted both discursively (by speeches, prayers, shouts, discussions, newspaper articles and books), and physically (by the symbolic re-grouping of participants into battle units and by their experiencing a sense of sacrifice comparable to those who gave up their lives for the cause). Here again I could not prescribe the relations between discourse and power: the ritual can by turns, or at one and the same time, be both legitimatory of, and legitimised by, those who attempt to control its performance; Carlist villagers, members of its elites, conservatives and progressives may all interpret its history and historical significance in their own ways, and may try (as they have, with varying degrees of success) to impose their interpretation of it. Once again, I had no recourse but to trace Carlist chronology, the historical record of its performances, in order to observe the evolution of these interrelations.

I hope that the foregoing has demonstrated the central ways that a fieldwork-based dialogue, married to a thoroughgoing concern with history, structures what I like to consider a modern ethnography. To this extent I disagree with Goddard et al. (1995: 34–5) who argue against the central role of fieldwork in the contemporary production of European anthropology. What we need, however, is not to dislodge fieldwork, but rather a more expanded, labile notion of its power and extension, where, for instance, the 'community' studied need not be a geographically circumscribed unit, where the fieldworker is alive to the restrictions, as well as the opportunities, provided by fieldworking. As I have argued earlier (MacClancy 1984), since the time of Malinowski, fieldwork has been the primary research method of our discipline: while its technological apparatus might have become somewhat more sophisticated, its nature has, to all intents and purposes, remained unchanged. We don't need less of it. If anything, we need more.

REFERENCES

Clifford, James (1980) 'Fieldwork, Reciprocity and the Making of Ethnographic Texts', *Man* 15: 518–32.

Goddard, Victoria, Llobera, Josep and Shore, Cris (1995) 'Introduction', in V. Goddard, J. Llobera, and C. Shore (eds) *The Anthropology of Europe*. Oxford: Berg, pp.1–24.

Lisón-Tolosona, Carmelo (1966) *Belmonte de los Caballeros: Anthropology and History in an Aragonese Community*. Oxford: Clarendon.

MacClancy, Jeremy (1984) 'Fieldwork Overseas' *RAIN* 64: 3–4.

—— (1993) 'Biological Basques, Sociologically Speaking', in Malcolm Chapman (ed.) *Ethnicity: Biological and Social Aspects*. Oxford: Oxford University Press, pp. 92–139.

McCabe, Colin (1995) 'Tradition, Too, Has Its Place in Cultural Studies', *The Times Literary Supplement* 4816 (26 May): 13.

Sherzer, Joel (1986) 'Language, Culture and Discourse', *American Anthropologist* 89: 295–309.

## 6 CULTURAL STUDIES AND SOCIAL ANTHROPOLOGY: CONTESTING OR COMPLEMENTARY DISCOURSES?

*Signe Howell*

Not long ago, at a dinner party I was sitting next to two people from a university Media Department. They presented themselves as adherents to cultural studies and one of them told me that he felt aggrieved at the indifferent, or even hostile, attitude of anthropologists. 'Why do I never get invited to speak at your seminars?' he asked, 'My colleagues and I do the same work as you. There are too many artificial disciplinary boundaries.' We got into quite a heated discussion. I maintained that the fact of extended fieldwork coupled with the holistic ambition which are central to the anthropological enterprise, mean *ipso facto* that our aims, attitudes and expectations with regard to the intellectual endeavour we engage in are uniquely different and that, consequently, so are the resultant understandings and texts. He retorted that this was nonsense because his is an ethnographic approach and, anyway, until anthropologists face the fact that 'primitive' societies no longer exist they are making themselves peripheral to the proper understanding of cultural processes. Post-industrialisation, postmodernism, consumerism and the capitalist globalisation of culture are rapidly rendering previous anthropological questions, methods and theories void, he said.

His remarks made me angry, but also, and more interestingly, it made me question *my* own understanding about what I am all about, and what anthropology is all about. Do anthropologists have to face the fact that we are redundant, the last remnants of colonialism in this postcolonial era? At any rate those amongst us who still persist in working in small-scale, distant and 'exotic' societies, where we try to figure out how people, who in many ways are so very different from ourselves, make sense of themselves and the world in which they live.

The time had come to familiarise myself more systematically with cultural studies. The best way to do so was to examine the products; that is, read their texts. The proof of the pudding is, after all, in the eating. I had already read some of the so-called 'globalisation of culture' literature. This had left me fairly critical, mainly because most of the theoreticians struck me as remarkably class-, gender- and Euro-centric in their assumptions, questions and, frequently, high-handed answers (Howell 1995). A brief overview of articles contained in some of the mainstream cultural studies journals confirmed this initial impression, but also showed that cultural studies is a very heterogeneous category. Much of their work is also very exciting. Before proceeding further, let me state unequivocally that I do not think that, from an intellectual point of view, social anthropologists need fear being usurped or encompassed by cultural studies. But, from an academic power-politics point of view, we may have to fight for a recognition of our unique contribution to the study of social and cultural institutions and processes, a contribution whose disciplinary roots are largely unacknowledged by exponents of cultural studies who seem to claim for themselves concepts, theories and methodologies which have long been integral to the practice of social anthropology. We could, however, play complementary roles. Before doing so, however, we would all need to examine our particular characteristics and relative strengths and weaknesses. Just as my media colleague was miffed about a lack of recognition from us, anthropologists have good reason to feel the same with regard to cultural studies. While adopting so many long-debated anthropological concepts, theories and methods and presenting them as their own, there is no doubt that in the process they are repackaging them very seductively. Much of the cultural studies literature has a heady feel; as a reader you feel that you are in at the cutting edge of social theory. Nevertheless, I think that there are several serious flaws in much of the literature. Some of these may be attributed to the fact that cultural studies is not a discipline with its own intellectual traditions which are brought to bear on actual research practices. Topics and subject matter, however interesting, cannot in themselves replace the reflexive mode of disciplinary anchored academic research. Thus, all the weaknesses (but also the strengths – primarily those of a freshness of approach and lack of inhibiting respect) of cross-disciplinary borrowings can be found in cultural studies.

In this chapter, I shall try to point out what, to my mind, constitute some major differences between social anthropology and cultural studies. It will not be an unbiased comparison, and not everyone will agree with my vision of anthropology. I shall end by giving a short account from my fieldwork with a hunter-gatherer group of people in the Malaysian rain forest and show how their notions about natural species challenge several deeply embedded Western ones, in order to argue for the inherent 'usefulness' of exotic fieldwork carried out within the disciplinary parameters of social anthropology.

## CULTURAL STUDIES: SOME CHARACTERISTICS

In his Introduction to the volume *The Cultural Studies Reader* (1993), During makes the point several times that whatever else cultural studies may or may not be, it has always been focusing on *people*, on a profound awareness of individuals' 'otherness' and their agency, as opposed to what he characterises as the dehumanising concepts and practices found elsewhere in the social sciences. Collectivities, collective representations, ideologies, world view and similar terms have dominated, resulting, he argues, in people being treated as undifferentiated categories. By contrast, the right of the multiple voices to be heard and taken analytic account of has found a champion in cultural studies. As a discipline, it has 'globalized itself through affirming otherness', that is, affirming the right of various sub-cultures to be accepted and – analytically and politically – to be accepted on their own terms.

Such statements surprised me. It could be argued that ever since Malinowski's programmatic Introduction to *Argonauts of the Western Pacific* (first published in 1922), the anthropological ambition has steadfastly been to 'grasp the native's point of view. . . to realize *his* vision of *his* world' (1978: 25, original emphasis). Anthropologists still continue to debate how best to achieve this. Be that as it may, multiculturalism with a built-in normative aim is now firmly on the agenda in universities throughout the United States.

The reported concern from anthropological circles – primarily in the US – that cultural studies is usurping anthropology deserves some reflection. In a recent article, Terry Turner puts the ball back in the anthropologists' court by telling us that we must not sulkily and passively wait to be invited to engage cultural studies, but challenge it on its home ground. For Turner, this means actively marshalling the anthropological premise of human *capacity* for culture 'as a collective power emergent in human social interaction', a capacity that, he reminds us, is inherently social in its character and which has 'virtually infinite plasticity' (1993: 426). Anthropologists have long been investigating manifestations of the capacity for culture in many parts of the world. He further suggests that as a more theoretical contribution to the study of multiculturalism, the insights gained could be used to argue for culture as a general human right (ibid.: 427–8). But is this enough? Should we just consider the challenge – if such it is – from cultural studies thematically, and with reference to 'modern Western' issues such as multiculturalism in its various manifestations of minority resistance and demands for recognition? Should we not also question their claims that what *they* do which makes them special is that they study contemporary culture and that they affirm otherness (During 1993: 25)? Do not anthropologists also do that? How we do this differently becomes the question. Contemporary culture is not, of course, synonymous with the post-industrial 'West', a fact that seems to pass many cultural studies researchers by. But even 'at home', a large number of the same themes have by now been studied by both groups: tourism, supermarkets, rock music and video, consumerism, mass media, soap operas, cinema are just a few areas where we have both engaged ourselves. There is nothing that inherently demarcates some sociocultural domains as social anthropology and others as cultural studies. There are, however, big differences in the methodologies and in the resultant studies.

In the editorial to the first issue of the journal *Theory, Culture & Society*, Featherstone sets out the main aims of the journal as, first: 'to encourage speculative and critical theory, encourage theory building and work towards a universal theory'; second: '[an] equally important aim. . . [to] encourage the substantive description and analysis of everyday life and popular culture. Seek to steer the difficult course between the superficiality of colour supplement sociology and the dangers of over-theorization' (1982: 1–2). My impression is that, thirteen years later, the editors have achieved the first aim stunningly well (with the possible exception of creating a universal theory, but perhaps in these postmodern days that is less desirable anyway), but that they have failed dismally in their second one. This impression is confirmed by another major journal, *Cultural Studies*. It is less heavily meta-level theoretical but, despite a more empirically grounded focus, nevertheless does not achieve the second aim above. I want to explore some reasons for this, and try to juxtapose what I perceive to be some major differences in our understanding of the nature and purpose of our research and its transformation into text.

My reactions to what I have read of cultural studies can be summarised as five main points which will be elaborated below. (1) They focus upon cultural representations to the exclusion of presenting contextualised indigenous views and practices. (2) Despite frequent assertions that they conduct ethnographic and qualitative research, it is difficult to accept these claims at their face value. The prevailing strength of social anthropology is precisely the extended fieldwork and the use of empirical data in theorising. (3) They frequently operate on a highly abstract, jargon-ridden, meta-level. Not being an academic discipline, their theoretical vocabulary is necessarily borrowed. This means that they frequently use it idiosyncratically (not necessarily a bad thing) while claiming generality. (4) Cultural studies focuses on the modern Western world. Social anthropology focuses on both alien and familiar sociocultural formations and is comparative in its aims. (5) Despite claims to the contrary, those working in cultural studies are not reflexive about their own theories and assumptions. Given the fact that they borrow and adapt concepts from other disciplines, this ought to be central. Ultimately therefore, the impression one is left with is an academic practice which easily becomes socio-centric and provincial.

## REPRESENTATIONS OR PEOPLE?

It is noticeable that in order to analyse aspects of contemporary Western society, the data used in much cultural studies research are cultural representations drawn from, *inter alia*, media, architecture, art, advertising, literature, pop songs, fashion. Anthropologists, by contrast, have an unavoidable commitment to people. By living amongst those they study for prolonged periods the aim is to try to understand what really is going on and why. They have sought to embed interpretations of representations within a study of social institutions and social life. On the whole, cultural studies, with a strong grounding in literary studies, has been about cultural products, representations and processes rather than social life – despite the claims made by During cited above. So while they base their research primarily on texts and other representations, they move from this to assertions about sociocultural life. In my view, this means that many of their claims remain unsubstantiated. This is not to say that representations are not social facts, but that they need to be grounded in social worlds. At the same time, much of the literature is enlightening.

But the absence of people becomes rather noticeable after a while. For example, in an article entitled 'The Shape of Things to come: Expo '88' (1991), Bennet analyses the semiotics of the lay-out, architecture, posters and design as if they in themselves have some intentionality. I miss some reference to his interaction with local politicians, designers and exhibitors in order to elicit their intentions and hopes for the Expo, as well as with the various categories of the public who attended. To base the analysis exclusively on the products, however ingeniously, ends up by being suspect because the reader is not given an *entrée* into the numerous deliberations which must have occurred in the creation, performance of and participation in the Expo. As a result, one has to take it or leave it.

Another example of focusing on representations, not social relations or institutions, is Urry's article on tourism (1988) in which he describes the decline of British seaside resorts graphically with reference to collapsing piers, decaying guest houses, etc., interspersing the analysis with reference to what 'people want.' But we are not introduced to any people, so we cannot judge whether what Urry says they want actually reflects what they want.

Even when the studies include people, these are often at a remove, such as in the often cited study on *Dallas* by Ang (1992), in which she uses letters received in response to her advertisement about people's attitude to *Dallas*. These clearly are important data, but an anthropologist would not trust them on their own and would wish to carry out some participant-observation in people's homes while they actually are watching the series. While no one method is perfect, I maintain that on the point of general methodology, there are some very good arguments for the anthropological version of fieldwork and for relating cultural products to their makers and users. A case in point is an article which appeared in a recent issue of *Cultural Studies* on a Brazilian soap opera. I read this with great pleasure. It displayed what I regard as good ethnography: long periods of hanging around in people's homes before, during and after the televising of the soap, watching behaviour, body language, and taking notes of people's comments; making sure that the homes represented different socioeconomic groups in Brazil; and following fieldwork up with informed interviewing; comparing and contrasting attitudes and behaviour, and explaining these with reference to sociocultural and economic factors, to the various contexts and to relevant anthropological literature (Lead and Oliver 1988: 81–99).

Even when there is a strong theoretical desire to ground their research in people, it appears in some circles to be difficult to achieve. An article entitled 'Let Us Return to the Murmuring of Everyday Practices: A Note on Michel de Certeau, Television and Daily Life' (Silverstone 1989) typifies much of this. The author's insistence that 'if we are to gain a more mature understanding of television's place in contemporary cultures, then we need to study in detail the mechanisms of its penetration into the warp and weft of everyday life; into the ways in which it enters, and is transformed by, the heterogeneity – the polysemy and the polymorphology – of daily life' (1989: 77–94) seems promising enough. Reading on, however, we never discover how this might be achieved, nor are we given any examples of this having been done and what findings have been made. Another example is an article by Lash entitled 'Learning from Leipzig – or Politics in the Semiotic Society' (1990) in which he starts off by positioning himself as a participant-observer in euphoric Leipzig on the day that the Berlin Wall fell. Being asked by an East German what he thought about the event, he at first could think of nothing. Safely back in his office, however, he could tell us what had been going on, namely: 'The logic of post-Fordism is indeed that of semiotic production. . . an increasingly large proportion of post-Fordist commodities (i.e. information and discursive goods) are post-industrial. And an increasing amount (i.e. images) of both post-Fordist and post-industrial commodities are postmodern' (1990: 147). Does this fulfil Featherstone's second aim referred to above?

The above quotes draw attention to what I regard as an unreflexive attitude to the use of jargon in much of the cultural studies literature. Authors appear to have a deep conviction both of its truth value and its infallible explanatory value.[1] This means that we are presented with the conclusions without being let in on the argumentation, nor given possible alternative interpretations. The process can easily become self-referential. I therefore would argue for a more radical interpretation of the 'reflexive mode and the flow of signs' (Lash and Urry 1994, see below) than we actually get from the thrust of many cultural studies analyses. If methodologies are not discussed, nor basic prejudices aired, then the much-heralded reflexivity does not reach one's own practices. This is actually where much recent anthropological writing tries to be open and honest; many anthropologists today position themselves as ethnographers, writers and interpreters. I find little of this in cultural studies. We are rarely told where the authors come from, what their formative influences, their explicit and hidden agendas are.

## THE ROLE OF EMPIRICAL AND COMPARATIVE RESEARCH

This leads to another major difference, one which arises out of the previous ones, namely the way in which we construct our papers. There is a time-honoured anthropological tradition to delineate a particular issue, or theoretical problem, at the outset of a paper, often drawing upon various grand theoreticians from both anthropology and other disciplines. Then some connotations, paradoxes and implications of the issue are explored through the presentation of detailed ethnographic material which supports, expands, questions or refutes the various meta-positions. Anthropologists try not to lose sight of the complexities of their own insights gained from the study of other forms of social life. If the theory does not fit the emerging map of a reality, the theory has to be altered, not the reality. This has led to accusations of Bongo-bongoism, that is, the use of a belief or practice from one little-known exotic social group studied by the anthropologist in order to refute any general point. I would retort, however, that particular empirical examples which question or highlight general theories should be used creatively (as they mostly are); and second, better bloody minded bongo-bongoism than grand assertions that can be grounded nowhere. Comparison is the name of the anthropological game. Only through contrasts can one discern patterns. Only through contrasts can we understand our own situation, institutions and values. As far as I can see, much of cultural studies is not hampered by the demands of relevant empirical material. An avowed liberal conscience does not, to my mind, make up for lack of rigorous fieldwork, contextualised and broad-based data collection.

An added bonus of the traditional anthropological method of writing is that those who come after us can use our empirical information in order to construct alternate interpretations. Recent debates in anthropology have alerted us to the problems of the 'realistic ethnographies'. It is now a commonplace to acknowledge that ethnographic texts are symphonic products created at the interfaces between the ethnographer as personality and intellectual being, the people studied and interacted with, and the texts of previous ethnographers and theoreticians. We have a duty to record as accurately as we can observed events, actions, utterances. Not because we believe – as perhaps our predecessors did – that this activity is scientific in a positivistic sense, but because careful descriptions represent one version of a reality; a reality which is there regardless of the presence of the anthropologist (cf. Howell 1994). As Rosaldo pointed out, we may not be able to identify progress in anthropological knowledge, but we do recognise a good ethnographic description when we read one (1989: 33). To write good ethnographies should be our aim. Larcom gives an example of how Deacon's work from Melanesia written 50 years prior to her own fieldwork in the same area gave her insights needed to make meaningful interpretation of social change. At first resistant to his interpretations, the experience of living in the field made her abandon her original theoretical focus in favour of an appreciation of central indigenous ideological principles. She rightly points out that her use of these principles served ends different from those of Deacon, but without his careful observations, her own interpretations would have been poorer (Larcom 1983: 190). I wish to suggest that this is an example of historical changes having taken place not just in the specific part of Melanesia, but also within the anthropological interpretative communities (cf. Fish 1980). One is not going to stop asking questions from the same material. As I have argued elsewhere (Howell 1994) reading culture (that is, the texts of others who came before us) self-consciously and reflexively is the catalyst in the development of knowledge. In other words, there is an aspect to the anthropological discourse which means that it may be regarded as a cumulative process whereby we continuously encompass our predecessors' ethnographies. There are no final answers, only twists and turns of understandings. However, these understandings from distant and near places can in themselves be regarded as a positive contribution to understanding the world we ourselves live in.[2]

## CENTRE OR PERIPHERY? OURSELVES OR OTHERS?

Difference can further be found in what constitute the topics and ultimate aims for research. So far, to my knowledge, there are no studies of geographically distant 'exotic' societies which have come out of cultural studies. I think here lies, if not *the*, then at least one, nub. Cultural studies practitioners are primarily interested in understanding cultural phenomena and processes within their own cultural domain, by which I (they) mean the industrialised capitalist 'West', a West which increasingly includes Japan and the Pacific Basin but without taking analytic account of the numerous local varieties. In other words, cultural studies is primarily concerned with analysing cultural phenomena within their own socio-historical and cultural configurations, often with an added normative function. Certainly, sub-groups and dissident voices receive attention, but primarily in terms of these being related to, or juxtaposed with, some form of dominant Western discourse. The majority of the studies that take on board non-Western cultural phenomena are dealing with the globalisation of culture, but, again, they do not display an inherent interest in alien forms of social and cultural life. One may detect relatively unquestioned assumptions of the inevitable and rapid encroachment of Western capitalism, mass culture and consumerism. The numerous edited volumes on global culture which have appeared in recent years are very marked in this respect. The few anthropologists (mainly Honers, Friedman and Appadurai) who are invited to participate, actually write very different papers in which they seek to show that indigenous attitudes to, and use of, industrialised products frequently are profoundly different from those of 'Western' consumers. The difference in their papers and the sorts of questions being posed can be traced to my points above concerning methodology. It is easier to make sweeping generalisations about cultural processes if one does not have to look too closely at the internal contradictions and plethora of counter-examples.

In so far as cultural studies has any identity at all, one is repeatedly told, this is through giving full analytic status to the other. Whatever that means in practice, it is true to state that ever since Boas and Malinowski, the anthropological project has been committed to some form of cultural relativisrn. Debates about how best to achieve this without collapsing all significant differences, creating radical alterity, or abandoning the psychic and cognitive unity of humanity are not similarly addressed in the cultural studies literature. I would further argue that living in close proximity to those we study, makes anthropologists hyper-sensitive both to the implications of creating 'the other' and to developing normative ideologies.

With an avowed denial of collectivities, by wishing to give full analytic status to individual agency and to empowerment, and with an ideological commitment to giving voices to the numerous others, there is a danger of losing sight of the constitutive significance of the cultural in culture, the social in society. Recently, exciting new evidence from developmental psychology substantiates the anthropological postulates about innate sociality and the intersubjective constitution of knowledge (for example, Meltzoff and Gopnik 1993, Trevarthen 1993). Their work shows that human being are in their very nature social; that meanings, values and symbols are created relationally. A theoretical separation between individuals and society becomes less tenable than ever, and the bounded, self-sufficient individual has little to offer social theory.

Unlike the majority of cultural studies practitioners anthropologists make a point of studying life-worlds different from their own personal experience. This does not exclude the study of social configurations within the Western world. However, the legacy from previously concentrating on the dramatically alien, has led to a methodological requirement to 'exoticise' the familiar in order to gain a distance and thereby question that which is experienced as normal. If this is not practised deliberately, a blindness can easily arise to genuine alternative social realities and to the theoretical implications of this. Anthropology has a long tradition of studying those socialities which have developed ontologies, epistemologies and cosmologies with little, or no, reference to those of Western traditions. We are a comparative discipline. If we abandon that ambition, we are in danger of losing the main contribution of anthropological practice, namely the presentation of the genuine alternative views of reality, humanity, cosmos, knowledge and of being in the world; the dramatically different social, political and cultural institutions. I would argue that it is only by fully accepting the importance of this fact that we, as reflexive individuals in the modern Western world, may realise the premises for choice and for change. If we focus only on ourselves and those within our own economic and political orbit, without debating our methods and theories, I suggest that there is a real danger that the very notion of reflexivity will become meaningless, and the research itself a closed system.

This obsessive interest in ourselves can therefore make us close in on ourselves and, in effect, exclude considerations of alternative ways of being and the theoretical challenges of how to account for sociocultural differences and similarities. Otherwise, despite the ever increasing sophistication of analysis, a certain inevitability creeps in when the focus is on particular cultural products or processes confined to 'modernity'.

In their recent, very interesting, book *Economies of Signs and Space* (1994), Lash and Urry exemplify some of these unintended consequences. At the end of the Introduction, after having told us what the book is about, namely a *Zeitdiagnostische Soziologi* which contains both 'a sociology of flows and a sociology of reflexivity' (1994: 6), they acknowledge the undesirable possibility of methodological individualism, and state that, despite an increasing detraditionalisation [in the West] there is nevertheless a structural basis for today's reflexive individuals which is not, they argue, social structures, but 'increasingly the pervasion of *information and communication* structures'. These are global (ibid.). However, as if to substantiate my point about self-focusing, Lash and Urry apologise for not discussing anything but 'the centre,' for including nothing about 'the periphery', such as Eastern Europe and the Third World. While claiming to speak about the global situation, by identifying it as 'peripheral' they dismiss the larger part of the globe at the stroke of a pen. Moreover, I am not convinced that everyone in the West perceive themselves as reflexive individuals living in a detraditionalised world. Many social scientists, artists and journalists probably do; but do the villagers in Austria or France, or inhabitants of urban British council estates? Nor am I convinced that the 'pervasion of information and communication structures' is understood identically in the same stratum of one society, let alone by all participants in Western capitalism.

The last sentence of the Introduction is very potent, very resonant, and yet at the end of the day, how do we know that it reflects an experienced reality of the main, or indeed subsidiary, actors? It reads:

People are in fact increasingly knowledgeable about just how little they in fact do know. Such increasingly uncontrolled economies of signs and space are inconceivable without extraordinarily complex and ever-developing forms of information, knowledge and aesthetic judgement. The unintended consequences of reflexivity – that is, the effect of reflexive agency on increasingly contingent structure – often lead to yet further disorganization. (1994: 11)

Until we are given examples that provide evidence that this is in fact how people (whoever they may be) think about the world today, this statement may reflect nothing more than a view from afar.

## CULTURAL STUDIES AND SOCIAL ANTHROPOLOGY

How does cultural studies threaten social anthropology? How do we threaten them? How should or could we work together? I can see no reason to feel threatened by cultural studies when it enters our home ground of ethnographic fieldwork, that of making other life-worlds seem meaningful by studying social and cultural institutions in their contexts. I can see very little evidence that they really do want to study human beings in their sociocultural settings; that they want to explicate upon indigenous categories and values in order to either make some interpretative generalisations about a particular form of social life, or use insights gained about the particular to theorise about the general.

The anthropological method of living in a community over a long period has been a prerequisite for providing knowledge about social and cultural institutions and processes. Although in recent years this has had to be modified in those cases where the anthropologists study complex institutions in industrial societies, the basic requirements of the method stand. These demands are: to interact in the local language; to participate in daily as well as special events; to pay particular attention to the minutiae of social action and interactions, to the institutional, cosmological and materiality of daily and ceremonial life, to the qualities of significant objects, to daily and ritual speech and the dissecting of local categories and indigenous ideas and values; to evaluate cultural representations; to elicit patterns and paradoxes, underlying structuring principles and the force of the normative, as well as interpretative significance of instances of breaches and idiosyncrasies. In principle, this is the approach adhered to whether we study hunter-gatherers in the Malaysian rain forest or rock groups and their followers in Oslo. I see little sign that cultural studies takes account of our findings, or gives the methodology credence. Indeed questions of method receive scant attention. This may perhaps be one reason for the superficiality of ethnographic accounts and the tendency to operate on a theoretical meta-level in much cultural studies.

I can see a danger of theorising replacing empirical research – an activity which is much too easily dismissed as empiricism. I can see a danger of students being seduced by the heady jargon. I am not sure, however, how much anthropologists in Britain and Europe need to fight back. Social anthropology is also a heady discipline and we are attracting ever increasing student numbers. Perhaps we need to formulate some clear arguments so that we can counter claims from students demanding a shift towards cultural studies and a desire to study a topic, or some cultural representations, not a form of social life. Arguments are not too difficult to find.

There is a tendency in many cultural studies texts to overvalue local (that is, those generated by cultural studies) theories and concepts. As a result it can become self-confirming to an alarming degree. It can also smack of self-righteousness which can lead to ideological dichotomi-sation. A study carried out on students' reactions to various cultural studies courses at the Open University shows that many students felt that, unless they toed the theoretical line, a line which many felt was extremely moralistically dogmatic about popular culture in its many expressions, they were given to feel that they were beyond the pale (Miller 1994: 427) . It is precisely intellectual dogmatism that anthropology can combat through the continuous marshalling of a multiplicity of alternatives, both theoretical and empirical.

On the other hand, much resonant theoretical apparatus has emerged out of cultural studies. It has not correspondingly emerged out of social anthropology. Beyond deconstructing every previously useful anthro-pological concept such as totemism, millenarianism, kinship, marriage, sacrifice, culture and even society, anthropologists' main contribution in recent years has been the elaboration of second-order – or middle range – theoretical concepts. The discipline can be characterised as going through a severe attack of timidity. This is bad timing in view of the interest taken in anthropology by other disciplines. By contrast, adherents to cultural studies do not suffer from any similar inhibitions. Their style of writing is noticeably strident and self-confident. Where anthropologists would put forward a tentative suggestion, the majority of cultural studies theorists make vigorous assertions. They have no hesitation in presenting first-order theorising, frequently extremely thought-provoking and taken up by anthropologists in their own research. Thus for example, Beck's notion of risk society opens a new way to analyse contemporary political economy. His argument is that we are moving from a social situation in which political conflicts and cleavages were defined by a logic of the distribution of goods, to one in which these cleavages are increasingly defined by the definition of 'bads', that is, of hazards and risks (Beck 1992: Ch. 1). Risk society knows no national boundaries; the effects of Chernobyl, of the destruction of rain forests and the ozone layer are felt across the globe. In place of the class-versus-class cleavage of industrial society, the risk society is more likely to put sector against sector. Giddens's notion of 'autopoetic system', whereby relationships become independent of external anchors of convention and institution (cf. Lash and Urry 1994: 42), and concepts such as globalisation (for example, Robertson 1992, Featherstone 1990) have helped our thinking about contemporary socioeconomic processes, as has Wallerstein's world system theory (1974). Anthropologists can counter with nothing of the same magnitude.

Lash and Urry have taken on board some of the criticism levelled against cultural studies. Concerning accusations of methodological individualism, they seek both to reinstate the 'we' and society. However, although one of their aims in *Economies of Signs and Space* has been to demonstrate significant differences between 'apparently similar advances in capitalist societies' (1994: 321), they disclaim any desire to return to what they have already critically dismissed as 'society centred' social sciences. Rather, they claim to have:

shown that such differences are the complex product of the interplay between each society's history *and* the current flows of capital, technologies, people, ideas, and images, where those flows are also seen as having a history and a geography and where there are certain local nodes in particular societies involved in the propagation or reproduction of certain flows. (ibid.)

It is hard to argue against such statements of intent. But is this not close to what anthropologists would claim that they are trying to do as well? There is no reason why we should not all seek these goals, but unlike meta-theoreticians like Lash and Urry, anthropologists should stick to their last and engage actively in a continuing critique of the generalised statements. Anthropologists could investigate what such 'flows' actually might mean, and how they might be constituted at any given time in any given place.

## THE VALUE OF EMPIRICALLY BASED
## CROSS-CULTURAL COMPARISON

I turn now to a short case study through which I shall seek to highlight some of the general points I have addressed above. The empirical material was obtained during extended and repeated fieldwork with the Chewong, a small group of hunter-gatherers/shifting cultivators who lived, until a few years ago, deep in the rain forest of peninsular Malaysia where they carried on a way of life largely undisturbed by outsiders, adhering to their particular view of reality.[3]

I wish to start on an anecdotal note. Throughout my original fieldwork I was intrigued by their classification of the 'natural world'. I tried systematically to grasp which animals or plants were thought of as conscious beings, what I call personages, and which were not. I tried to elicit what criteria allocated them to either grouping. Chewong individuals got pretty fed up with my asking whether every encountered natural species was 'like humans'. I inquired whether it had *ruwai* (soul, consciousness – I return to this below), whether it spoke a real language, whether it had the same social institutions as they and observed the same prescriptions and proscriptions, and other obsessive anthropological concerns. After some time, I began to appreciate that their natural environment, their social world and their cosmological understanding were best interpreted from the point of view that they were coexistent (Howell 1989a).

When I returned to the Chewong some years later, much of the jungle had been cut down and someone had bought a television set which was run off a car battery. People particularly enjoyed watching nature films and programmes that included animals. They also liked to watch cartoons, of the Walt Disney variety, of animated animals dressed in clothes and living in houses where they behaved according to North American human standards. Once as we sat watching such a film, my old mother turned to me and asked:

Why were you always asking if pigs, dogs, monkeys, snakes, bananas or whatever were personages or not? You told us that in your country they could never speak; that they did not behave like humans when they were in their own lands. But here we see that they do all those things. There is no difference between us in the jungle and you in England.

From a certain perspective this throws us right back into nineteenth-century anthropological animistic speculations, or to Lévy-Bruhl's notions of the pre-logical. In a more cultural studies mode, the incident could be used to study the impact of television on a social group hitherto unexposed to modern media. Neither is my intention here. I want to use the incident to discuss how an appreciation of an ontology and epistemology based on dramatically different premises to those of Western science can assist in thinking about our own notions and practices reflexively. Mine is a defence of the comparative approach and of the anthropological method. I wish to make a claim for the superior strength of the ethnographic method in eliciting essential details about existential matters. We cannot predict what may be regarded as problematic or unproblematic in social situations. Neither is there a 'predictable correspondence between specific ecosystems and specific schemes of practice' (Descola 1992: 111). We forget this at our peril. In my opinion, it is an anthropological truism that, minimally, people are committed to a description, or sets of descriptions, of their world and that every description presupposes some (often implicit) theory. Our job is to discover and interpret the descriptions and the theories. Only then can we begin to make generalisations about human life.

## CHEWONG IDEAS OF SPECIES: QUESTIONS OF CONSCIOUSNESS AND MORAL IMPERATIVES

In Western moral philosophical terms, since Classical times, humans have been set apart from – and usually above – all other animals according to some essential criteria. This separation has been justified on grounds of moral superiority and was reinforced by the Cartesian separation between mind and body. These pairs have not been held to be of equal value: humans are superior to animals, the mind is superior to the body just as thinking is to feeling. Furthermore, the mind and mental processes have been regarded as characteristically male qualities and the body and emotionality as female ones. From the anthropological point of view, these ideas are, of course, to be regarded as just one ethnographic example of how humans may construct meanings and morals about their own identities and realities. They represent, however, a view with universalistic ambitions, and it has proved peculiarly resistant to challenges. My argument here is that the

Chewong constitute an empirical counter-example to several of the above Western universalistic models and therefore warrant serious consideration (Howell 1996).

Animals (and other natural kinds such as trees, plants, rivers, stones) are included in Chewong understanding of humanity and personhood. Their ideas of species and natural kinds are integral to their world view, to their views of themselves and others.[4] Simplified, everything in their environment is divided into two major categories: those animals, trees, plants, rivers, stones and objects which are personages and those which are not. The class of personages is constituted on the basis of presence, or absence, of consciousness in the sense of language, reason, intellect, emotionality and moral conscience. From the point of view of principle, all these qualities are necessary and the social and moral codes are identical for all personages, but each species has its own parameters of actual manifestations. What is acceptable and unacceptable behaviour is species-bound. Human beings, as one species of personage, stand in interactive and intersubjective relationships with all other personages.

I have argued elsewhere (Howell 1989a, 1989b, 1996) that the body is to be understood as part of Chewong notions of species-bound consciousness. While it is possible in trance to move between bodies of other species, this can only be done for short periods, and it is a risky business. It is vital that the *nuwai* returns to the correct body. Chewong notions thus contradict a basic premise of Johnson's in his discussion about embodied knowledge, namely 'that our bodies are a stable given from which we are never separate' (1987: 206). To the Chewong, bodies are *part* of a bigger whole that constitutes the person as a member of a species. Epistemologically, there is thus a very real sense in which one may talk of mind/body/emotion fusion.

TO CONCLUDE

Chewong views cannot in any sense help Western scientists or moral philosophers in their quest for understanding essential differences and similarities between humans and other animals. Western boundaries between nature and culture are embedded within Western ideology and philosophy and have a long intellectual history. They cannot be changed, moved or removed except by posing the questions and arguments within concepts and categories of Western philosophical and scientific discourses. Chewong views can, however, dismantle Western-centrism, and open possibilities for a new reflexivity towards Western academic intellectual givens.

This fairly traditional anthropological summary of some classificatory ideas, and their social ramifications, amongst this small pre-literate, pre-industrial, pre-modern, pre-Fordist group of people, does therefore represent a genuine contribution to knowledge; a contribution which, according to my argument, is unlikely to have emerged from cultural studies. I do not intend to reiterate the points already made about what I regard as some major differences between the two approaches to the study of social and cultural phenomena. My point here is to draw attention to the kind of empirical detail that anthropological fieldwork gives rise to as this practice is predicated upon debated methodological and theoretical premises, detail that it would have been well-nigh impossible to obtain through interviews or through the observation of cultural representations alone; detail without which any statement about Chewong understanding about themselves and their reality would be spurious. By extension, any attempts to generalise from the Chewong material would be equally spurious.

I do not claim that my interpretation of Chewong values and practices is in any sense 'correct'. There probably is no one correct version. I do maintain, however, that it is recognisable to Chewong individuals. My insights were obtained mostly by being present in daily and ritualised life when tiny, semi-automatic, acts were performed that no one thought worthwhile telling me about because, to them they were completely 'natural' while to me, they were filled with unexpected meanings. I learnt from being told their myths and legends in ordinary social settings and listening to children's questioning about their meaning; from recording their shamanistic songs and obtaining native commentaries on them. I learnt by being taught how to behave according to the numerous seemingly mundane prescriptions and proscriptions which, I came to appreciate, were cosmologically derived and thus infractions had cosmological consequences.

Focusing, as I ended up doing, on indigenous categories of species, on emotionality, and on their cosmologically constituted mundane and ritual practices, meant that I have had to be extremely careful about the concepts used when writing about them. Questions about translation become particularly pertinent when we find ourselves in the domain of the cognitive, the psychological, the symbolic. Words like 'fear' or 'proud' or 'angry', like 'right' and 'wrong', like 'grandmother' or 'mother's brother', for example, may connote different meanings to different sociocultural groups using the same language. How much more difficult then, meaningfully to translate such words from unrelated languages and cultures. I would maintain that only sustained involvement with many different people within a sociocultural group over a long time gives the analyst any legitimacy for pronouncing upon such delicate matters. Contextualisation and thick description become of utmost importance. In places where more familiar cultural representations, such as literary texts and art practices exist, these should of course be incorporated into the analysis, but not instead of 'the murmuring of everyday life' (Silverstone 1989).

I also wish to make the point that I did not set out to study the themes I ended up with. They were forced upon me by the empirical situation that I found myself in. Species qualities, illness and health, spirits and the handling of emotionality were what the Chewong themselves were preoccupied with. I therefore allowed my investigations to be dictated by what was significant to the people themselves. The explicit theoretical questions that I subsequently addressed emerged out of the themes and conundrums of seeking to understand elusive indigenous concepts. Some of the theoretical vocabulary that I subsequently employed has been drawn from non-anthropological sources, including cultural studies. However, I would argue strongly for the inductive anthropological tradition. It is only by arriving in the field without clear-cut problems to be solved, theories to be tested, that we may still have something to contribute to the social sciences. By allowing that which is important to the people we study to dictate our questions, and by the rigorous exploration of the how, what, where, when, who and why, we can still claim to be a discipline that is genuinely interested in people – and in the cross-cultural comparison of social institutions and processes. Anthropologists should seek to keep hold of a continually constitutive relationship between theory, method, empirical data and theme. By separating them, one runs the danger not only of separating what people join, but also of losing premises for meaningful debate with the practitioners of other disciplines.

These aspects of social anthropology should be of interest to adherents of the cultural studies paradigms. They might do worse than include some anthropological journals in the list of 'other journals in the field of cultural studies' that appears in each issue of *Cultural Studies*. The editors state: '[the journal] wants to keep its readers informed of the work being done by these journals. After all cultural studies is a collective project.' My sincere hope is that it will become so.


## NOTES

1. The level of jargon and unsubstantiated abstractions found in much cultural studies provokes many. The *New York Times* of 17 May 1996 gleefully reported the revelations in the latest issue of *Lingua Franca* of Alan Sokal, a New York University physicist, that being fed up with what he regarded as 'the academic left's gibberish' wrote a parody on cultural studies entitled 'Transgressing the Boundaries: Towards a Transformative Hermeneutics of Quantum Gravity' which was accepted for publication by *Social Text* (May/June 1996). 'I structured the article around the silliest quotes about mathematics and physics from the most prominent academics, and I invented an argument praising them and linking them together,' he said. 'All this was very easy to carry off because my argument wasn't obliged to respect any standards of evidence or logic.' And so on. Needless to say this has created a furore and is doing the rounds on the Internet. (I am grateful to Thomas Hylland Eriksen for bringing it to my attention.)
2. An added bonus of careful ethnography is the constructive use to which it may be put in development projects – be these in the Third World or in deprived urban areas of North America or Europe.
3. Fieldwork was conducted for a period of eighteen months during 1977–79, for three months in 1981, and briefly in 1990 and 1991.
4. It is not appropriate in this paper to discuss the details of Chewong perceptions. As a result, I may give an impression of a reified culture imprisoned temporally and spatially by me. However, I have published the details elsewhere, so that those who want to test my argumentations may do so (Howell 1981, 1989a, 1989b, forthcoming).


## REFERENCES

Ang, I. (1992) 'Dallas and the Ideology of Mass Culture', in S. During (ed.) *The Cultural Studies Reader*. London: Routledge.

Beck, U. (1992) *Risk Society: Towards a New Modernity.* London: Sage.

Bennet, T. (1991) 'The Shape of Things to Come: Expo '88', *Cultural Studies* 5 (1): 30–51.

Descola, P. (1992) 'Societies of Nature and the Nature of Society', in A. Kuper (ed.) *Conceptualizing Society.* London: Routledge.

During, S. (ed.) (1993) *The Cultural Studies Reader.* London: Routledge.

Featherstone, M. (1982) 'Editorial', *Theory, Culture & Society* 1 (1): 1–2.

—— (ed.) (1990) *Global Culture: Nationalism, Globalization and Modernity.* London: Sage.

Fish, S. (1980) *Is There a Text in This Class?* Cambridge, MA: Harvard University Press.

Howell, S. (1981) 'Rules not Words', in P. Heelas and A. Lock (eds) *Indigenous Psychologies: Towards an Anthropology of the Self.* London: Academic Press.

—— (1989a) *Society and Cosmos: Chewong of Peninsular Malaysia.* Chicago: Chicago University Press.

—— (ed.) (1989b) with R. Willis *Societies at Peace: Anthropological Perspectives.* London: Routledge.

—— (1994) 'Reading Culture: Or how Anthropological Texts Create Fieldwork Expectations and Shape Future Texts', in E. Archetti (ed.) *Exploring the Written: Anthropology and the Multiplicity of Writing.* Oslo: Scandinavian University Press.

—— (1995) 'Whose Knowledge and Whose Power? A New Perspective on Cultural Diffusion', in R. Fardon (ed.) *Counterworks: Managing the Diversity of Knowledge.* London: Routledge.

—— (1996) 'Nature in Culture or Culture in Nature? Chewong Ideas of "Humans" and Other Species', in P. Descola and G. Palsson (eds) *Nature and Society.* London: Routledge.

Johnson, M. (1987) *The Body in the Mind: The Bodily Basis of Meaning, Imagination, and Reason.* Chicago: University of Chicago Press.

Larcom, J. (1983) 'Following Deacon: The Problem of Reanalysis, 1926–1981', In G.W. Stocking (ed.) *Observers Observed: Essays on Ethnographic Fieldwork.* Madison, WI: University of Wisconsin Press.

Lash, S. (1990) 'Learning from Leipzig – or, Politics in the Semiotic Society', *Theory, Culture & Society* 7 (4): 145–58.

Lash, S. and Urry, J. (1994) *Economies of Sign and Space.* London: Sage.

Lead, O.F. and Oliver, R.G. (1988) 'Class Interpretation of a Soap Opera Narrative: The Case of the Brazilian *Novela* "Summer Sun"', *Cultural Studies* 5 (1): 81–99.

Malinowski, B. (1978) [1922] *Argonauts of the Western Pacific*. London: Routledge and Kegan Paul.

Meltzoff, A.N. and Gopnik, A. (1993) 'The Role of Imitation in Understanding Persons and Developing a Theory of Mind', in S. Baron-Cohen, H. Tager-Flusberg and D. Coehn (eds) *Understanding Other Minds: Perspectives from Autism*. New York: Oxford University Press.

Miller, R.E. (1994) 'A Moment of Profound Danger: British Cultural Studies Away from the Centre', *Theory, Culture & Society* 8 (3): 417–37.

Robertson, R. (1992) *Globalization: Social Theory and Global Culture*. London: Sage.

Rosaldo, R. (1989) *Culture & Truth: The Remaking of Social Analysis*. Boston: Beacon Press.

Silverstone, R. (1989) 'Let Us Return to the Murmuring of Everyday Practices: A Note on Michel de Certeau, Television and Everyday Life', *Theory, Culture & Society* 6 (1) 77–94.

Trevarthen, C. (1993) 'The Self Born in Intersubjectivity: The Psychology of an Infant Communicating', In U. Neisser (ed.) *The Perceived Self: Ecological and Interpersonal Sources of the Self*. New York: Cambridge University Press.

Turner, T. (1993) 'Anthropology and Multiculturalism: What is Anthropology that Multiculturalists Should be Mindful of It?' *Cultural Anthropology* 8 (4): 411–29.

Urry, J. (1988) 'Cultural Change and Contemporary Holiday-Making', *Cultural Studies* 5 (1): 35–55.

Wallerstein, I. (1974) *The Modern World System*. New York: Academic Press.

# 7 METAPHORS OF EUROPE: INTEGRATION AND THE POLITICS OF LANGUAGE
*Cris Shore*

## DISCIPLINES, DISCOURSES AND RELATIONS OF POWER

One of the key differences between anthropology and cultural studies lies in their respective methodologies. If this is a conclusion reached by many of the contributors to this volume, it is also one shared by some writers within cultural studies. 'What is fundamental to a discipline', as Colin McCabe (1995: 13) says, 'is not this or that picture of the world but the practices that sustain it.' In other words, a discipline is characterised not only by its style, ethos and origins, and methods – and the implications of those methods for defining its field of inquiry – but also by the way its practitioners are trained and educated. All this seems axiomatic. To many outside observers, however, the division between anthropology and cultural studies often seems more a matter of academic politics and the maintenance of disciplinary boundaries than of content or substance. The very fact that laments about 'academic imperialism' and being 'shut out', 'silenced' and 'excluded' abound on either side of the disciplinary boundary (Rosaldo 1994: 526) appears to support this argument: after all, neither side protests about being excluded by chemists, statisticians or psychologists. As Rosaldo (1994: 525–7) observes, senior anthropologists complain about the loss of the 'discipline's crown jewel' – the concept of 'culture' – which they argue 'has been ripped off by cultural studies', while graduate students 'feel oppressed by cultural studies agendas, which they regard as the new hegemony'.

What is interesting about these remarks are the metaphors of un-neighbourly behaviour ('shut out, silenced, excluded'), theft ('ripped off') and colonialism ('imperialism, hegemony'), that characterise the relationship between these supposedly 'cognate' disciplines. In this chapter I want to explore an area where anthropology and cultural studies can complement each other both in terms of theory and method. Rather than engage in sterile disputes over intellectual property rights and academic turf-wars, I want to highlight the advantages of a multi-disciplinary approach – in this case one that draws together anthropology, cognitive linguistics and cultural studies. In a curious way, the relationship between anthropology and cultural studies, and the way this is expressed in metaphors, provides a useful starting point for thinking through the way language, ideology and power intersect in shaping and mediating social relationships. What I want to do in this chapter is develop this insight to analyse relationships between the European Union and its member states. Here too, accusations of 'hegemony', 'colonialism', 'exclusion', 'un-neighbourly behaviour' and stealing the 'crown jewels' (in this case, national sovereignty and identity) abound in debates over European integration.

My focus is political discourses on European integration and their implications for international relations, state-formation and policy-making in the European Union. The starting point is ethnography, but the analytical framework and research questions take much of their inspiration from writers commonly situated within the genealogy of modern cultural studies, most notably, Raymond Williams (1976), Antonio Gramsci (1971), Michel Foucault (1980) and Benedict Anderson (1983). My argument is that studying discourses on European integration – particularly metaphors – can reveal a great deal about the cultural differences and ideological rifts underlying current debates and disagreements between member states over the future shape and direction of the European Union. They also provide valuable insights into the deeper cognitive or classificatory schemas through which Europe is perceived in different member states. Far from being simply window-dressing used to embellish the political process with colourful imagery, I suggest that these metaphors are central to the process of imagining and conceptualising Europe. They are also key weapons in a struggle to direct and control the European agenda. This chapter asks, whose interests are served by these metaphors of Europe? To what extent do they work as instruments of power? How do they lend legitimacy and authority to particular conceptions of Europe, while imposing silence or closure on other conceptions? How are these metaphors received and interpreted by different audiences, and why do they sometimes fail to impart the messages intended by their authors? And how do problems of cross-cultural translation sometimes give these metaphors new or unintended meanings?

What I would like to propose here is that debates within anthropology and cultural studies can help us answer these questions. Anthropologists have long been interested in analysing indigenous systems of classification and thought and deconstructing the normative categories of 'other societies' – even before the term 'deconstruction' was rendered fashionable by the literary turn of post-structuralist theory. Anthropology's record of achievement in what has come to be called 'anthropology at home', however, is less impressive. Here cultural studies, particularly the work of cultural Marxist thinkers including Antonio Gramsci, Raymond Williams, E.P. Thompson, Stuart Hall and writers within the British 'New Left' and Foucauldian traditions, has made a particularly useful contribution to our understanding of the relationships between culture, ideology, human agency and modern forms of power. Although sometimes criticised for its populism,[1] its emphasis on 'texts' rather than ethnographic 'context', and its preoccupation with the politics of 'race', 'class' and 'gender' – often to the exclusion of other cultural forms and practices (see Howell and Werbner, this volume)[2] – this critical strand of cultural studies has, nevertheless, provided a valuable corpus of work in the analysis of those normative concepts and categories that structure cultural life in Western societies – precisely because of its concern with power relations and the politics of difference. As Handler (1993: 992) states: 'With respect to theory, anthropology has much to learn from cultural studies about the analysis of modern systems of power and how these intersect with categorizations of persons and with social class.'

Among the most interesting and unambiguously 'political' of modern categories of thought are concepts which provide the raw material of international relations, including such imagined geographies as 'the West', 'the Orient' and 'the nation-state'. Much attention has been given to analysing the *ideological* nature of these geo-political constructs and the way they are created through discourse and power, symbols, invented traditions, the re-writing of history and other cultural devices (Anderson 1983, Foucault 1980, Hall 1992, Hobsbawm and Ranger

1983, Said 1978). Relatively little critical attention has been paid, however, to that other important geo-political concept: 'Europe', or to the ways in which these concepts are embedded within and expressed through cultural forms and practices. Furthermore, what *meanings* these categories hold for the actors and subjects of such discourses is a question often glossed over or ignored in much of the non-anthro-pological literature.

## CULTURE AND COMMUNITY AT 'THE HEART OF EUROPE': EUROPE'S POLITICAL ELITE

The actors I am concerned with in this chapter are those European Union (EU) officials and politicians who are often described as Europe's 'political class' or 'technocratic elite' (Delanty 1995: 6). If Europe is often defined as a 'construct' by critical social scientists, for those politicians and civil servants who work for the EU's institutions in Brussels, Luxembourg and in the European Commission's numerous overseas delegations (sometimes termed pejoratively as 'Eurocrats'), it is typically experienced and perceived as part of their everyday, concrete reality as well as a political ideal: 'working for Europe' and 'building a new Europe' (*la construction européenne* as it is referred to in EU parlance), is their goal and their *raison d'être*. I refer here particularly to those 28,000 or so permanent officials (*fonctionnaires*) who have made the European Union their vocation and career. Since 1992 my research has focused on these people and the institutions they serve, especially the European Commission and its staff. Apart from its extraordinary range of functions and powers, what makes the European Commission unique among international organisations, and of particular interest to students of culture, is its claim to be 'forging a new model of public administration' (Hay 1989: 51), and its description of itself as a 'supranational' civil service. Unlike national administrations, the Commission is a modern institution – barely forty years old – which its creators consciously sought 'to endow with a supranational ideology or mission' (Spence 1994: 64).

From an initial pilot study of European Community information policy and its campaign to promote a 'People's Europe' (Shore 1993), my research expanded to include the question of whether a 'European consciousness' and 'European identity' can be created to underpin the integration process, and whether there is any evidence of a new kind of distinctly 'European' subjectivity emerging within the European Commission itself. Seeking answers to these questions I embarked upon a further two-year anthropological study of EU civil servants and cultural policies, including six months of intensive fieldwork spent living and working in the so-called 'European Quarter' of Brussels.[3] As often happens during anthropological research, however, the fieldwork encounter opened up new areas for investigation, including the question of language and its implications for European integration.

What struck me during the many long interviews and conversations with EU officials was the discourse they used to describe themselves and the process of European integration. In their everyday speech, as well as in their official texts, Commission officials continually referred to European unification using journeying motifs and travelling metaphors. The process of European integration was variously characterised as a 'journey', 'road' or 'path', leading inexorably 'forwards'; away from a 'Europe of nation-states' towards a harmonious, post-nationalist future characterised by 'peace', 'progress', 'prosperity' and a more federal system of government. This was what some officials called Europe's *vocation fédérale* or 'federal destiny'. Commission officials frequently spoke of their institution as the 'dynamo of European integration' and 'heart of the Community process'. Significantly, these metaphors deviated very little from those found in the EU's official texts and public statements. According to these narratives, the Commission's legal role as 'guardian of the Treaties' legitimates its claim to being the 'conscience of the Community' and, more controversially, defender of the 'European interest'.

Equally striking was the way these conceptions had become internalised by officials and had shaped their self-image. Some clearly saw themselves not as 'mere administrators' or public servants, but as intellectuals and pioneers. If the Commission was the 'engine' of integration and 'custodian' of the Community interest then these *fonctionnaires* were its 'engineers', 'architects' and 'guardians' whose job is to oversee the integration process and make the Union work. The Commission and its staff were therefore at the forefront of the project for 'building Europe'. Indeed, a common expression used by officials as a shorthand for European integration was, '*la construction européenne*' ('the European construction') – a phrase which, significantly, has no clear meaning in English. '*Construction européenne*' was a root metaphor of European integration used both to explain the European Union's political objectives and to justify the Commission's role as vanguard and 'agent of history' within that project. This sense of mission was summed up by former Commission president Jacques Delors. Speaking on French television in 1990, he declared that he and his colleagues in the Commission were 'the trustees of European history' (quoted in Grant 1994: 136). These are bold and controversial claims, particularly for unelected civil servants who have little public support. Nevertheless, many Commission staff saw the 'ever-closer union of the peoples of Europe' envisaged in the Treaties as an irreversible process; part of the trajectory of European history – perhaps even its apotheosis. The member states were depicted as passengers on a train; moving forward together towards what the founding treaties called 'a destiny henceforward shared' (CEC 1983: 15). The alternative to European integration was typically construed as nationalism, barbarism and war (an argument often prefaced with the phrase, 'Look what happened in the former Yugoslavia!'). This idea of a stark alternative between 'progress' or decline was epitomised in the memorable image used by former Commission president Walter Hallstein, who compared European integration to riding a bicycle: the choice being either to move forward or fall off.

A third fieldwork observation was that while officials were clear about their own objectives and sense of self, they were curiously ambiguous about the destiny or definition of this entity called 'Europe', either in terms of boundaries and borders, or in terms of its institutional arrangement – although most subscribed to a broadly federalist plan of the kind promoted by the German government. 'Europe' was therefore an 'evolving' organism, 'in the process of becoming'. Like Christianity and Marxism, both of which subscribe to an eschatological vision of an idealised society in the distant future or at the 'end of history', so the ideology of European integration envisages a future-oriented, 'supranational' utopia[4] based on a (so far undefined) 'post-national citizenship'.[5]

This vagueness in defining Europe arose from pragmatic as well as ideological factors. The problem of defining Europe became much more complicated during the late 1980s, particularly after the collapse of Communism, German reunification and the liberation of Eastern Europe. These events had an unravelling effect on traditional conceptions of Europe. Having arrogated to itself the term 'Europe',

and having grown accustomed to equating 'Europe' with Western
Europe, the European Community now found itself without a clear
eastern border. The disappearance of the old Communist adversary –
which had helped unify the countries of the European Community
as bastions of liberal democracy – was gone. The absence of the
'barbarian at the gate' left the European Union with an identity crisis.

A notable phenomenon during the early 1990s was the number of
speeches by European political leaders, including Thatcher, Kohl,
Mitterrand and Delors, setting out their respective 'visions' of Europe
in the run-up to the start of the 1996 Inter-Governmental Conference
(IGC). From these and the various draft reports published by the different
governments, a number of alternative perspectives on the future shape
and direction of European integration began to emerge. Perhaps even
more interesting than their content was the style of these documents
and speeches, particularly the metaphors used to represent each
particular vision of Europe. These ranged from high-speed trains, cars,
motorways, pillars, temples and human anatomy to restaurant menus,
wedding-cakes, marriages, geometry and naval convoys. Equally
striking were the number of governments making contradictory claims
that 'their' policies or country were 'at the heart of Europe'. Some
went further and tried to suggest that their country and its people were
the 'true' heirs of Europe's cultural and ethnic heritage.[6] Stepping back
from this it seemed that after four decades of Cold War rigidity,
'Europe' had once again become an open political field: a semantic
and conceptual space lacking fixed contours or content, and therefore
ripe for appropriation and colonisation. Standing up for Europe,
claiming to represent the 'European interest' or simply campaigning
on a platform of 'Britain or France or Italy in Europe', had become
politically fashionable. In many respects the idea of Europe was
functioning in a similar way to what Edwin Ardener (1971: xliv) called
'blank banners': symbols which are not linked to specific programmes
but which can become, when appropriate situations arise, icons under
which a number of different causes and movements can be mobilised
and united. What interested me, however, were the questions: How
does a particular definition of Europe become the dominant one? How
do some discourses become powerful and authoritative while others
are rendered silent? And what effect does the language of European
integration – particularly the metaphors mentioned above – have on
the policy process?

## THE SIGNIFICANCE OF METAPHORS FOR COGNITION AND COMMUNICATION

One approach to these questions is to adopt Foucault's insights into the close relationship between power/knowledge and ask, how do these discourses influence subjectivity? As Foucault (1977, 1982) has shown, the language of specialists is part of the disciplinary technology by which human subjects are made objects of power. The labels and classifications of experts such as doctors, psychiatrists, therapists, priests, social workers, educationalists (or in the case of European integration, lawyers, economists, statisticians, journalists and marketing consultants) become critical instruments of normalisation and stigmatisation. These 'dividing practices', as Foucault calls them, exert a powerful influence over the way individuals are categorised and controlled. However, the most insidious of these dividing practices involves 'subjectification', or the process by which individuals come to actively discipline their own thoughts and conduct (Foucault 1977: 201–9). In this way, discourse works through individuals by re-configuring their sense of self so that external norms and constraints become internalised and integral to one's sense of selfhood and identity. Foucault's work concentrated mainly on the way such processes of self-formation work as political technologies to control – or render 'docile' and therefore more manageable – dominated and marginal groups, including psychiatric patients and prisoners. Similar processes can be detected in the self-formation of elites, however. Language is a powerful agent of consciousness that not only shapes the identities and subjectivities of those populations over whom European political elites aspire to govern; it also actively colludes in the subjectification of those elites themselves.

Metaphors of Europe are therefore integral components of discourse. Those metaphors used by Commission officials both reflect and, in turn, engender of a sense of elitism and mission among EU officials. The way the Commission represents itself through metaphor is only one example of the way language can influence the politics of European integration. Equally important are the metaphors of Europe found in the discourses of different member states and their governments. Raymond Williams's work on language offers a useful starting point for thinking through the social and political implications of this metaphorical language. 'New kinds of relationship', he writes, 'but also *new ways of seeing* existing relationships, appear in language in a variety of ways: in the invention of new terms (*capitalism*); in the adaptation and alteration (indeed at times reversal) of older terms (*society* or *individual*); in extension (*interest*) or transfer (*exploitation*)' (Williams 1996: 22, my emphasis).

Williams also charts the way many contemporary keywords were created or acquired new meanings with the onset of industrialisation and the rise of the nation-state. This poses the question of whether, in an increasingly 'post-industrial', globalised world, European integration might exert a similar galvanising effect on everyday language? The extent to which European integration has been a catalyst for the creation of new kinds of relationship and new 'ways of seeing' is an important consideration. The concept of 'European citizenship' created by the 1992 Maastricht Treaty was certainly a political and legal innovation, even if it has not yet translated into a coherent sense of identity or community at the level of popular consciousness. The European Union has also given rise to a whole new vocabulary, replete with invented, arcane, legalistic terms such as 'subsidiarity', 'additionality', 'commitology', '*acquis communautaire*', '*rapporteur*' and '*construction européenne*'. Many of these words have no direct equivalent in English and have been incorporated wholesale into the English language, with the result that they are often quite ambiguous or incomprehensible even to those who use them.[7] In many ways, these concepts do entail new ways of thinking and talking about Europe, although this vocabulary is only slowly being adopted beyond the confines of EU specialists and political elites. What *has* entered the wider public domain and does influence perceptions of Europe beyond the level of elites, however, are the metaphors and images of European integration. These metaphors play a crucial role in mediating between perception, communication and understanding.

The argument that categories of language reflect processes of thought, particularly the 'cultural part of cognition' as D'Andrade calls it (1984), has been well established in anthropological writing ever since the pioneering work of Benjamin Lee Whorf (1956) and his immediate intellectual ancestors, Sapir and Boas.[8] Within British anthropology, the links between language and systems of classification have been amply explored in ethnographic studies of dietary taboos (Douglas 1975), animal taxonomies (Leach 1964, Tambiah 1973 ) and cultural notions of purity and pollution (Douglas 1966, Okely 1983). Without venturing into the complex debates within linguistics over how one might separate the 'cultural part of cognition' from individual or innate aspects of cognition (cf. Hill 1988), a key question for the present discussion is the extent to which metaphors shape or influence thought and, if so, what the political implications of this might be for understanding the process European integration?

I suggest that metaphors play a far more significant role in shaping the political debate than is commonly recognised, and that they constitute a site of critical importance and contestation in the struggle for political hegemony in Europe. I shall return to this theme in more detail below. The point to emphasise here is simply that metaphors are cognitive tools that provide people with a means for grasping new concepts and ideas. As Lakoff (1987) argues, metaphors are a means of understanding a new, unknown realm ('target domain') in terms of a familiar realm ('source domain'). By mapping the familiar onto the unknown, '[m]etaphors provide the necessary schemata for producing new thoughts about. . . complex or abstract phenomena' (Schäffner 1996: 32). They are therefore cultural facts which serve as conduits for thinking and talking about new objects and ideas. More than this, metaphors are models for thought processes; crucial devices not only for cognition (understanding a phenomenon) but also for communication. To the extent that they embody modes of conceptualisation, practices of thinking and habits of speech, metaphors 'provide the cultural forms that make ideas communicable' (Strathern 1992: 5). In short, they are a fundamental yet highly contested aspect of cultural practice.

## HOW METAPHORS INFLUENCE POLICY: TWO EUROPEAN EXAMPLES

What, then, are the cultural forms that make the idea of Europe communicable and to what extent do they affect European integration or influence policy-making? I would like to focus on two examples which, in different ways, address this question. Both involve metaphors of Europe coined by political leaders which subsequently provoked, or at least facilitated, the emergence of new kinds of policy discourse.

The first was President Mikhail Gorbachev's controversial metaphor of the 'common European house' coined in a French television interview in October 1985. For Gorbachev, this phrase encapsulated an important element of the 'new thinking' in Soviet foreign policy, and was intended to depict a new model of peaceful coexistence across the Iron Curtain. However, Gorbachev's model was rejected by French political leaders largely because the French translation of 'our common European house' (*la maison commune européenne*) suggested an intimacy too close for comfort. It was also seen as a 'device to exclude America, but include Russia, by dangling the mirage of German unity before West German eyes' (Chilton and Ilyin 1993: 16). The basic idea for Gorbachev's use of the metaphor was the term *dom*. For Russian speakers, the prototypical referent of *dom* is a multi-story apartment block with several entrances, in which several families live their own lives, without interference from their neighbours, but with common norms or rules of conduct that make stable communication and cooperation possible. By contrast, the French prototypical *maison* has connotations of conviviality and is based on the one-family house, with free movement from one room to the other (Chilton and Ilyin 1993: 23; Schäffner 1996: 34). Gorbachev's common European home metaphor also contrasted with the British stereotype based around the idea of detached or semi-detached houses – as illustrated in *The Economist* response that 'good fences make good neighbours' (*The Economist* 23 April 1988, cited in Schäffner 1996: 34).

The second exemplar occurred shortly after I had begun fieldwork in Brussels. In February 1996 the German Chancellor, Helmut Kohl, delivered a lecture on the future of the European Union at the Catholic University of Louvain. His speech urged Europe's leaders to turn their back on the nation-state (whose day was over) and resist efforts by Britain to slow down the pace of closer European integration. In language intended to curb the growing tide of Euro-scepticism he argued that 'the policy of European integration is in reality a question of war and peace in the twenty-first century'. Recalling Germany's invasion of Belgium in two world wars, he echoed the late President Mitterrand's comment that 'nationalism is war', and declared: 'we have no desire to return to the nation-state of old. It cannot solve the great problems of the twenty-first century. Nationalism has brought great suffering to our continent.' He reassured his audience that building

Europe did not mean creating a 'European super-state', but warned that 'a set-back now on the road to Europe' and to deeper integration at the Inter-Governmental Conference (particularly on the issue of a common foreign and security policy) would 'put Europe back a generation'. In a comment aimed at the British government he warned that those individual partners 'unwilling to move forward' would not stop the others from doing so, adding that 'the slowest ship in the convoy should not be allowed to determine its speed'.[9]

Kohl's speech is a fairly typical example of the discourse on European union that prevails among EU officials and supporters of closer political integration. What is interesting about Kohl's comments is not only his argument about the urgency of further integration to prevent the spectre of regressive nationalism and war, but the tropes used to portray this process. In previous speeches, Kohl's preferred imagery for European integration involved railway metaphors, with frequent emphasis on phrases such as 'keeping to the timetable', getting negotiations 'back on track', warnings about the dangers of 'missing the train' or being 'left behind on the platform', and concerns about the 'European train' becoming 'derailed' or 'hitting the buffers' (Schäffner 1994, 1996). Trains and railways are a potent source of imagery and symbolism. As Foucault (1986: 23–4) notes, 'a train is an extraordinary bundle of relations because it is something through which one goes, it is also something by means of which one can go from point to another, and then it is also something that goes by'. More importantly for the European debate, a train has a fixed endpoint or destination and its passengers travel *together* at the same speed, even if they occupy different carriages. Equally significant in terms of its symbolic associations, as Darian-Smith (1995: 210–15) points out, is the historical connection between the expansion of railways and the spread of colonialism.[10]

Kohl's convoy metaphor was therefore a departure from the usual railway trope, yet consistent with the 'federal destiny' and Europe-on-the-move motif. However, given that his criticism about the 'slowest ship' was directed against Britain, the convoy metaphor was an unfortunate choice. For many Britons, this implicitly evoked memories of the war and of Atlantic shipping convoys and their role in feeding the nation at a time when German U-boats were blockading their country.[11] Furthermore, the metaphor seemed curiously misplaced as the whole point of a convoy is that it *must* travel at the speed of the slowest ship for the safety and protection of all, otherwise the 'convoy' ceases to exist – a point spelt out in the robust retort to Chancellor Kohl by Britain's Foreign Secretary, Malcolm Rifkind (quoted in Castle 1996: 2). Despite this apparent contradiction, Kohl's speech was interpreted by some journalists and politicians as a veiled threat and coercive tactic. The convoy metaphor thus became the focus for a heated debate in Britain over government policy towards Europe and monetary union, and was referred to repeatedly in subsequent political speeches, either to be supported or rebuffed (see, for example, Aylott 1996: 14, Howe 1996: 18).

If, to paraphrase Marshall McLuhan, the medium is also part of the message, then Kohl's choice of venue was also significant. Belgium, with its world war battlefield sites and graveyards was symbolically an appropriate place to deliver a sermon on war and peace and the death of the nation-state. From Chancellor Kohl's point of view, the city of Leuven may have seemed an especially appropriate venue as its university is one of Europe's oldest and most famous, boasting among its former teachers such illustrious figures as the great humanist Erasmus of Rotterdam and Justus Lipsius. Furthermore, German occupying armies had rased the town and set fire to the university library in 1914, and then again in 1940. However, whether by accident or by oversight, Kohl's venue was not the ancient (Flemish) University of Leuven, but the new Université Catholique de Louvain. This was an unfortunate decision as the new Catholic University of Louvain is a problematic site for lending crediblity to Kohl's message about reconciliation and the transcendence of nationalism. Its origins are much more recent, stemming from 1968 when the old university became a flashpoint in the ethno-nationalist conflict between Walloons and Flems. That ethnic conflict – which continues to be the single most important factor in Belgian politics – resulted in the division of the university in two as the francophone teachers and students broke away to establish their own exclusively francophone university in the new town of Louvain-la-Neuve a few kilometres away.[12] Kohl's arguments about the end of the era of nationalism – which is a central theme in the Europeanist discourse of German and EU policy-makers – therefore appeared curiously at odds with the historical experience of most of those attending his lecture.

## METAPHORS TO FIGHT WITH: THE FUTURE OF EUROPE AND THE IGC DEBATES

What these illustrations show is the way metaphors not only create new ways of thinking and talking about basic political issues, thereby providing the key references or focal points for political debates, but the subtle ways in which they can also influence those debates. At the same time, they also indicate some of the complexities of talking across cultures and language groups. The problems of translating between cultures, particularly the transferral of meaning in metaphors, is also highlighted in the debates which foreshadowed the start of the 1996 IGC.

The purpose of the IGC, as stated in Article N of the Maastricht Treaty, was to evaluate the functioning of that Treaty, consider possible revisions to it, and more generally, to provide a forum for discussion of the future shape of the 'European construction' (including such questions as institutional reform, enlargement and monetary union). The two major issues of controversy concerned the pace of European integration and its shape or structure. Not surprisingly, the dominant metaphors used in these debates typically involved, on the one hand, images of movement and speed ('fast track', 'slow lane', 'the European train', 'progress towards a common defence policy', 'further steps forward on the road to political union', 'fear of being *left behind*'), and on the other, building or construction ('blueprints', 'houses', the 'pillars of the Treaty', the 'Community's complex architecture', 'building a fortress Europe'). According to Chilton and Ilyin (1993: 11), 'there is a general metaphor available in English-speaking culture that compares institutions to buildings, and talks of their construction'. However, this also seems to be a characteristic of the ideologies of most new states. As the Russian linguist Ilyin noted in a survey of the basic metaphors in the standard ideology handbook of his school years in the early 1960s, 'nearly half the total occurrences of structural metaphors involved schemata of building, preparing ground, placing cornerstones, and so forth'. In short, the metaphor of 'building communism' became the key political formula of the discourse and ideology of the Soviet system in all its years of existence (Chilton and Ilyin 1993: 7–8). The same metaphor, it would seem, has become part of the ideological formula for the European Union.

Other metaphors of Europe included containers ('entering the
ERM', 'going into Europe') gastronomy ('France says "no to à la carte
Europe"'), weddings ('the ERM marriage'), mathematics ('variable
geometry', 'concentric circles') illness ('healing Europe's wounds') and
rites of passage (the 'death of the ERM', the 'birth of the a new
currency', the 'christening of the Euro'). To this list John Major
added 'sport' when he summed up the 253 pages of the Maastricht
Treaty signed in February 1992 as 'Game, set and match to Britain'
(Davidson 1994: 27). What is significant about these metaphors is the
way they are used to set the terms for debate and provide discursive
models for promoting alternative scenarios. In each case, use of these
metaphors can be linked to rival and often conflicting visions of
Europe, and reflect attempts by different political agents to exert
hegemony over the European debate.

*Europe à la Carte*

'Europe à la carte' literally means accommodating the diversity of Europe
by allowing member states to pick and choose the policies that suit
them and opt out of those that do not. The first references to this phrase
in public debates in Britain appeared in newspaper reports in early 1989.
The origin of the phrase is attributed to the book, *The Challenge of
Europe*, written by one of Britain's leading 'Euro-enthusiasts', Michael
Heseltine (1989). In it, Heseltine argued that 'to pick and choose from
Europe's programme, to dine à la carte, is to risk quenching the
enthusiasm that British managers must display if the opportunity of
1992 is to be grasped' (quoted in Rogaly 1989: 21). While the idea
of ordering off the set menu appeals to many British Conservatives,
it is vehemently opposed by pro-integrationist member states and EU
officials.[13] They accuse Britain of not embracing the *spirit of the
Community* (another Euro-federalist metaphor) in opting out of parts
of the Maastricht Treaty, namely the Social Chapter and commitment
to the final stage of economic and monetary union. The lawyers'
argument is that such opt-outs make the EU legally unworkable
because they undermine the clarity of the European integration
process, and therefore its legitimacy (Davignon 1995: 19). Most
member states, however, have obtained special protocols on matters
of particularly national sensitivity, such as the definition of nationality

in Germany, the purchase of second homes in Denmark, and monetary relations between Italy, San Marino and the Vatican City.

What is particularly interesting about the à la carte image is its conflicting messages about status and sociability. The metaphor of Europe as a dinner or fixed-menu meal evokes the idea of commensality, which has powerful semantic and symbolic resonance for most Europeans given its associations with morality, sitting down together and sharing. Whereas ordering à la carte is often a statement of individuality, affluence and high status, in this context it has few, if any, of these meanings and is widely interpreted as an act of bad manners and selfishness. The metaphor is therefore most commonly used to emphasise this pejorative sense and is seen by its detractors, including the German Commissioner for industrial policy, as a tactic for the 'renationalisation' of European Union competencies (Carvel 1993: 4).

## Variable Geometry

'Variable geometry' covers a range of views on the development of the European Union and assumes that since not all members can achieve harmonisation at the same pace, there should be special arrangements whereby some forge ahead while others follow more slowly with long, Community-aided transition periods. The metaphor appears to have acquired popular usage around the time of the EC Summit in Birmingham in October 1992 – shortly after the French and Danish referendum verdicts on the Maastricht Treaty. The major concern of European political leaders at that time was to recapture momentum for European integration and halt the declining support among the European (and particularly Danish) electorate. The Summit Declaration therefore contained a series of new watchwords about citizens' rights, subsidiarity, respect for national identity and the need for more 'openness' in the Community's arrangements (CEC 1995b: 33). While it made no mention of 'flexibility' or 'variable geometry' and emphasised again the need for 'strict adherence to the principles of sound economic management, as set out in the [Maastricht] convergence programmes' (CEC 1995b: 32), the idea of 'variable geometry' to accommodate the less enthusiastic member states was clearly on the political agenda (Morgan 1992: 18). Most governments adhere to their own versions of this idea. Germany, France and the Benelux countries, however, are adamant that they will not allow one country to 'block progress' for the others. As Gunter Rinsche, the German Christian Democrat leader, argued, 'the Union should use flexible formulas as the cement constructing integration', but 'standing still' was unacceptable (Gardner 1994: 3).

The term 'variable geometry' is consistent with the root metaphor of 'building', but subverts the metaphor of an architectural blueprint by introducing the idea of a plurality of variations on the basic design. According to the *Shorter Oxford English Dictionary*, geometry is 'the science of properties and relations of magnitude' which concerns the rational 'ordering of objects in space'. The logic of this metaphor is that the 'European construction' can be worked out mathematically, but according to flexible formulae based on an effective 'piecing together' of the component parts. As one observer described it, this is 'Europe as Meccano (or Lego, for Danish sensibilities). Not everyone wants to, or can, do the same things. . . So a way of organising the EU has to be found that permits different permutations – which has been happening since Maastricht anyway' (Marshall 1994: 11).

*Concentric Circles*

The 'concentric circles' theory was set out by former French Prime Minister Edouard Balladur in an interview in *Le Figaro* on 30 August 1994. Balladur described a Europe of three concentric circles structured like a wedding cake (a metaphor also used to portray the 'architecture' of the Maastricht Treaty). The European Union represents the top, or centre circle; the middle circle is an intermediate phase similar to the current European Economic Area but called the Organisation of European Integration, and the outer circle or bottom layer includes prospective members which currently have association status with the Union. For Balladur, the first circle would be a free market economic union of core members. The second would involve a smaller number of states with a more organised monetary structure. The third circle would consist of non-EU members with which the EU would establish diplomatic, security and commercial links, similar to what the Conference on Security and Co-operation in Europe (CSCE) is doing already.

Although widely attributed to Mr Balladur, the idea for a Europe of concentric circles was contained in an earlier report for the European Commission published in April 1994. The report, written by Richard Baldwin of the Centre for Economic Policy Research, originally mentioned only two circles and addressed the problem of how to integrate the countries of Eastern Europe (Baldwin 1994). Balladur's inclusion of a third, 'inner' circle, was a more controversial proposal as it raised the much-criticised idea of a 'multi-track, multi-speed' Europe proposed by John Major. However, under Balladur's model, the outer circles would be only temporary; a transitional phase to allow those weaker member states to catch up while allowing 'an efficient central core' of countries to press ahead (quoted in Miller 1994: 9). The imagery of a Europe of concentric circles naturally provoked comparisons with Dante's vision of Hell, with 'good Europeans' at the centre, the uncertain and incapable in the middle, and the unwilling flung to the outer cantons (Marshall 1994: 11), or worse, lost in the vestibule where, as Dante (1980: 85–6) has it, the 'forlorn' and 'wretched spirits' of the Futile – those who 'to self alone were true' – run perpetually after a whirling standard.

## Two-tier and Hard Core

'Two-tier' and 'hard core' metaphors are variations on the 'variable geometry' idea and find their clearest expression in the controversial plan put forward by the German Christian Democrats (CDU) and their coalition partners in the Bundestag in September 1994. The plan envisaged that an inner group (or *feste Kern*), including France, Germany and the Benelux countries, would proceed with rapid political and economic integration whilst the others followed at their own pace. Unlike the à la carte or variable geometry proposals, this staggered, two-tier approach does not allow for flexibility in signing up to some parts of the Treaties but not others: all member states would be bound by the Treaty provisions. The common fear this proposal provoked was that those unable to join the 'hard core' would subsequently be bound by legislation that they had little or no part in formulating. Here, it is claimed, lies another example of the problem of intercultural translation. The term *feste Kern* in the German document means 'solid, firm'. '[T]o translate it as "hard [core]" introduces associations of exclusiveness and of an unsympathetic attitude to outsiders not present in the original, and it was these associations at least as much as the idea itself which occasioned resentment' – although not in France, where its translation as *noyau dur* carries positive associations of durability and germination (Bainbridge and Teasdale 1995: xi). In Britain, 'hard core' typically carries negative meanings often associated with extremism and violence, for example in phrases like 'hard core of football hooligans' or 'hard core of prisoners/troublemakers', and 'hard core pornography'.

This idea was rejected as divisive by John Major and also by the French and German foreign ministers, Alain Juppé and Klaus Kinkel, but for very different reasons. While the latter favour 'moving together at the same speed' (in a way similar to Kohl's convoy metaphor), Britain favours what it calls a 'multi-track approach', an idea which challenges not only the concept of convergence, but also questions the federalist 'direction' the EU wishes to head towards.

### Multi-track, Multi-speed

The metaphors of 'multi-track' and 'multi-speed' suggest that while member states follow the same path towards free trade, deregulation and open markets, they would be free to continue in more flexible ways, following national policies rather than harmonised and common policies. This transport imagery construes Europe as a giant motorway system in which all are subject to the same basic traffic rules (including free trade, open markets, deregulation and fair competition) but beyond that they are free to do as they please. These metaphors, coined by John Major and later endorsed by Douglas Hurd, challenged Kohl's popular metaphor of Europe as a high-speed train by suggesting there might be a number of different lanes and speeds for the member states to follow, rather than just one, with first-class and economy-class passengers riding in different carriages. Critics say that a 'multi-track Europe' would mean a 'return to a Europe of nation states', which would dangerously weaken the EU institutions as law-making bodies and put their role into doubt. Supporters indicate that this would be a desirable outcome. Shifting metaphors from roads to sartorial styles, however, Michael Howard gave an interesting twist to this theme in a speech in June 1994. 'What we need', he declared, 'is a made-to-measure Europe in which the institutional arrangements comfortably fit national interests, not an off-the-peg standard size Europe, ill-fitting and splitting at the seams' (quoted in Marshall 1994: 11).

## THE EFFECTIVENESS OF METAPHOR IN SHAPING POLITICAL THOUGHT

These illustrations support Raymond Williams's argument that language is a site in which new relationships and ways of seeing emerge. However, new categories may also close down, as well as open up, avenues for thought. As Steven Lukes (1975: 301) observed in his analysis of political ritual, 'every way of seeing is also a way of not seeing'. Foucault's (1980) work in particular has helped sensitise anthropology and other social sciences to the fact that questions of language are inextricably linked to questions of power. The key question for critical anthropology of Europe is *whose* meanings prevail? How are these images made authoritative? And what do these competing metaphors reveal about the dynamics of European integration? For Andrew Marshall (1994: 11) the proliferation of images reflects extraordinary uncertainty over what the picture that emerges from 1996 will look like. 'Try to imagine a piece of fruit with pillars made of Meccano bowling down a motorway built in concentric circles and you can see the problem.' I would go further than Marshall and argue that this proliferation of images also reflects the power struggle being waged over Europe as different governments compete for control of discourses about the future shape and direction of European integration. As Philip Schlesinger notes (1994), 'Europeanness has itself become a new cultural battlefield.' Gramsci understood this years ago in his analysis of language, ideology and 'common sense'. Philosophical activity, he wrote, is 'above all. . . a cultural battle to transform the popular "mentality" and to diffuse the philosophical innovations which will demonstrate themselves to be "historically true"' (Gramsci 1971: 348).

The metaphors of Europe described above provide valuable insights into the alternative conceptions of European integration and various meanings European Union has for different actors. As Franklin (1993) and others have observed, the key expressions that recur in the main European languages reveal quite clearly the contours of the European debate. Britain's Conservative government wants a 'wider, looser

Europe' which means that it wants to put a brake on any 'federal blueprint'. It prefers the inter-governmental model to supranationalism. It supports the common market but rejects measures that erode national sovereignty (including the national veto). It tries to subvert the Euro-federalist metaphors about 'peace', 'progress' and 'harmonisation' by raising the spectre of bureaucratic centralisation and a 'European super-state', and by invoking metaphors of Europe as a de-personalised machine or conveyor belt, determined to impose uniformity through regulation, thereby crushing individual freedom and destroying national culture and identity. Supporters of a federal Europe speak of the coordination and convergence of national laws and legislation as 'harmonisation' – a term which, as Dembour (1996: 2) reminds us, is a metaphor culled from music, evoking the idea of pleasing or concordant melodies. British Euro-sceptics reply with metaphors of 'identikit Europeans' and Orwellian images of a totalitarian state dominated by Germany (Cash 1991). Their task is made considerably easier by the pejorative connotations in Britain that surround terms like 'federalism' and 'blueprint', not to mention the popular disdain that attaches to words with the prefix 'Euro' or 'European'.

German policy-makers, as they themselves readily admit, like to have an overall plan; a *Gesamkonzept*, or 'total concept' (Franklin 1993). Their blueprint is a democratic, federal Europe based on the model of the German constitution. They reason that federalism has worked for Germany, so it must work for Europe too. More importantly, Europe needs a federal constitution to protect it from the dark, 'centrifugal' forces of nationalism that threaten to plunge European nation-states back into protectionism and war. Interestingly, the prospect of a revival of German nationalism seems to be feared as much by Germany's current political leaders as it is by Germany's neighbours. For Germany, federalism means political decentralisation and stability. The relationship between Germany's federal government and its powerful *länder* could find its counterpart in a 'Europe of the Regions'. For German policy-makers European political union must happen: the task for the IGC is to fix the timetable and get the integration process back on track.

For the French government, a key phrase is *la préférence européenne* (preference for Europe) which generally serves as a euphemism for protectionism. France would like to extend its protectionist farm regime to industry and defend itself against foreign imports from those countries which use sweat-shop labour. It also denounces American cultural imperialism (*le défi americaine*) which, it argues, not only undermines the French audiovisual industry, but poses a threat to French culture and civilisation. The Spanish government emphasises *la cohésion* – which generally stands for European Community aid to poorer countries, a cause which Spain has often championed. For Spain (and for many of the less economically developed member states) the European Union is perceived as a source of modernity, civilisation and money in the form of EU subsidies, regional funds and the specifically named 'cohesion' funds.[14] What these different cultural expressions also show is that, like metaphors, political thinking and political model-building also entails similar cultural practices of mapping unfamiliar or new domains of knowledge on to familiar schemas to produce new forms of knowledge. The result is that different governments construct their rival 'visions' of Europe not only in self-conscious ways to suit national self-interests, but also unconsciously as they interpret European events through the prism of their own historical experiences, and as they project their indigenous models of what constitutes the good society outwards and on to the European canvas. In many respects, therefore, 'Europe' functions not only as a 'blank banner', but also as a kind of blank screen on to which different member states project their individual fantasies and meanings.

## Setting the Political Agenda

How do metaphors 'work' as instruments of power? A central aspect of the power of metaphors lies in their ability to shape the parameters within which discussions occur. As most politicians and experienced committee members know, an effective way of influencing decision-making is to define in advance the terms of reference for debate. 'The agenda is the key to controlling the argument', as Hutton (1995: 25) observes. This is what Alex de Waal (1994: 8) calls controlling the 'meta-discourse', or the argument about what the argument is about. Creating or appropriating powerful metaphors, like dressing oneself up in the popular symbols of prestige and power, can be a potent way of accruing political authority and making one's definition of a problem and its solution stick, while eclipsing or excluding other possible ways of seeing. Metaphors play a key role in this process, particularly in the mobilisation of bias and in the way they work to classify or redefine objects, subjects, places or policies in emotive ways so as to promote a particular political agenda.

The power of metaphors also lies in their invisibility to the native speakers who use them and in their ability to naturalise social norms and conventions in such a way that they are accepted uncritically. As Foucault (1978: 86) observed, power 'is tolerable only on condition that it mask a substantial part of itself. Its success is proportional to its ability to hide its own mechanisms.' A good example of this is what in sociolinguistics is called the 'realm of the unsaid'. As Jane Hill (1988: 22) observes, 'a vast and unspoken source of human cultural meaning derivable primarily only by inference, lies not only in the conditions of pragmatic interaction, but in the patterning of grammar itself'. Thus, the sentence 'leaders of the EU "determined to lay *the foundations* for an ever closer union"' (CEC 1983: 113) suggests that there is likely to be a whole team of construction specialists – architects, planners, surveyors, lawyers, economists, structural engineers, stonemasons, site managers, machine operators, building workers, planning inspectors and security guards – who will be involved in digging, laying and securing those foundations. The phrase *to lay the foundations* does not mention these experts: they are the 'covert category' implicit in the building metaphor – just as the 'train' metaphor invariably suggests the covert category of a driver and a track. In each case, the spoken and the unspoken help to reinforce and 'naturalise' the idea that European integration has a logical outcome or destiny which is being safely managed and carried forward by competent specialists.

Bloch's (1975) work on political oratory provides further insight into the effectiveness of metaphors as instruments for exercising political and cultural hegemony over a population. For Bloch, much of the power of political oratory derives from its use of certain 'formalised codes'; cross-references that are customary and accepted sources of legitimacy. These political references (images, anecdotes, concepts, metaphors) are all drawn from a fairly precise set of sources that are restricted to 'a body of suitable illustrations, often proverbs or scriptures' which tend to be fixed, eternal and orthodox (1975: 15). Once political discussion has been shifted into this formalised code then the discourse (and consequently the speaker) become imbued with the source of traditional authority and its power. The effect of shifting debate into this register has the effect of endowing the speaker's

arguments with an almost sacrosanct quality. As Bloch (1975: 16) states:
'The most important social effect of this merging of the specific into
the eternal and fixed, is that it moves the communication to a level
where disagreement is ruled out since one cannot disagree with the
right order.'[15]

The European Commission follows a similar tactic by linking itself
and its project for European integration to the ideas of 'peace',
'progress' and 'civilisation' – all of which are potent, mobilising themes
in the history of Western thought. To 'block progress' towards deeper
union is defined as 'turning the clock back' to a Europe of nation-
states, nationalism and war. This is the message clearly conveyed by
Pascal Fontaine (1993: 6) in his statement about European Union being
'an attempt to establish between States the same rules and codes of
behaviour that enabled primitive societies to become peaceful and
civilized' and in his claim that European citizens must choose between
political union or a return to nationalism, insecurity and war. According
to this discursive frame, to oppose the ideals of the European Union
is not only to pit oneself against the trajectory of history, it is also to
position oneself outside the boundaries of 'civilised society' and
morality. The Maastricht Treaty is similarly worded so as to rule out
disagreement. Its Common Provisions (Articles A and B) look forward
to a 'union among the peoples of Europe in which decisions are taken
as closely as possible to the citizens'. Who would object to that, or to
seeing relations between member states 'organised in a manner
demonstrating consistency and solidarity'? And what objective could
be more laudable than to 'promote economic and social progress
which is balanced and sustainable'? (Article B, Treaty on European
Union). The power of discourses, therefore, lies largely in the way
they can link institutions or individuals to objects that are 'sacred' in
the sense that these are symbolically set apart, and command authority
and respect.

## CONCLUSION

As I have argued, metaphors are powerful instruments for directing
and shaping thought. Like symbols and rituals, they provide the
cognitive tools which structure our understanding of the world. They
are not, therefore, a residual component of supposedly 'real' politics,

nor can they be reduced to a peripheral status as epiphenomena of political struggles waged elsewhere. Rather, they play a key role in defining and organising people's experience and understanding of political reality. As Lakoff and Johnson observe (1980: 56), '[o]ur normal conceptual system is metaphorically structured; that is, most concepts are partially understood in terms of other concepts'. It is largely through metaphor that political concepts such as 'state' or 'nation' acquire a tangible reality. As the political scientist Michael Walzer wrote, '[t]he state is invisible; it must be personified before it can be seen, symbolised before it can be loved, imagined before it can be conceived' (Walzar 1967, quoted in Kertzer 1988: 6). Metaphors make it possible for Europe to be imagined. Their influence is greatest, however, when they appear natural and normal, thereby escaping our attention. This happens often because, like the structures of grammar, the most frequently used metaphors tend to be 'referentially transparent and essentially undiscussable' to those native speakers who use them (Hill 1988: 23).

Writing in a different context, Emily Martin argues (1991: 501) that the challenge for anthropologists is to 'wake up such sleeping metaphors' and thereby 'rob them of their power to naturalise our social conventions'. I suggest that this is a challenge for both cultural studies and anthropology. This chapter has tried to combine insights from Williams, Foucault and Gramsci with the work of sociolinguists and anthropologists in order to explore some of the ways that metaphors can influence policy and politics. Not only are metaphors used by European elites as weapons to control the agenda for debates over the future of Europe, they also function as instruments of ideological incorporation at the level of the masses; those ordinary European citizens whose interests these rival discourses on European union profess to serve. Recent shifts in the arcane language of European integration, however, suggests that some significant changes are occurring in the way Europe is being constructed. As both Marshall (1995: 14) and Schäffner (1996: 57) note, the current style of Euro-speak makes much greater use of metaphors concerned with relationships rather than the old mechanistic, architecture metaphors. This is giving rise to a new vocabulary of European integration which includes terms such as 'social model', 'transparency and openness', 'collective solidarity', 'feelings of belonging', 'in-out cohabitation', 'structured dialogue' and 'coalition of the willing'.[16] To some extent, this linguistic shift is illustrative of a way European integration is being reconceptualised as a more 'humanistic' and cultural enterprise, rather than the traditional neo-functionalist idea which tended to construe integration as a predominantly technical and rational process concerned almost exclusively with economics and law.

Like other authors in this volume, I have also tried to illustrate the key role that anthropological fieldwork – with all its characteristic 'untidiness' – has played in shaping, and then reshaping, my research agenda. The value of intensive, long-term participant-observation in 'the field' (however one chooses to define that concept)[17] lies not in the supposed 'authority' it gives to authors, nor simply in its capacity to provide empirical answers to preconceived research questions. Rather, it is the unpredictability of fieldwork and its capacity to challenge and unravel those preconceived assumptions and research questions, and throw up new ones, that makes it such a useful, 'reflexive' methodology. Without the experience of living and working among EU officials in Brussels, and the constant exposure to *their* narratives about 'European construction' that this provided, I would never have been able to understand either the significance of these metaphors and discourses for European integration, or the complex cultural meanings they hold for these political actors. Of course, one could extend this line of inquiry further, with a more complex and theoretically imaginative 'decoding' of the metaphors detailed above. This chapter has focused primarily on the metaphors and discourses of European institutions and elites: much more research is needed to understand how these discourses are received and 'decoded' by wider audiences beyond the confines of Europe's 'political class'. Anthropologists, I suspect, have much to learn from cultural studies here.

By emphasising the discursive as well as the cognitive nature of metaphors, I have tried to show how they can be studied not simply as 'webs of meaning', but as tools of domination and 'snares for thought'. This is why they are so politically and strategically important to the governance of Europe. In order to create and diffuse its vision for a federal Europe, it is first necessary for the institutions of the European Union to create a common language for imaging this new Europe. The problem, however, is that European politicians and officials sometimes become ensnared by their own rhetorical allusions and metaphorical constructions and fail to realise that their visions and values are not shared by the wider community. The discourse of

Europeanism promoted by the Commission encourages Europe's technocratic elite to see itself as 'custodian of the European interest' and agent of history, whose mission is to 'civilise Europe' by creating a political system that somehow 'transcends' the nation-state. 'Europe' will continue to be a contested geo-political concept well into the next millennium, I suspect. The challenge for supporters of a federal Europe is whether they are capable of extending their supranational ideology beyond Brussels and Europe's technocratic elite. That will depend on whose political agenda becomes the dominant one – and on whose metaphors prove to be the most potent and compelling.

## NOTES

1. For useful critiques of the politics of cultural studies see McCabe (1995), Mulhern (1995) and Turner (1993).
2. These criticisms are not unfounded, as several recent text-book definitions of cultural studies (for example, During 1993, Hartley 1994) would seem to indicate.
3. The research upon which this chapter is based is part of an ongoing anthropological study of the European Union and the politics of 'European identity'. I would like to thank the Economic and Social Research Council for sponsoring this research, and Chris Caswill and the staff at the UK Research in Higher Education European Office (UKRHEEO) for their support during the period of fieldwork in Brussels.
4. As Leicester (1996: 8) notes:

   this more or less explicit commitment to eventual federalism [is] the central legitimating idea on which the Community was based. Instead of an inherited myth about a nation forged in past battles, the Community is based on 'a myth of the future.' It is only in contemplating the eventual goal of federation, or 'ever closer union' as it became in the Treaty of Rome, that the peoples of Europe might discern a vision of their participation in a wider polity. That vision, however remote, has helped keep democratic doubts about the nature of the evolving European institutional structure at bay.

5. For discussion of the idea of post-national citizenship, see Delanty (1995: 156–63).

6. See, for example, Dietler's (1994) excellent analysis of attempts by the French government and by French nationalists to exploit the idea of the Celts as the first Europeans.
7. The term 'subsidiarity' is a good case in point. As Theodor Schilling (1995) notes, subsidiarity was an ambiguous notion seized upon primarily as a device to save the Maastricht Treaty in 1991. Yet despite its continuing lack of clarity and contested meaning, it has now become the second most cited principle of the European Treaties, after the prohibition of discrimination.
8. The principle enshrined in the 'Whorf hypothesis' – that the language of a people shapes their way of thinking and perceiving and, to some extent, structures and encodes their world view – has an even longer ancestry. As Jane Hill points out (1988: 14), it was first formulated at the beginning of the century by Wilhelm von Humboldt. Humboldt, in turn, built upon the work of Kant, Herder and Hegel in developing his notion of language as the embodiment of a *Weltanschauung* which mediates between the nature of reality and human understanding.
9. For a summary of Kohl's speech see Bremner (1996: 1) and Helm (1996: 1).
10. Darian-Smith (1995) uses this argument to explain much of the fear and hostility she encountered among Kent residents to the building of the Channel Tunnel during the 1990s.
11. This point was amplified in the British media. As Karacs (1996: 14) noted with irony:

    Helmut Kohl should have known better than to 'mention ze war'. . . Only in Britain, it seems, was the Chancellor's sinister message – the Panzers are ready to roll unless you accept EMU – correctly decoded and amplified to the level of a major international incident.

12. In a further act of 'ethnic apartheid', the books from the ancient library were divided between the old and new universities on the basis of odd and even shelf-marks (Baedeker 1993: 262).
13. According to the 1995 Commission Report for the Reflection Group, the Commission 'is utterly opposed' to the prospect of an 'à la carte' Europe (CEC 1995a: 8).
14. Informants reported that the Spanish government refused to sign the 1992 Treaty on European Union (or Maastricht Treaty) until

the Treaty had made provision for these so-called 'cohesion funds'.

15. Although Bloch's theory is criticised by Parkin (1984) and others for its over-deterministic view of linguistic rituals, we may agree with Chilton and Ilyin (1993: 12) when they say that 'the desire of conversants to cooperatively maintain conversational and social cohesion may constitute pressure to remain within a metaphorical frame that has been established in the discourse'.

16. Many of these terms can be found, for example, in the Commission's White Paper on *Growth, Competitiveness, Employment* (CEC 1994).

17. For an appraisal of what constitutes 'the field' in anthropology, see Shore and Wright (1997).

REFERENCES

Anderson, Benedict (1983) *Imagined Communities: Reflections on the Origins and Spread of Nationalism*. London: Verso.

Ardener, Edwin (1971) 'Introduction', in E. Ardener (ed.) *Social Anthropology and Language*, ASA Monograph. London: Tavistock, ix–cii.

Aylott, Nicholas (1996) 'Letters to the Editor: Nothing Hysterical in British Reaction to Kohl', *Financial Times* 8 February: 14.

Baedecker (1993) *Baedecker's Belgium*. London: Prentice Hall.

Bainbridge, Timothy and Teasdale, Anthony (1995) *The Penguin Companion to European Union*. Harmondsworth: Penguin.

Baldwin, Richard (1994) *Towards an Integrated Europe*. London: Centre for Economic Policy Research.

Bloch, Maurice (ed.) (1975) *Language and Oratory in Traditional Society*. London: Academic Press.

Bremner, Charles (1996) 'Nation State's Day is Over, Britain Told', *The Times* 3 February: 1.

Carvel, John (1993) 'No à la carte Warning for Britain', *Guardian* 13 February: 4.

Cash, William (1991) *Against a Federal Europe: The Battle for Britain*. London: Duckworth.

Castle, Stephen (1996) 'Rifkind Hits Back at Kohl', *Independent on Sunday* 4 February: 2.

Chilton, Paul and Ilyin, Mikhail (1993) 'Metaphor in Political Discourse: The Case of the "Common European House"', *Discourse and Society* 4 (1): 7–31.

Commission of the European Communities (CEC) (1983) *Treaties Establishing the European Communities* (abridged edition). Luxembourg: Office of Official Publications of the European Community.

—— (1994) *Growth, Competitiveness, Employment* (Commission White Paper). Luxembourg: Office for Official Publications of the European Community.

—— (1995a) *Commission Report for the Reflection Group*. Luxembourg: Office of Official Publications of the European Community.

—— (1995b) *The European Councils. Conclusions of the Presidency, 1992–1994*. Brussels: European Commission, Directorate General for Information, Communication, Culture and Audiovisual.

D'Andrade, Roy (1984) 'Cultural Meaning Systems', in Richard Schweder and Robert Levine (eds) *Culture Theory: Essays on Mind, Self and Emotion*. Cambridge: Cambridge University Press.

Dante, Alighieri (1980) *The Divine Comedy, 1: Hell*, trans. Dorothy L. Sayers. Harmondsworth: Penguin.

Darian-Smith, Eve (1995) 'Landscapes of Law: The Channel Tunnel and English Legal Identity in the New Europe', unpublished PhD Thesis, University of Chicago.

Davidson, Ian (1994) 'Bizarre British Novelty', *Financial Times*, 8 June: 22.

Davignon, Etienne (1995) 'The Challenges that the Commission Must Confront', in E. Davignon, N. Ersbøll, K. Lamers, D. Martin, E. Noël and F. Vibert, *What Future for the European Commission?* Brussels: Philip Morris Institute: 12–19.

Delanty, Gerard (1995) *Inventing Europe*. London: Macmillan.

Dembour, Marie-Bénédicte, (1996) 'Harmonization and the Construction of Europe: Variations away from a Musical Theme', *EU Working Paper, Law No. 96/4*. Florence: European University Institute.

De Waal, Alex (1994) 'Meta-conflict and the Policy of Mass Murder', *Anthropology in Action*, 1 (3): 8–11.

Dietler, Michael (1994) '"Our Ancestors the Gauls": Archeology, Ethnic Nationalism, and the Manipulation of Celtic Identity in Modern Europe', *American Anthropologist* 96 (3): 584–608.

Douglas, Mary (1966) *Purity and Danger*. London: Routledge and Kegan Paul.
—— (1975) *Implicit Meanings*. London: Routledge and Kegan Paul.
During, Simon (ed.) (1993) *The Cultural Studies Reader*. London: Routledge.
Fontaine, Pascal (1993) *A Citizen's Europe*. Luxembourg: Office of Official Publications of the European Communities.
Foucault, Michel (1977) *Discipline and Punish: The Birth of the Prison*. Harmondsworth: Penguin.
—— (1978) *The History of Sexuality*. *Volume 1*. Harmondsworth: Penguin.
—— (1980) *Power/Knowledge*, Colin Gordon (ed. and trans.). New York: Pantheon Books.
—— (1982) 'The Subject and Power', in Hubert Dreyfus and Paul Rabinow (eds) *Michel Foucault: Beyond Structuralism and Hermeneutics*. Chicago: University of Chicago Press.
—— (1986) 'Of Other Spaces', *Diacritics* 16 (1): 22–7.
Franklin, Daniel (1993) 'Survey of the European Community', *The Economist* 328, 3 July.
Gardner, David (1994) 'Multi-speed EU Rejected by Strasbourg', *Financial Times* 29 September: 3.
Gramsci, Antonio (1971) *Selections From Prison Notebooks*. London: Lawrence and Wishart.
Grant, Charles (1994) *Delors: Inside the House that Jacques Built*. London: Nicholas Brealey.
Handler, Richard (1993) 'Anthropology is Dead! Long Live Anthropology!', *American Anthropologist* 95 (4): 991–9.
Hall, Stuart (1992) 'The West and the rest: discourse and power', in S. Hall and B. Gieben (eds) *Formations of Modernity*. Cambridge: Open University and Polity Press: 275–320.
Hartley, John (1994) 'Cultural Studies', in T. O'Sullivan, J. Hartley, D. Saunders, M. Montgomery and J. Fisk, *Key Concepts in Communication and Cultural Studies*. London: Routledge: 71–3.
Hay, Richard (1989) *The Europoean Commission and the Administration of the Community*, Luxembourg: Office of Official Publications of the European Community.
Helm, Sarah (1996) 'Kohl Warns of War if European Union Fails', *Independent* 3 February: 1.

Heseltine, Michael (1989) *The Challenge of Europe*. London: Weidenfeld and Nicolson.

Hill, Jane H. (1988) *Language, Culture and World View*, in F.J. Newmeyer (ed.) *Linguistics: The Cambridge Survey*. Cambridge: Cambridge University Press: 14–36.

Hobsbawm, Eric and Ranger, Terence (1983) 'Introduction: Inventing Traditions', in E. Hobsbawm and T. Ranger (eds) *The Invention of Tradition*. Cambridge: Cambridge University Press: 1–14.

Howe, Geoffrey (1996) 'Personal View: No Longer Part of the Convoy', *Financial Times* 11 March: 18.

Hutton, Will (1995) 'Is this Man Really so Dangerous?', *Guardian* (Supplement) 17 February: 24.

Karacs, Imre (1996) 'Why Kohl Could be Britain's Best Friend in Europe', *Independent on Sunday*, 11 February 'The World': 14.

Kertzer, David (1988) *Ritual, Politics and Power*. New Haven and London: Yale University Press.

Lakoff, George (1987) *Women, Fire and Dangerous Things: What Categories Reveal about the Mind*. Chicago: Chicago University Press.

Lakoff, George and Johnson, Mark (1980) *Metaphors We Live By*. Chicago: University of Chicago Press.

Leach, Edmund (1964) 'Animal Categories and Verbal Abuse', in E.H. Lenneberg (ed.) *New Directions in the Study of Language*. Cambridge, MA: MIT Press: 28–63.

Leicester, G. (1996) 'A Pragmatic Approach to the Construction of Europe', in M. Herrero de Miñón and G. Leicester, *Europe: A Time For Pragmatism*. London: European Policy Forum: 6–19.

Lukes, Stephen (1975) 'Political Ritual and Social Integration', *Sociology* 9: 289–308.

McCabe, Colin (1995) 'Tradition too Has its Place in Cultural Studies', *The Times Literary Supplement* 4816, 26 May: 13.

Marshall, Andrew (1994) 'Mixed Metaphors Spell Out Post-Maastricht Doubts', *Independent on Sunday* 8 September: 11.

—— (1995) 'A Little In–Out Cohabitation: New Generation of Jargon' *Independent on Sunday* 2 July, 'The World': 14.

Martin, Emily (1991) 'The Egg and the Sperm: How Science has Constructed a Romance Based on Stereotypical Male–Female Roles', *Signs* 16 (3): 485–501.

Miller, Vaughne (1994) 'The 1996 Intergovernmental Conference: Background and Preparations', *Research Paper 94/115*. London: House of Commons.

Morgan, James (1992) 'As They Say in Europe: GATT and the EC', *Financial Times* 17 October: 18.

Mulhern, Francis (1995) 'The Politics of Cultural Studies', *Monthly Review* July–August: 31–40.

Okely, Judith (1983) *The Traveller Gypsies*. Cambridge: Cambridge University Press.

Parkin, David (1984) 'Political Language' *Annual Review of Anthropology* 13: 345–65.

Rogaly, Joe (1989) 'The Europe of the Saloon Bar', *Financial Times* 19 May: 21.

Rosaldo, Renato (1994) 'Whose Cultural Studies?', *American Anthropologist* 96: 524–9.

Said, Edward (1978) *Orientalism*. Harmondsworth: Penguin.

Schäffner, Christina (1994) 'The Concept of Europe – A Network of Metaphors', in David March and Liisa Sato-Lee (eds) *Europe on the Move. Fusion or Fission?* Finland: Sietar Europa: 117–25.

—— (1996) '"Building a European House?" Or at Two Speeds into a Dead End? Metaphors in the Debate on the United Europe', in Andreass Musolff, Christina Schäffner and Michael Townson (eds) *Conceiving of Europe – Diversity in Unity*. Dartmouth: Aldershot: 31–60.

Schilling, Theodor (1995) 'Subsidiarity as a Rule and a Principle, or: Taking Subsidiarity Seriously', *Harvard Jean Monnet Working Paper 10/95*, Cambridge, MA: Harvard Law School.

Schlesinger, Philip (1994) 'Europeanness – A New Cultural Battlefield?', in J. Hutchinson and A.D. Smith (eds) *Nationalism*. Oxford: Oxford University Press: 316–25.

Shore, Cris (1993) 'Inventing the "People's Europe": Critical Perspectives on European Community Cultural Policy', *Man* 28 (4) (December): 779–800.

Shore, Cris and Wright, Sue (1997) 'Policy, a New Field of Anthropology', in C. Shore and S. Wright (eds) *Anthropology of Policy: Critical Perspectives on Government and Power*. London: Routledge.

Spence, David (1994) 'Staff and Personnel Policy in the Commission', in G. Edwards and D. Spence (eds) *The European Commission*. Harlow: Longman: 62–94.

Strathern, Marilyn (1992) *Reproducing the Future*. Manchester: Manchester University Press.

Tambiah, S. (1973) 'Animals are Good to Think and Good to Prohibit', in M. Douglas (ed.) *Rules and Meaning*. Harmondsworth: Penguin: 106–19.

Turner, Terrence (1993) 'Anthropology and Multiculturalism: What is Anthropology that Multiculturalists Should Be Mindful of It?', *Cultural Anthropology* 8 (4): 411–29.

Whorf, Benjamin Lee (1956) *Language, Thought and Reality*. Cambridge, MA: MIT Press.

Williams, Raymond (1976) *Keywords*. London: Fontana.

# 8 THE PROBLEM OF CONSCIOUSNESS IN POLITICAL RHETORIC

*Alexandra Ouroussoff*

Taken generically, the Corporation has come to institute a conjunction of ideas about how the world ought to be composed, and the transactions within it conducted and reckoned, which has sought and won dominion over the lives of more people than any other, including, probably Islam. (Engberg 1976)

Turning to write the introduction for this chapter, I was confronted with what seemed like an insurmountable problem: the rhetorical strategy which I knew was required to engage the reader's interest in an ethnographic account of corporate polemics would seriously undermine the thesis underpinning my argument.

The source of the problem is the unspoken collective agreement which has emerged within anthropology over the last decade or so to study Western culture either in terms of the conscious lived experience of individuals or to begin *post festum* with the supposed results of this consciousness and discuss the relation between particular dominant ideas – as though one could deduce actual social outcome from the explicit manifest meaning of law, social policy, the division between subjectivism and objectivism, etc. What is being offered, in effect, is a choice between two forms of idealisation both of which obscure the epistemological connection between conscious intention and the specific relations through which social outcome is achieved.

There is no mystery about the rhetorical strategy underpinning this rupture, it is to deflect attention from the relatively stable and enduring social relations which structure Western society as a whole. Giving inadequate weight to the consequences of these relations preserves an image of a society constantly renewing itself, one determined by consciousness rather than by history.

160

The ideal view of the West has taken such a hold on the discipline that it now actually shapes the procedure of inquiry. And herein lies the difficulty, because if the aim of a study is to understand what the ideal leaves unsaid, then one is stuck with having either to deny, through various abstract stylistic subterfuges, what the chapter is really about or risk alienating the very audience with which one would like to engage.

What is really required is a full programme of ethnographic studies designed to recover the social relations which have either been misrepresented or rendered invisible; a programme tacitly discouraged by the prevailing ethos. This chapter, then, is a rudimentary attempt to demonstrate ethnographically that an anthropological interpretation of the morphology of Western culture has to advance a far more effective conception of political causality than has hitherto been offered. The chapter is based on an ethnographic study of a British multinational corporation. I chose to study a public corporation partly because it is one of the primary institutions of capitalism but also because critical relations to property and wealth in the wider society are well represented within the hierarchies characteristic of the public company.

I am primarily concerned in this chapter with the way directors and managers spontaneously and imaginatively order reality to conceal the concentration of effective corporate power. This activity is most intense in the context of their relations with outsiders, a focus of this chapter which follows from my working in the company as well as taking it as an object of anthropological analysis.

Managers and directors are skilled in masking contradictions between the power structure through which the corporation pursues its economic goals and the idealised version of this structure which they assume their various audiences wish to see.

The main stipulations of this ideal are fairly familiar. They portray the corporation as an entity that serves the interests of the individuals who constitute it as a whole, rather than just the interests of its shareholders; an institution that promotes autonomy rather than dependence, that protects the rights of individuals to equal self-development rather than fostering inequalities and one which strives to achieve this on the basis of moral principle (conscious intention) rather than legal or social coercion (external constraint).

It follows from this that, as well as their acknowledged economic function, managers fulfil a political function which is to ensure that

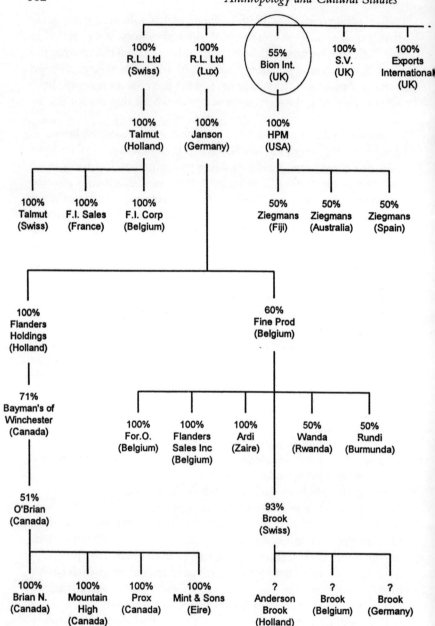

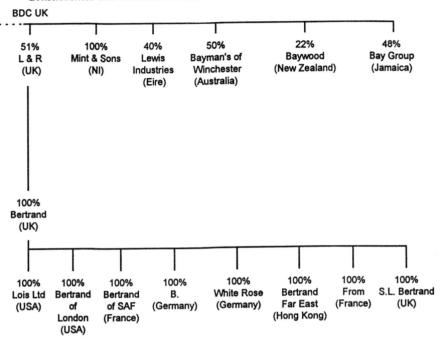

Figure 8.1 Bion Int. (UK): Corporate Links Through Ownership

the structure on the basis of which the corporation accumulates wealth appears compatible with the aims of a liberal political economy.

What is important in the context of relations with outsiders is to make access to the Company nominally possible, yet in actuality strictly controlled so that elements of experience that do not conform with the liberal ideal are hidden from public view.

This skill is not a conscious one. The complex task of adjusting liberal principles to the concrete circumstances which contradict them is not a problem managers consciously set out to solve either as a collective or as individuals. From their point of view, the problems they routinely discuss and need to solve are defined primarily by economic, not political exigencies. In other words, their political role is integrally interwoven with their economic role in such a way that they do not consciously experience their routine concealment of corporate power as a separate sphere of activity. This, I believe, is one of the reasons why their rhetorical strategy is so effective.

The examples I describe below explore how lack of conscious intention in this area of their activity helps shape the operations of thought and behaviour that are allowed to be witnessed by outsiders as 'objective' relations of the Company.


## THE COMPANY AND ITS HIERARCHY

A brief description, first, of the context in which this occurs. Bion International's Head Office is located in Oxfordshire where 320 managers (3 of whom are women), 98 secretaries and 104 clerical workers are employed to coordinate the production of the Company's five factories and manage product distribution.

Head Office is a five-storey concrete block, purpose-built in 1974. It sits in the middle of a green field a few minutes drive from the nearest town. The eight directors and the chief executive occupy the top floor and ranks descend in succession, albeit rather loosely, to the basement, where telephonists and photocopyists do their work. Senior executives and visitors enter through the front of the building where two women in their early twenties sit behind a reception desk in a mahogany panelled reception area. They are slim, with short blond hair and wear identical light blue suits.

The 'girls' as they are affectionately known, greet visitors, issue them with identity cards and ask them to be seated. The *Financial Times*, *The Times*, the *Daily Telegraph* and *The Economist* are set out on a Danish teak coffee table which stands in front of a matching teak settee.

With the exception of Company directors whose chauffeurs drop them off and collect them at the front of the building, employees park at the rear of the building and come in through the back entrance where a security guard checks all passes. The chief executive has no chauffeur and parks his Land Rover on the back lot. He uses the back entrance though he is not required to show his security pass. His choice of car and his reluctance to enter by the front of the building are regarded as highly idiosyncratic by directors and managers alike, though it does not appear to lower him in their esteem. It is thought to reveal lack of pretension rather than affectation.

Eight divisions make up the overall Company hierarchy. If you ask, in a formal context, managers will say the divisions are parallel, but in practice – and everyone recognises this – there is a hierarchy of divisions, with manufacturing at the top and personnel at the bottom. Relations between managers within divisions are also structured hierarchically; every manager knows his hierarchical position *vis-à-vis* his divisional colleagues. Ranks include managers of all divisions in the same depth of 'reporting relation' to a director.

Bion International is itself owned by Bion Development Corporation, which controls 55 per cent of its shares. Financial control is centralised through BDC, which has a portfolio of 45 related businesses. The main function of its Board is the coordination of financial resources among its businesses.

Bion's chief executive, John Holmes, is the only chief executive of a subsidiary to sit on the Board of BDC, a consequence of Bion's economic importance to the group as a whole.

With the exception of the chief executive and the financial director, who occasionally attends BDC's Board meetings in Cadogan Square, the managers and directors of Bion have never seen and are never likely to see the men who ultimately control the operations of their Company. Neither the chairman nor members of the BDC Board visit Bion's Head Office or factories. It was impressive that managers below the level of director did not know that BDC's Board includes a number of titled persons.

I was not in a position to find out BDC's rationale for maintaining a low profile, but one can speculate that it is a consequence of accepting the conventional wisdom that financial information offers an objective measure of a company's performance combined with the social and cultural distance which separates the members of the two Boards. The BDC Board is made up of people far removed from the social world of Bion.

In contrast to BDC, Bion International has a high public profile and its name, which is easily identified with its product, is familiar. Managers at all levels of Bion International participate in maintaining the Company's public profile. All managers contribute at some time or another to the vast number of formal documents that are produced by the eight Company divisions, from recruitment brochures to financial reports to Company policy documents. These documents are consistent in portraying the Company as based on egalitarian principles.

One example is the job description. Every manager in the Company has to approve his own job description which forms part of the legally binding contract of employment. In the idiom of the Company, the document 'clarifies the reciprocal obligations between Company and employee' – formally approving the ideal of equality before the law. The document also expresses the most concrete and absolute denial of Company hierarchy.

## DENYING HIERARCHY

In all job descriptions from chief executive to supervisor, subordinates are not described as persons but as resources. While at senior levels the number of people over whom a manager has authority is expressed in terms of the salary or wages bill; at factory level, middle and junior management jobs are defined in terms of supervision over product, with no mention of the people a manager directs in order to produce this product. Hence, the authority a manager has over people is subsumed conceptually under personal responsibility for the property of the Company. In this way the fact that managers, at all but the lowest level, hire people, direct their labour, appraise them, promote them and occasionally dismiss them is neatly deflected and relations within the Company take a purely economic form.

Writing job descriptions is a specialised skill and two managers have responsibility for drafting them. I knew the more senior of the two quite well. I had worked with him when I was asked to draft a job description for a newly created post in my department. When I returned to the Company in the capacity of researcher, I asked him why job descriptions omit to take into account managers' authority over people. He responded by slowly and patiently explaining the process by which he calculates people as resources. When he saw I was not convinced by this, he referred to the authority of the two organisations which advise this Company and others on drafting job descriptions. When he saw I was still looking doubtful he produced from his desk a pile of brochures that had been given to him by these organisations saying that I was free to take them home and read them at my leisure. In other words, his answer was, this is the way it is done.

This manager is concerned with the function of his specialised task which, given his response to my question, I believe he takes at face value. He did not try to explain or attempt to rationalise the omission but repeatedly told me how he makes the calculation. He did not deny that relations of authority are eclipsed by the document; he did not try to convince me that managers have no authority over people nor did he deny that this method of defining a manager's job makes for a less than comprehensive definition of what managers do. The omission simply had no meaning for him. It did not constitute a problem even after I pointed it out. As the point I made had no meaning, he was not motivated to reflect on the implication of the language he used: that turning subordinates into resources implies choice and not constraint because each manager stands out as individual, not subject to the will of his superior.

In this example, the denial of constraint through the denial of authority is reproduced by a manager who is simply being unreflective while doing his job. He is apparently doing no more than applying himself to the task at hand. I say 'apparently' because his intentional dissembling of the reality of hierarchy – the masking of constraints on individual choice through unreflective compliance – only raises a more interesting question, what are the social/psychological forces which stand behind his (I would argue, unconscious) decision not to reflect, that is, to conceal from himself the social and political implications of his role?

Unreflective compliance is only one of a range of ways that managers reconcile the ideal of egalitarianism with the reality of hierarchy. But whatever the underlying motive, the identification of the Company with the ideal is reinforced on a routine basis. Every time a manager is recruited or promoted he is required to approve his own job description and each time a job description is approved without question the manager is participating in the rhetoric of political economy.

Managers do not come under pressure from any quarter to justify the representation of the Company in terms of individuals. However, changes in legislation (the Sex Discrimination Act and the Employment Protection Act both passed in 1975) were placing considerable pressure on managers to demonstrate that the category 'individual' was open to women as well as men.

The passing of the 1975 Sex Discrimation Act itself was not, in fact, enough to pressure managers into widening their pool of selection to include women. It was several years later, when the Company was threatened with prosecution for racial discrimination that, worried about their public image, it began to take anti–discrimination laws seriously. This created the opportunity to observe how managers reconcile divisions within the Company based on gender and class with the ideal of equal self-development.

I was working with Bob Taylor in his office when Kate Arnold, an executive from a well-known employers' association, telephoned to say that her organisation was sponsoring a course for secretaries who wanted to move into management. Taylor is personnel controller, and reports to the director of personnel. Taylor knew Kate quite well. They had previously worked together on a project.

Taylor and Kate discussed the course at some length, he congratulated her on her achievement in setting it up saying how important it was for secretaries to be able to change careers if they had the ability. He said that to keep people working below their capacity was a ridiculous waste of Company resources. She asked if the Company would let secretaries attend. He said of course it would and she asked for the names of secretaries who might be interested. He said he would get back to her.

A few minutes later Taylor's own secretary came into the office to give him some papers and he told her sarcastically, 'Now the association wants to send secretaries on a management course!' She said, 'That sounds interesting.' Then taking up his paper work and indicating that he wanted to get back to the job at hand, he said to Pat, 'Remind me to call her on Thursday and tell her we haven't got anyone.' As soon as Pat had left the room, I asked him why he was not going to ask around, suggesting he begin by asking his own secretary. He replied, 'Secretaries here are happy with their jobs, they are very well paid. They have families and don't want the responsibility of a management job. If you don't believe me talk to Pat, you'll see that I'm right.'

The next day I waited for a moment when Pat was on her own before asking her what she thought about the course. She said she would be very interested in attending but 'knew' that her boss would not give her the time. I should say a few words about Pat. She is a highly regarded, full-time secretary who has been with the Company for five years. She is 30 years old and married to a middle manager who works in a nearby Company. She has two school-age children. Apart from longer hours, which would be compensated for by higher pay, there was no advantage in her remaining in a secretarial position. Having said this, she was not dissatisfied with her job, either in terms of salary, terms and conditions or treatment by her boss, nor did she feel inherently diminished by being a secretary.

On Thursday Taylor reminded Pat to make the call to the association to say that no secretaries were interested. A call from a secretary would add weight to his claim that no secretaries in the Company had ambitions to move into management. His assumption that he could take Pat's loyalty for granted was not misplaced. Pat made the call.

Taylor believed he was acting in the best interests of the secretaries, and that he knew where their true interests lay. What he was intent on hiding was that he had not been systematic in canvassing opinion on a question to which he already had the answer. He did not have the skills required to make this 'intuitive grasp' of secretaries' needs sound as if it were derived from hard evidence without resorting to a lie. Taylor's justification for deceiving the woman from the employers' association was his conviction that secretaries do not want to be managers – 'They do not want the responsibility of a management job' – a conviction so powerful he did not hear Pat's tentative but positive response, 'That sounds interesting.'

For Taylor, the other side of the rhetorical line is not a wish to prevent secretaries from becoming managers - 'over my dead body' so to speak; it is the wish to avoid unnecessary work which would be a waste of his time – Company time – and which may also be disruptive to other managers. He knows full well that they share his conviction.

But Taylor's conviction, that secretaries do not want the responsibility of management jobs (a claim made on behalf of 98 women) rests on a bit of self-deception – that he knew what secretaries wanted. He is not conscious of the fact that this so-called knowledge arose out of historical fact and prejudice: secretaries do not become managers. Nor could he be aware that his prejudice excluded Pat from communicating her desire to him in more assertive terms. This left him free to make decisions on her behalf *in all consciousness*.

Taylor's prejudice contains a constellation of values in relation to class and gender that permeate the Company as a whole. In Bion International, secretaries are working class. Managers are middle class. Female managers, in order to compensate for their gender inadequacy, not only have to be middle class but perceived to be a notch above the managers to whom they report. This was true of the three women managers in the Company. (Because of my accent I was perceived as an American and therefore stood outside traditional class categories.) In this Company a secretary could no more become a manager than could become a male clerical worker. Believing that his views are based on evidence, Taylor has no way of comprehending that his privately and unconsciously held views are profoundly social in character, corresponding to a set of collectively held beliefs which create a structure on the basis of which relations within the Company are determined.

Apprehending the origins of Taylor's lack of insight into his own predisposition to put what he perceives to be the interests of the Company before the interests of its secretaries would require a detailed study of his family history and the social conditions of his upbringing. But whatever the conditions that account for his motive, the political effect of his action is to ensure that Kate can never be informed enough to make a valid judgement. Taylor has effectively ended all discussion. Kate is not in a position to put a case for the secretaries or to question his judgement. (That she works for an employers' association, of which Bion International is a member, means she would be unlikely to be allowed to use institutional pressure against Bion International in any case.) One can see here how the issue of whether secretaries should be promoted into management masks the concentration of effective corporate power that underpins Taylor's authority to lie with impunity.

Three months later, I was sitting on a panel with Taylor and two other managers, addressing the sixth form of the local comprehensive on the role of industry in Britain. During question-time, one of the sixth formers asked if the Company practised equal opportunity for women. Taylor said yes and pointed to me as an example. No fool, the sixth former then turned to me and asked me if I thought the Company practised equal opportunity for women. Taylor, who operates on all six cylinders, took an instant to see my hesitation and cut in saying that just recently he had canvassed secretaries in the Company to see how many wanted to attend a course on moving into management. He said that no one had taken up the opportunity: 'You must realise, that not every woman is ambitious.' He spoke to her patronisingly, as though this were one of those home truths that can only be learned by experience.

Kate had done Taylor an unexpected service. She had provided him with a means of proving to his audience that the Company was voluntarily adapting to the changing aspirations of women where there is a genuine demand.


## THE RHETORIC OF INDUSTRIAL RELATIONS

Bion's public position, was and still is, that there is a fundamental harmony of interests between the role of the unions (five unions represent 4700 workers ) and that of the Company. When managers discuss conflict of interests between the Company and the trade unions with outsiders, they speak as if it were limited to superficial economic disagreements which, in each case are reconciled to the benefit of both parties. Despite the public posture of harmony, Head Office managers see the trade unions as external to the Company and they assume, incorrectly, that shop floor workers identify with their respective unions and not the corporation. The workers' quarrel is with the local factory managers whom they believe to be incompetent in their jobs and dishonest in their dealings with workers. From their point of view, were the Company to recruit competent factory managers, their problems would be solved.

The public projection of Head Office managers is in sharp contrast to the way they discussed the role of the unions with one another. In this context, conflict of interest was seen as grounded in the very system of the organisation, that is, as essentially political. Negotiations for wages and conditions were not regarded as temporary disagreements, but as part of a long-term union strategy to rob the Company of its resources. At the time of the original study managers believed that the unions posed a fundamental threat to the stability of the Company. And because public knowledge of endemic instability can lead to loss of investor confidence and a fall in share value, they were careful to hide the perceived threat from outsiders.

The chance encounter described below illustrates managers' skills in concealing the considerable tensions that existed between unions and factory management. A PhD sociology student carrying out research on the attitude of senior managers in manufacturing industry towards trade unions was given permission by the Board to interview 25 senior managers. She was to carry out open-ended interviews over a two-week period.

While she was interviewing Roberts, the industrial relations manager, I happened to drop in to see his secretary on some other business. Seeing me through the glass window of his door, he came out and asked me to join them. I had missed most of the interview, but he carried on, 'People think we are anti-union, we're not. What people don't realise, is that unions have to be the body through which wages are negotiated. They make management's job easier. Can you imagine having to negotiate wages and conditions every year with each employee?'

What he was saying was sheer nonsense and he knew it. Non-unionised companies set wages, they do not negotiate with individual employees. It's the collective power of the trade unions that forces management to the bargaining table.

The industrial relations manager is a large man. As he was talking to the sociology student, he leant forward across his desk, folded his hands and lowered his voice, as if he were letting her in on some secret. It struck me then that he was acting a part. When he had finished speaking to her, he looked at me as if to say, have you anything to add? He knew I had just spent four weeks on the shop floor of the Company's most conflict-ridden factory where machine sabotage and walk-outs were weekly occurrences (a problem that is not disputed by any factory or Head Office manager). Not for one moment did it occur to him that I might disagree. He was right. I said I didn't have anything to add. Not only that, I said so cheerfully though I was in fact feeling quite perturbed by the ease with which he was relating this tale. *I* was acting. Yet I have little doubt that the sociology student believed my agreement was genuine and sincere.

Before she left, the student asked if she could have access to data on strikes and stoppages throughout the five factories. The industrial relations manager gave her a sheet of figures which were being drawn up for the benefit of the unions. I knew these figures were pure fiction. I return to this below. The point here is that this young woman was sent off to reconcile her 25 interviews with senior managers – all of whom are experienced rhetoricians – with her misleading statistics.

In this context Roberts was consciously hiding what he knew to be the true state of affairs. He was also well aware that he was engaging in rhetoric that his counterparts across the country engage in, on a daily basis. His motive was to disguise what he believes to be a weakness – that trade unions pose a significant threat to Company stability – and he deftly achieved this, or so he believed, by describing relations in terms of a balance of economic interests.

The rhetorical device of portraying relations in purely economic terms in order to mask what is perceived to be a deep political division is not a tactic he has worked out from first principles. As in the case of the personnel controller's prejudice, the predisposition to identify with the interests of a particular group is rooted in family history and the social conditions of his upbringing. However, the tactics he uses to appeal to his audience are slowly absorbed by observing what other managers do in similar circumstances.

The political consequence of the industrial relations manager's rhetoric was to prevent the student from becoming entangled in the industrial relations issues which were of real concern to Roberts himself, and indeed to a majority of senior managers. She was not therefore given the opportunity to make sense of these entanglements and present them in her PhD. And whether due to ignorance, naivety or a lack of social confidence, she was unable or unwilling to challenge his story. In any case, she would only have been given permission to carry out the research in the first place because managers could see that they could rely on her passivity to protect their position. In other words, they saw her coming.

It is important to separate the two different kinds of effects of managers' rhetorical strategy. The first is a result of a broad strategy designed to conceal instability because of its potential effect on share value. This is a conscious strategy to protect the Company's economic viability. The second effect goes unacknowledged; it obscures the social conditions that determine industrial relations practice in this Company. In terms of political effect, whether or not the student believes the industrial relations manager is irrelevant. She does not have the information that would enable her to make sense of the conditions that determine industrial relations practice – conditions that include the power of the Company to delegate authority to managers to engage their various audiences, including the trade unions, in misrecognition of the facts.

When examining the context within which managers project the ideal of harmony of interests between labour and capital, one has to keep in mind their presuppositions *vis-à-vis* their audience. Thus far, I have described managers as they relate to women, whom they assume to be more gullible than men. The presumption of a more sophisticated audience requires a different approach.

A senior manager from the Finance Department and myself were having lunch with the director of a large and well-known biscuit company, which has a reputation in the business community for its progressive industrial relations policies.

The conversation turned to industrial relations in the two companies. The manager of Bion International 'candidly' explained that he believed the industrial relations problems in his company were partly caused by the cynicism of certain senior managers towards the unions and their rank and file. He went on to describe their attitudes, how they were 'set against' the unions and could not accept the unions' legitimate role in industry, implying he himself believed they had a legitimate role. By admitting that there were a number of poor managers and showing himself willing to criticise his own company, he gave the impression that he was making an impartial and objective assessment of Head Office management. But what he referred to as cynicism is characteristic not of two or three managers but of the values that dominate Head Office as a whole, and of the manager who was seeking to defeat this impression.

In this case the manager was telling the truth as he saw it at that time. As I was listening to him it was easy for me to understand the picture he had in his mind. The cynics he was referring to were the two or three managers who most loudly and insistently expressed their dislike of the unions. At the time he was speaking he forgot that they are merely voicing an opinion which he has expressed on a number of occasions and on which the majority of managers, including him, *act*.

In other contexts, when he was with his own colleagues, the manager was openly hostile to the unions and would vigorously justify and defend his anger. For example, on hearing what the latest acts of machine sabotage had cost the Company in terms of lost output – 'Those bastards!' said, not off the cuff, but in anger. During this period demand was exceeding supply and lost revenue was unlikely to be recovered. The misplaced assumption was that union influence was the cause of the problem.

My own perception of the manager's reaction to his colleague from the biscuit company was that he temporarily believed he shared his colleague's convictions, in other words, he was not engaging in conscious hypocrisy. And further, that this temporary self-deception made his claim all the more effective.

Without having to think the question through, he knew there to be no advantage in trying to mask what he took to be the conflicting interests of capital and labour to a manager in another manufacturing organisation – who also takes this for granted. He also knew there would be a great deal of advantage in claiming that the problems that do exist stem from the irrational views of one or two individuals rather than the ethos of management as a whole.

## A REPORT TO STAKEHOLDERS

An example of a coordinated effort by Head Office managers to protect Company interests was the production of the 'Report to Stakeholders'. At the time of the study, the Company was under legislative pressure to provide a wide range of information to the trade unions for collective bargaining purposes. One of my briefs was to write the report to stakeholders. In January 1977 the Board made the decision to publish a yearly report and accounts. The decision was taken in order to pre-empt the unions' legal right to financial information. The law obliged companies to provide proof of financial status and other information deemed useful to the unions for collective bargaining purposes, should the unions request it. Managers believed that for the Company to be seen to be voluntarily providing sensitive information would pre-empt a demand by the union.

The personnel director who had overall charge of the project also had a personal ambition which was to win the Report to Employees Award given by yet another employers' association. This would not only give him prestige but would be good publicity for the Company. To prove the Company's goodwill the report was to contain information defined as sensitive, including detailed information about the Company's income; its allocation into profits, wages and capital investment; the number of products produced annually at each location and the number of accidents and injuries at work. The project took three months to complete.

Over the weeks there were many discussions and disagreements about the content. For example, no director wanted to include information on days lost due to management absenteeism, but only days lost by manual workers. (The average number of days lost for workers was 7.2 while for managers it was 7.9.) I argued that people might find the absence conspicuous and imagine the days lost by management to be more than they in fact were; having spent a considerable amount of time on the shop floor I knew this was exactly what people would think. Or it might even lead some people to question the validity of the entire report (again, a real possibility). But I was overruled. 'We are not going to publish it. It isn't that we have anything to hide. If anyone asks, we'll tell them', said the director of manufacture for Northern Ireland.

At that time there was a great deal of demand on the shop floor for comparative figures of stoppages and strikes in the five factories. Factory managers were aware of this demand and, at my insistence, reluctantly agreed to provide them. They were slow in coming, so I finally went to the largest factory to insist personally. The factory manager sent me to the accountant and I sat and watched as he fabricated a set of numbers. 'This'll do', he said, handing them over. I looked at it. More walk-outs took place in a month than he claimed took place in six months. I believed it was still worth pursuing because the unions were interested in relative figures, but the only honest account came from the factory that had had no industrial disputes during the past year.

I collated the figures as given me by the five factory accountants and sent them to the Board, which instantly rejected them. The argument was that employees in the factory with no industrial disputes would find it disconcerting to know there were problems in the other four factories. The real reason was that unions would use the information to compare levels of productivity for negotiation purposes, which is exactly what the legislation had intended.

With the help of an agency which specialised in the layout of financial reports, at the end of eight weeks I had worked out a rough format for the 'Report to Stakeholders'. From this format emerged a serious problem. The financial information did not tally. I took the report to the Company's senior accountant to sort out. He looked through it carefully and when he reached the end he suddenly burst out laughing. He really found it very funny. He got up to close the door to his office and then returning to his seat he explained, 'When a company fixes its figures year after year there comes a point when you just can't make them add up any more. I'll do what I can to patch it up but I am not making any promises.' I asked him what exactly was the problem? 'Years of exaggerating the amount of money spent on reinvestment and wages and benefits.' He added that the Board's decision to use value added instead of a profit and loss statement would be useful because it would make it extremely difficult to compare this report with the report and accounts of BDC. He did sort out the problems and I then took the report to the financial director for his final approval. He checked it, commenting, 'Very imaginative', then he added, 'You realise these figures have nothing to do with the finances of the Company?' (These were the figures given to the PhD student.)

The following day I took the report to BDC's London office to have it approved by its financial director. He read it through and said he thought it was 'Excellent'.

The report was published, widely distributed not only to employees but to other institutions, it took second prize in the competition; the results were reported in the financial pages of the national press. This illustration of managers' collective willingness to break the law not only raises important issues about democratic process and the authority of managers to determine the content of policy unhibited by 'democratic' checks, but in terms of the theme of this chapter the collective breach of the law also raises a number of questions with regard to how managers perceive their relation to the Company.

Managers take for granted the institutional powers that enable them to ignore the law. They do not discuss or question the source of the authority that leaves them free to maintain an unfair advantage in negotiation while at the same time raising the prestige of the Company in the eyes of the public by being seen voluntarily to provide unions with 'sensitive' information.

Although at one level it seems fairly obvious that managers should take their authority for granted – they are after all employed to represent Company interests – one can well imagine an alternative scenario, where managers less inclined to identify with these interests share a sense of discomfort with regard to the demands being made upon them. A sense of discomfort would be likely to be reflected in managers' discourse, if not during actual working hours then in more informal circumstances, for example in the bar after work, during long train journeys to and from their factory in the north, over dinner, etc. But even in these less formal contexts what was routinely emphasised was pride in their achievements, rather than any discomfort with the means of that achievement.

This is not to suggest that managers were never critical of the Company. Criticism was a routine feature of Head Office life when outsiders were not present, but with one exception managers' criticisms were limited to the personalities of colleagues and problems of economic inefficiency. The exception was Davis, a manager who genuinely wanted to pressure the Company to adopt liberal reforms. Davis believed that trade unions have a legitimate role and that women should be promoted according to their ability. For three years he campaigned for Day Care facilities to be introduced into the Company's five factories – an idea initiated by the trade unions. He met with union leaders, progressive women's groups, and MPs. He produced statistics to show not only that costs would be met over a 5-year period, but that Company profits would actually increase. He rewrote his own secretary's job description and tried to get her moved up into a management grade. From his point of view, he worked at the boundary of what is acceptable and attempted to influence institutional policies in so far as his position would allow. In his 15 years with the Company, however, he has never succeeded.

The personnel director provided him with the resources to carry out these activities and sanctioned the time he spent away from his desk pursuing his various causes. The director was seen by other managers as giving in to the whims of a do-gooder and wasting Company resources; but despite their misgivings Davis is not shunned by his colleagues, either professionally or socially. The director's rationalisation for giving in was that he does not want to lose him – in his own field Davis is considered an excellent manager.

Despite his ostensibly adversarial stance, the unintended consequences of Davis's activities are beneficial to the Company. Though criticised from within, his activities are highlighted by other managers who can, in all honesty, tell trade unions, women's groups and other interested bodies that the Company is in the process of looking into issues that are of concern to them. Needless to say, his lack of success in producing a result is not brought into the public domain.

Davis believes he is being hard-headed and realistic about his colleagues' convictions and what it is he is up against. But he does not see that in relation to the wider context his activities strengthen the rationalised corporate vision that he is striving to change.

Where Davis differs from his colleagues is in his belief that a closer alignment of corporate values with liberal principles is in the long-term interests of the Company. But, like his colleagues, he does not question the source of the authority that enables managers to limit threat, whether by liberal or by other means; an authority ultimately rooted in a much broader organisation of power from which these managers are excluded and over which, as individuals, they have no control.

In each of the examples described above managers are careful to mask the institutional power that delegates them the authority to project a false image of the Company, thus creating the social fiction that managers are the source of their own authority. This fiction is politically necessary if the liberal ideal is to appear compatible with the concentrations of effective corporate power which in reality contradict it. What I want to suggest is that managers themselves believe in this fiction and, moreover, they do so unconsciously.

As individuals, Bion managers have very little power. There is no security of employment; managers live on their wages and have limited personal capital. Even in times of high employment, for many managers there is no guarantee that their skills will be transferable; and the upheaval that change entails with regard to wife and family means that they have a serious, vested interest in this particular organisation. Since managers do not avail themselves of the collective support of a trade union, which would include both financial and legal support in the event of a disagreement with the Company, in his relation to the Company, each manager is dependent on his own resources. It was impressive that the terms of dependency did not form a part of management's discourse. Unlike workers, who routinely discussed the power of the Company to affect their lives, this concern did not form a part of the idiom through which managers discussed their relation to the Company.

What I have attempted to show here is that this lack of collective expression reflects a lack of conscious, collective awareness of the source of their own authority, a lack of awareness that may be linked to a pressing desire to deny their own vulnerability.


CONCLUSION

The question of why managers should share in this collective myopia raises issues far beyond the remit of this article and the research project of which it is a part, but it is hard to defer the matter entirely.

A tentative explanation, drawn from psychoanalytic literature would suggest a predisposition among Bion managers to internalise the power of the Company and believe that they possess in themselves the source of corporate power. Through this means, the insecurity generated by dependence and powerlessness would be converted into security and each manager would be able to treat the power of the Company as if it originated from his own personality and strength of character. Once power is internalised it would no longer pose an external threat and this would explain why the source of power is not experienced as an external social or political reality.

If this interpretation is accepted then it follows that the integrating structure of motivation within management as a whole is grounded in this shared illusion, and through this illusion the Company, that is capital, is sustained as an abstract entity.

Whatever the limitations of this particular interpretation, in terms of the anthropological ethnographic brief, it seems obvious that the dimensions of the problem (how do corporate managers accommodate the discrepancies between self-definition and corporate exigency?) could not even be identified, much less accurately analysed without recourse to a methodology that obliges the researcher herself to enter the actual, lived world of the manager, and enter it not with the expectation that the 'data will present themselves' and be dealt with in due course, but enter it with the recognition that the rhetorical strategies employed in the corporate domain are burdened with interest. The PhD student referred to in the text represents the shortcomings of a research strategy that does not take into account that rhetorical strategies do not merely 'come with the territory'. They are not devices employed in order to achieve conscious goals, but are strategic in the grander sense: they ensure the apparent naturalness of corporate structures which pretend to accommodate the broader social good while emphatically defeating precisely such aims.

## NOTES

The original study took place between 1978 and 1980. Since then I have returned to carry out short-term research projects on a number of occasions, the last one being in 1994.

I would like to thank Dr Stephen Nugent whose constructive comments have clarified many points in this article.

## REFERENCES

Engberg, Edward (1976) *On Civilising the Corporation*. Santa Barbara, CA: Capra Press.

# 9   TIES: THEORETICALLY INFORMED ETHNOGRAPHIC STUDY

*Paul Willis*

*Long before the relationship between anthropology and cultural studies came to be addressed as an issue of serious disciplinary territoriality (or shotgun marriage),* Paul Willis, through Profane Culture *and* Learning to Labour[1], *stood out as a non-anthropologist whose ethnographic practice was the match of – if not better than – much of what passed as 'normal' anthropological ethnography. As ethnography emerged as a centre-piece in cultural studies' programmatic claims for a new synthesis, however – and following the academic respectability achieved by the Birmingham School (in all its variants) – there was not a lot of it, and Willis's bore an inordinate responsibilty for representing what cultural studies ethnography stood for despite the fact that, as he himself notes, he is hardly a typical cultural studies ethnographer.*

*From the point of view of anthropologists sceptical of the possibilities of transferring the anthropological project from the periphery to the centre, Willis was (inadvertently) politically useful: for those, the argument went (and still goes), wishing to practise – in that instransigently unedifying phrase, 'anthropology at home' – the way to do it was via cultural studies, as Willis showed; not via anthropology.*

*In the epilogue which follows, Willis shows himself unmarked by the petty rivalries which have afflicted so much of the discussion around the real or putative relationship between anthropology and cultural studies, not least because of his down-playing of the idea that ethnography* per se *represents – either for cultural studies or anthropology – a methodological cutting edge: it happens to be useful for helping to answer certain kinds of questions, but probably in itself does not represent a particularly interesting epistemological stance (although that is hardly precluded).*

*Willis's contribution to this volume is drawn from comments he offered at a GDAT conference in Manchester, November 1996. The motion debated*

182

*was: 'Cultural studies will be the death of anthropology', and while some serious divisions were evident, none of the debaters was a credible adherent to an uncompromised position. Indeed, at times they seemed to fall over themselves in the interest of ensuring that shades of grey were given their due.*

*It seems particularly appropriate to close the volume with Willis's comments, not least because they suggest the fruitfulness of possible collaborations rather than a hardening of territorial positions. The comments were transcribed by Peter Wade, subjected to minor revisions by Paul himself, and rendered in the form below by the editors.[2]*

One of the problems we have to deal with is that of deciding what cultural studies is. The account of the anthropological ethnographic project as an approach to complex living forms is really not far at all from what I would describe as the project of cultural studies, and rather than oppose cultural studies and anthropology and subscribe to the notion that they are fundamentally at odds, I would argue that anthropology and cultural studies need each other and are constituting an ongoing mutual critique.

Instead of the proposed motion, I'd ask you to try to think of another scenario – fitting in to the motion to some extent – in which a dreadful struggle results in the death of both parties. And that would be no bad thing – I'm not interested in proclaiming the everlasting life of cultural studies, and some of the arguments within cultural studies are more lethal and a lot ruder than the arguments deployed on this occasion.

And out of this mutual deathly struggle, I would like to see the phoenix arise of theoretically informed, critical, comparative ethnographic practice. Let's simply think of it as theoretically informed ethnographic study, which happens to make an acronym of 'TIES'. So, whether in death or birth throes, I would like to tie these disciplines together through mutual critique, a mutual critique which apppears almost obligatory given that the two fields already do in some ways mirror each other's weaknesses.

What does cultural studies, or my version of cultural studies, teach us about anthropology? How is it that I'm still generally speaking, I suppose, within a cultural studies camp, rather than having jumped ship and joined an anthropology department? Well, in the (Anglo-American) anthropology I've seen, and in discussions over the years,

I think that anthropologists are still troubled by some fundamental theoretical issues. I'd summarise them as empiricism and humanism.

What do I mean by empiricism? The same as everyone else: that the meaning of reality is indeed simply written on its surface. It is certainly refreshing that, for you, it might not be a matter of *simple* discourses which can be detached and studied in the ivory tower, the plague of cultural studies. But there seems to me a continuing sense in anthropology that you go to the field, preferably as far away as possible, in some sense to come to an unmediated, real, authentic reality, and that in some way, you can then make a report of that, based on the immediate senses of your own experience. All that you need to know to understand about the field is in some way *in* the field.

In the same way, the associated problem of a centred humanism still seems to me to be a problem in anthropology. That is, since you've travelled so far to the field, and you have a bounded notion of the field, despite protestations to the contrary, you see the agents involved in that field as in charge of their own destiny in some way or another. It might look traditional, irrational, old-fashioned, religious or whatever, but your job is to show the real truth, to show that ultimately, another people's culture is human and rational, with centred human beings in some way controlling their own forms.

In my view – and admittedly this is a very compressed critique – you're still in need, as it were, of political economy, of history, and of taking seriously what I think of as theoretical cross-cutters – something akin to those issues around discourse referred to by the other participants today. But it seems to me that even in these sympathetic allusions to the centrality of questions of discourse, we still get from anthropologists rather more agency (and the specialness and definingness of human powers) than we get of historically given conditions and intractable discursive and symbolic material. We get rather more human control and centredness over the use of those things than we do respect for, and understanding of, the connected nature of those conditions which help to structure a particular field, and those conditions which decentre aspects of human agency, by which I mean precisely those things which you can't discover directly in the field: the history, political economy and context which determine a lot of behaviour in a particular site, as well as the discursive forms – from the power of the state, through to types of gender, fetishism, commodity cultures – and the limits set by an overwhelming commodity relation, especially in the developed countries, but also elsewhere. Actually, everywhere.

It seems to me that by not taking seriously these things, things which would have limited or mollified your empiricism and humanism, anthropology has indeed sold the pass to cultural studies, a cultural studies which has charged rather indecently and rather quickly – and, for my own personal taste, in rather too continental a way – into the theoretical issues of the actual symbolic, discursive, material, commodity forms, and the specific political, economically defined aspects of the field in which you are already accustomed to pursue your studies.

Associated with this empiricism and humanism is, for me, a continuing lack of discursive self-consciousness. I think this relates to empiricism and humanism again, that assumed sense of ethnographic authority. If the field is as far away from the metropolitan centre as possible, is bounded and separate, you can perhaps become the expert on it and, with few mediations, report on 'the truth' of the relations of the field. The continuing and obvious links with an imperialist past, despite the protestations, still make me – and many anthropologists, I know – uneasy, in terms of the whole notion of ethnographic authority; who are you, indeed, to poke your noses into others' business? I am also made uneasy by the way in which that ethnographic authority is often carried at the level of discourse for it is within the rhetorical devices and within a reproduced authority within the written text, rather than in any scientific claim to really know about the field, that that ethnographic authority often resides.

Look, I know there's been an internal critique. I'm a fan of Marcus and Clifford,[3] I like *Writing Culture*; I know Rosaldo's *Culture and Truth*;[4] I know about the impact of postmodernism on anthropology; I know the attempts to take seriously political economy; I know Daniel Miller's stuff on consumption – which, mysteriously, he seems to claim as an anthropological domain, whereas in fact I would argue cultural studies has made most of the running in this area. I know these internal debates and critiques, but I come back to a simple point, and it is 'the field'.

James Ferguson – who may or may not just have been speaking at the AAA on this and whom I heard at the large Tampere [Finland] cultural studies conference – is producing a jointly edited critical book on 'the field' in anthropology,[5] but it still seems to me, despite all of your protestations and despite all of the interesting internal critiques

– from which cultural studies, and certainly I, have learnt – that there is still, as Ferguson argues, something reified about 'the field'. In terms of institutional practice and the question of whether or not you're a real anthropologist and whether I, who am doing very similar things in many ways, could be considered as a real anthropologist, a lot of it comes back to whether or not you've done fieldwork – and still, I fear, the further away the better.

Despite, then, the fact that problems have been widely acknowledged, they haven't been adequately addressed. I think it is still the case that you're trapped in empiricism and humanism and in an imperial past and, specifically, by too bounded a notion of 'the field'. It's something you 'do' virtually for itself. It's your institutional and professional rite of passage. If you haven't been through that rite of passage you're not really an anthropologist, and no matter what the sophistication with which you can describe and analyse the baggage you seem obliged to take with you, your main orientation and set of definitions still revolve around 'the field'.

So, don't I believe in the field? Of course I do, but I think in my work that I have not reified the field. I haven't gone to the field because it's a field, the thing for itself. I've gone to different fields because of a puzzle or a problem that seemed directly relevant to me in political-economic, social and cultural terms. I've tried to indicate the theoretical kind of universe within which I was operating, why the puzzle turns into a puzzle, rather than the leftovers of the automatic obviousness of why you should go to a thing called the field, which still carries with it a whole set of imperial baggage and social relationship as well as the notion that you can describe a whole world.

In my own work – and I am bending the stick of argument somewhat, but I think the point is clear – I am trying to make a 'theoretical confession', saying what kind of world it is, then going to the field to make some kind of intervention.[6] I have a problem, say, in terms of why working-class kids get jobs; I have a problem in terms of how commodities are used; I have a problem in terms of how unemployed kids accept their fate. I go to the field as the second phrase in the construct, in order to try to get more knowledge about a specified issue, and to bring back that knowledge to give more adequate theoretical and thickly descriptive understanding. I am not arguing that the field is in a purely theoretical relationship to developed theory. There is clearly a theoretical case, which I'll get on to in a moment, for kinds of thick description; nevertheless, the approach to the field, the reasons you go to the field, the chain of logic that leads you to the field, what you admit to knowing and being before you're in the field – all these things are far more contingent and related to, in my own version of cultural studies, some form of intervention, rather than to a continuing assumption that the field can stand by itself, a position which, in my view, is still open to primary and non-trivial charges of empiricism and humanism.

OK, what are the mirror-image charges against cultural studies? The arguments are in many ways rather simple and straightforward. To start with, it hasn't really had a genuinely ethnographic tradition. If you look at the Birmingham Centre for Contemporary Cultural Studies, although it is assumed to be the heart of cultural studies and assumed to be responsible for having done much ethnography, in fact a lot of such work boiled down to people reporting on their own lives, what they overheard in pubs, quite short conversations with people – fieldwork, in other words, that didn't involve any disruption at all. I remember Jean Lave coming to Wolverhampton last year and saying that if you didn't have eighteen months in the field, and she definitely meant a long way away from where you normally lived, then you had no chance of beginning to present an ethnographic case or argument. I don't think any cultural studies text has ever had a really serious long-term field presence. Perhaps my *Learning to Labour* is most unusual in that way.[7]

My general case, though, about cultural studies, is that it has lost touch with some of its original premises – and which I would hope to hang on to and recycle – which lay in open projects, engaged projects, empirically based in some way. These were certainly evident to a significant extent in the early stages of the Centre for Contemporary Cultural Studies. Stuart Hall, after all, in those early days was looking at media and TV in specifically policy-oriented ways and aiming to produce work which was engaged in a public debate about the future of broadcasting. The early ethnographic work, if it was ethnographic, was nevertheless about recognising and responding to immediate change, the world around it, in an open and interventionist theoretical and political project. Much of that has now disappeared into theoreticism and scientism. I think there is truth in the charges heard against cultural studies to the effect that it has come to be about the subjects of study being aspects of discourses and how subjects are spoken by language and symbolic forms, rather than subjects in some way acting for themselves. I think a lot of the continental theoretical imports have basically been about withdrawing from an engagement and a struggle with contemporary issues and retreat into a theoretical argument about the formation of subjectivity and, from a variety of angles, an understanding of subjectivity as a function of the relation of differences of signifiers in discourses – removing the agent into discourse and therefore, to an extent, from history itself. After all, if the problem is to understand the discursive formation and limits of subjectivity, why bother with ethnographic study since all of the answers will be in the internal discursive relationships, not in what people do?

I accept that criticism. Despite the original engagement of cultural studies with contemporary reality – started, of course, at the Centre for Contemporary Cultural Studies by Richard Hoggart within the English Department [at Birmingham University], rather than Stuart Hall, who was the Centre's first research fellow – this engagement was, even in its heyday, not sufficiently empirical, not sufficiently ethnographic. It lacked a firm basis of extensive fieldwork, a methodology, a commitment to leaving the Muirhead Tower[8] – which really was a tower – to go out into a sensuous engagement with local cultural change and reality. It was that lack of, in a word, an anthropological root. Cultural studies did not grow out of anthropology. It grew in large part out of English studies and out of the Culture and Society tradition critiqued through the work of Raymond Williams – another story. The lack of a really genuine ethnographic root in cultural studies, I think, has allowed it to drift into a theoreticism which has removed it from the engagement from which it originally grew.

I'll rush on to specific strands – although I've touched upon them already – which particularly worry me in cultural studies. There is within it, after all, a tradition that calls itself ethnographic or qualitative, and that is media studies: it's what has happened to original cultural studies ethnography, in short. But I think that audience studies do not actually produce ethnography, but more exactly fraudulently trade on an assumed hinterland of ethnography and apparent anthropological knowledge of the communities, the groups, the cultures that are taking in the media messages under study. There is very little throughout the media texts, from Morley to Ang and onwards, which gives you an anthropological or detailed understanding of the receiving cultures as constellations of daily practices in the main sites of existence and exchange of those who are absorbing media messages.[9] At bottom there is, in my view, a kind of simple theory of reproduction going on which is that in the immediate decodings of messages, which you pick up through asking people what they think of TV or radio – and sometimes observing them in the immediate context – it is possible to build theories about how ideologies are reproduced, how people accept or reject those messages. As an ethnographer, in my view there's another very important loop that is missing from all this, a loop that goes from those decodings, and the sites of media consumption, back through into the practices and cultures and struggles of everyday life, especially around what continue to be the main sites – despite the claims of postmodernism: work, school, family and the street. I think it is certainly very true that there are new resources being pumped by globalism and commoditisation into people's lives, and that those resources are increasingly the means through which people make sense and come to an identity within the main sites of their lives. But in order to understand that use, we need to go back to what Raymond Williams called 'the relationships between elements in a whole way of life', by which he precisely meant as 'elements' the main sites, the main struggles, the main interests, the main issues that confront people in their lives.[10] Watching TV or listening to records may be one of them. What are the others? Where's the relation? The media tradition of ethnography has truncated ethnography whilst claiming its authenticity and power.

The other main strand of cultural studies I'd like to look at briefly concerns discourse and identity – from the state, through gender and different forms of symbolic systems and their differences – and the way these discourses produce meaning as well as 'subject-positions' for their users and participants. I do think this is a theoretical area vacated and still not taken seriously by anthropology, but in cultural studies it has become a slightly insane domain. This is especially so with regard to the postmodern gloss of absolute multiplicity, which then transmogrifies into an assumed impossibility of social agents' coming to any kind of selfhood or lived subjectivity, and ultimately the apparent provision for all of us of multiple subject-positions which never meet – multiple parallel railtracks to infinity – and which can be discussed solely and severally in terms of the respective discursive resources of a particular approach. It is posed as an advance that discourses 'suture' or 'articulate' in the production of identity, but this is still at *infinity as theory*, never in the study of real people or their actual practices in the multiple trafficking of everyday life at its main sites and material/social intersections.

What I argue, amongst other things, in my forthcoming book is that part of the way forward for cultural studies must be to look at the ethnographically observable interaction and relationship of those 'subject-positions', the comparative *uses* and rubbings off, on and against each other, the articulations of different discourses within a compressed life space or situation, giving us some theoretical scope and content for the creativity and 'agency' that both anthropology and cultural studies have an interest in rescuing.[11] Being formed as a woman, for example, might bring some critical resources to bear around schooling or state formations. Masculinity, certainly in *Learning to Labour*, became a vehicle for resisting a certain kind of mental inculcation. It is precisely in trying to see how those discourses and subject-positions combine through *practice* that you can get a better view of reality, and also some way out of the banal humanism that I'm afraid much of anthropology still falls into. But we won't get to that theorised sense of agency and subjectivity by keeping these discourses entirely floating, separate from each other or joining only in the abstract. It is in the study of ethnographically observable and identifiable forms of relationship that we will make theoretical and human progress.

What cultural studies needs is the 'surprise' factor I described long ago in the article 'Notes on Method'.[12] You can't get 'surprise' sitting in your study looking at discourses. You have to get into the world to see how discourses are used *in combination*. I would make a plea again for the contextual study of how the new resources of cultural meaning − commoditisation, globalisation and all the rest of it − are used, not in truncated audience studies, but in terms of understanding the relationships of the continuing main important sites of life. We won't come up with the old homogeneous groupings (working-class culture or whatever), but we will find observable new groupings that will help both our understanding and politics. We may also, through what I hope will be a renewed ethnographic practice in cultural studies, come to recognise the theoretical advantages of thick description, in which relationships not yet theorised − as in our race, class and gender mantra − nevertheless still appear in and are still somehow represented in the raw material of messy history, which is always beyond the naming of particular discourses. Like anthropologists, I do accept that in thick description are materials for the dialectical development and combination of new and existing theorisations, for the discovery and understanding of kinds of binary divisions and their relations other than those of our well-used mantra. I think humour is very important; creativity is very important; different kinds of languages and register use are very important; the relations of fetishism and authenticity are very important. There are many things yet to be clarified and theorised in fast-changing human cultures. Depending on your 'theoretical confession' and the type of intervention, a range of behaviours, a range of thick descriptions, are possible which are going to throw up relevantly messy data in order to develop your theory in specified ways – not in terms however, remember, of trying to discover, as it were, the whole world. There is a desperate need within theoreticised cultural studies for a theoretically informed fieldwork practice which allows for 'surprise', and which gives scope for thick description to produce data not prefigured in theoretical starting-positions.

So I finish very simply. Anthropology is dead. Long live 'TIES', theoretically informed ethnographic study.


## NOTES

1. P.E. Willis, *Profane Culture*, London, Routledge, 1978; *Learning to Labour: How Working-Class Kids Get Working-Class Jobs*, Aldershot: Gower, 1977.
2. We are grateful to the members of the University of Manchester Department of Social Anthropology for organising the GDAT session and for allowing us to use Willis's remarks. The other debaters on the day were John Gledhill, Mark Hobart and Nigel Rapport.
3. J. Clifford and G. Marcus (eds), *Writng Culture: The Poetics and Politics of Ethnography*. Berkeley: University of California Press, 1986.
4. R. Rosaldo, *Culture and Truth: The Remaking of Social Analysis*. Boston: Beacon Press, 1989.
5. A. Gupta and J. Ferguson (eds) *Anthropological Locations: Boundaries and Grounds of a Field Science*. Berkeley: University of California Press, 1997.

6. See P.E. Willis, 'Notes on Method', in *Culture, Media, Language*, S. Hall et al. (eds). London: Hutchinson, 1980.

7. P.E. Willis, *Learning to Labour*.

8. The Muirhead Tower was the Centre's home at Birmingham University.

9. D. Morley, *Family Television: Cultural Power and Domestic Leisure*, London, Comedia, 1986; I. Ang, *Desperately Seeking the Audience*, London, Routledge, 1991.

10. R. Williams, *The Long Revolution*. London: Pelican, 1965, p. 63.

11. P.E. Willis, *Life as Art*. Cambridge: Polity Press, forthcoming.

12. In *Culture, Media, Language*, S. Hall et al. (eds). London: Hutchinson, 1980.

# INDEX

*Index by Auriol Griffith-Jones*